From Bedford to the Somme

The Letters and Diaries of Denzil Heriz-Smith

BY THE SAME AUTHOR

Coward's War: An 'Old Contemptible''s View of the Great War (Matador, 2005)

From Bedford to the Somme

The Letters and Diaries of Denzil Heriz-Smith

edited by
Tim Machin

Matador
9 De Montfort Mews
Leicester LE1 7FW, UK
Tel: (+44) 116 255 9311 / 9312
Email: books@troubador.co.uk
Web: www.troubador.co.uk/matador

ISBN 978 1906221 188

Typeset in 11.5pt Times by Troubador Publishing Ltd, Leicester, UK
Printed by Cromwell Press, Trowbridge, Wiltshire

Matador is an imprint of Troubador Publishing Ltd

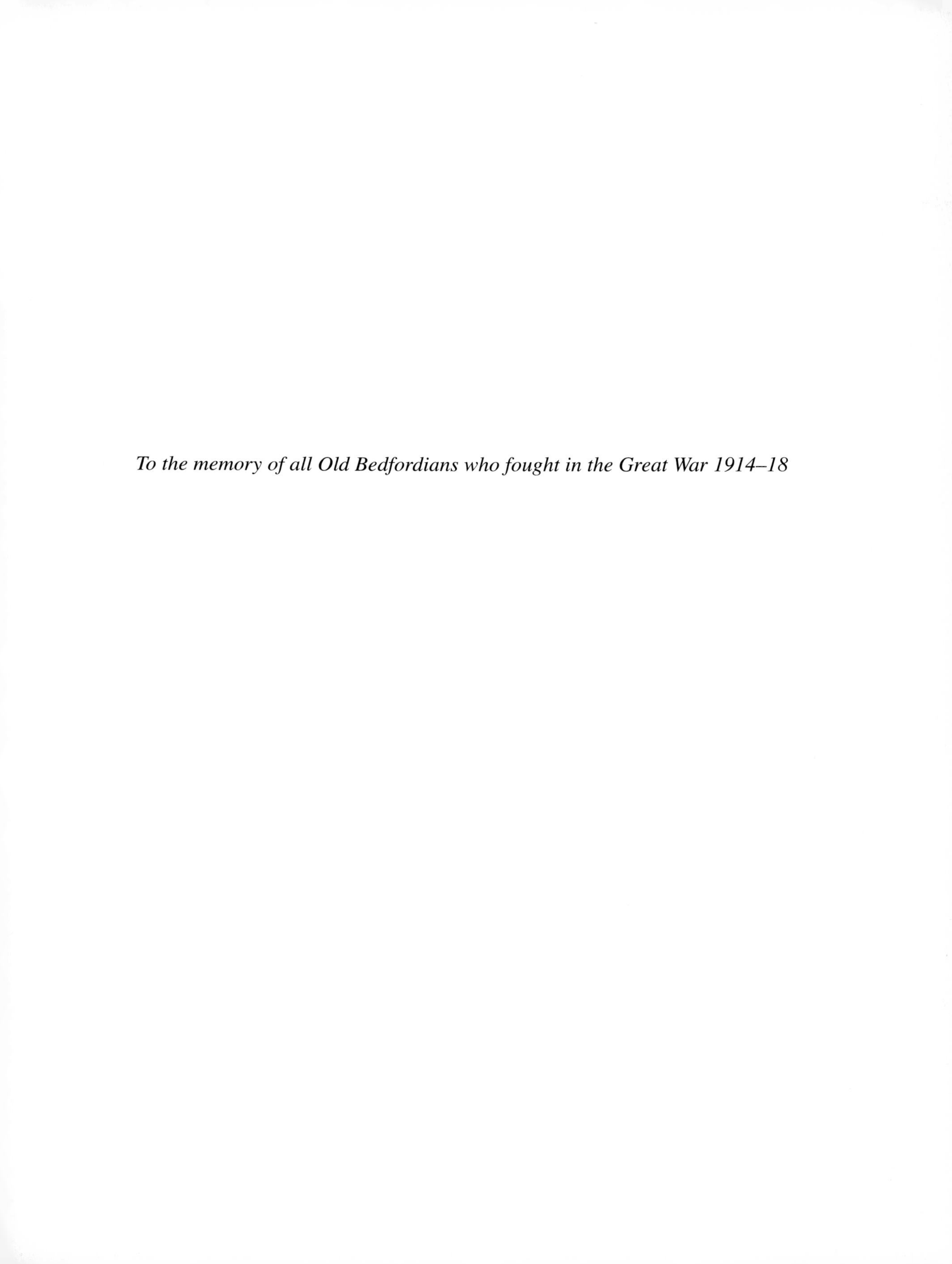

To the memory of all Old Bedfordians who fought in the Great War 1914–18

Contents

Preface

As you enter the large upstairs hall of Bedford School's Memorial building – the "Memorial Hall" - you are immediately confronted by a wall of names in gold on a contrasting blue background. The workmanship is immaculate, the sight arresting; but after a moment's reflection, the significance of the names, the hall, the building itself starts to take over, and the predominant emotions - in a mix of emotions, if the observer has any sensitivity - are ones of sadness, pride and resignation of "man's inhumanity to man". The board, of course, gives the names of all the former pupils of Bedford School who were killed in action in the Great War. There are four hundred and sixty three of them.

Underneath this memorial board (reflected incidentally on the opposite wall by names from the Second World War) are five blue-bound volumes summarising the circumstances of each death, but also giving some School and onward history of all these former pupils. One of the longest entries in volume two of these books is given

View of the School from the top of the Chapel Tower, Summer 1913

over to Denzil Heriz-Smith OB, late of the Northamptonshire Regiment and former Head Boy of Bedford School, 1913-1914. He looks out impassively from the page: Lieutenant, killed in action, February 17th 1917; buried at Regina Trench Military Cemetery, now impeccably kept by the Commonwealth War Graves Commission.

Apart from the fact that he was Head of School, and hence part of our own history; apart from the fact that he was holding a confirmed place at Queen's College, Cambridge; apart from the fact that he wished to be an Anglican priest; is another dimension to our knowledge of him – and that is the fact that his family left his copious diaries and personal memorabilia to the School. Denzil, for soon you will feel you know him well, was a prolific diarist, as were so many at that time. We have volume after volume summarizing his time at School and afterwards: a mix of "domestic" detail – trivia even – sharing pages with momentous international events. We have snowball fights at School in which the Head Master ("Chief" to Denzil, as he was to all in the early twentieth century) is involved, choir practice in the "Glee Club", debating in the School's Victorian Great Hall; but we also have declarations of war of one country on another, "cruisers steaming north" in one of innumerable memorable word-pictures and more. We also have his sword, his officer's whistle and his "Flander's Cross", erected by his comrades in the mud where he fell, with penciled-in names still visible near the base after all these years.

In his highly readable yet sensitive style, Tim Machin, a former member of staff at Bedford School and historian, tells the story of Denzil Heriz-Smith. In one sense a well-researched biography, it is in another sense much more, for it captures the time – and by looking at this cataclysmic period through the eyes of one man who was very closely involved – opens up the tragedy and humanity of the time in equal and compelling measure. What was it like to be there? What was it like to see your world and the world of others turned upside down as political events overshadowed the ordinariness of life. What was it like to sense, week by week, that issues totally beyond your control were impacting in the most unforeseen way on your own life and time?

If you read this book you will find out; and you will also be changed. You will gain, through reading it, a personal insight into one of the most tragic, unnecessary and influential four years in our own history; you will gain an idea of what it was like to be alive and living where and when the storms raged. But most of all, you will be enriched.

Dr Philip Evans OBE
Head Master, Bedford School
March 2007

1

Introduction and context

The stark truth is that Denzil Heriz-Smith, former pupil and Head Boy of Bedford School, died of his wounds on 17th February 1917 at Miraumont, part of the Somme. He was in the 6th Battalion of the Northamptonshire regiment, and he was one of the 463 lives lost in the Great War by former pupils of the School, a total only exceeded by two other schools in the carnage of 1914-18. He was hit by either shell or mortar in the battle of Boom Ravine, a fight that was not really necessary, as the Germans were about to pull back from their position. Though evacuated from the field, he died in No 545 Field Ambulance at about 5pm. He is buried in Regina Trench Cemetery.

What makes his death "special" is not that he was more brave or deserving than the other victims, but that the school possesses very large archives left by his family and that we can trace a career that extends through school and the army. In writing about him, we are paying homage to all the others who fell on foreign fields, at sea, or in the air.

As I write this, we are now in the ninetieth year since the tragedy of the Somme and the biggest military loss of life in a day in British history, and this might be a good enough reason to embark on this project, but the war continues to fascinate even those teenagers who go on the annual trenches trip to Ypres and the Somme. They return with a memory that will always be with them, and the names on the boards in the Memorial Hall[1] take on more meaning.

Denzil was born in 1894, a time when Britain was still seen by many as being the dominant world power, though that dominance was fast being eroded by Germany and the USA. The latter Victorian era and the Edwardian age are sometimes portrayed as a Golden Age that was to be sent crashing by the Great War.

This period is associated with commercial power, the Empire, the dominant middle class, a certain aura of being British and the confidence and certainty that brought, a huge Navy and the belief that Britain did not need continental alliances.

To what extent did Heriz-Smith reflect all or many of these characteristics?

He never mentions Darwin and the survival of the fittest but he undoubtedly thought that Britain had an exalted place amongst nations and that this gave her advantages and obligations. He was proud of being English and did think that her institutions and systems of law were things that the other countries could learn from; she may not be destined to rule but others could learn from her way of doing things. Politically, Denzil never was too explicit. I first thought that he was a supporter of the radicalism of Lloyd George and the Liberal party, but he seems to have been a Conservative all along. Perhaps we should not be surprised at this as it was a time of great fluctuation in party politics with the Liberals about to implode. He may have been a conservative but he supported Home Rule for Ireland. Teasingly, he gives advice to another OB not to get too close to the working classes, but he was worried about the rise of Socialism. He was a bit of a snob, but I think there was an assumption he followed that he must give something of his life to the betterment of others, either politically, or more likely by a career in the Church, not as a parish priest but someone who could influence from the Church hierarchy; but even this idea may have been prompted by his failure to get into the Civil Service. [He tried twice but was let down by Maths!]

Imperialism did have some ennobling attraction to him and it did not mean military despotism. One must remember that he came from a relatively prosperous and old family and that his father worked in Madras in the Indian Civil Service, in the Department of Public Works. His imperialism would have been far less emotive than that of Kipling and based on the dualism of English know-how and Indian development. He did not think England had been selected to rule, but there could be worse outcomes! He was a patriot but not a Jingoist, although he held strong views about other countries, not least the USA and Germany, whom he thought were afflicted by greed in the first case, and capable of barbarism in the second.

To some extent, Bedford School was for the sons of the prosperous middle class, those from the town on bursaries, and from those in the armed forces and in colonial government.

His father obviously was hard working, erudite, conscientious and committed to his job. These are qualities that could apply equally to his son and one must consider the role of education in this, in other words the part played in his life by Bedford School. The very large growth in the School in the last two thirds of the 19th century was connected to outstanding Head Masters, but also to the coming of the railway and commuting to London, and as an institution that took in many of sons of the bureaucracy as well as of the prosperous middle class living in or around Bedford. Heriz-Smith went to school with this in the background, and his parents would have made him aware of academic excellence and the opportunities it gave. Certainly a quick glance at the diaries he kept whilst at Bedford Grammar School[2] shows just how involved he was in every sphere of school life, and what cannot be contested is that he dearly loved the place, to the extent of wanting the Ousel[3] to be shipped out to him even when in the trenches! He did see the School as a community.

Tom Brown's Schooldays was written considerably before the life of Denzil, but there were qualities expressed there that he would have recognised; Godliness and good learning, good behaviour, the role of sport, manliness and setting the right example. He played just about every sport that could be played at School, with most success at rugby, in which he was in the first XV. My instinct tells me that he was a very competent sportsman but that he succeeded through endeavour. He recognised the qualities of teamwork, courage and fair play. It might not be quite what a contemporary said, that the best proof of a man's fitness to rule India was to be Captain of Games at school, but successful games players were like icons at school, and to an extent still are. Interestingly enough, Denzil never mentions girls apart from his own sisters and very few acquaintances. He was educated and worked in a very masculine world. He went straight from a single sex school into the army.

Much of the discipline at school seems to have been done by the senior boys, with a relatively light touch I hope, but this was seen as part of the preparation for later roles in public and military service. This was mirrored by public schools in the Commonwealth, and it is of interest that one of the most prolific architects for some of those schools was Sir Herbert Baker, who also designed the Tyne Cott Memorial at Ypres.

As Head of School, he had a close working relationship with the "Chief", as the Head Master was called. He seemed to be consulted about just about everything, and his word or otherwise was the clue to promotion to Monitor or to remaining on the "backbenches". He seems to have been brought back to the School to be Head Boy as he was 20 when he left. Traditionally Prefects had a lot of authority at Boarding Schools, some would say too much, but I doubt he was a bully and he does seem to have gone out of his way to look after the interests of juniors, particularly at sport.

He was hugely suited to the dominance in the School curriculum[4] of classics, the humanities and religious lessons, as well as physical education. At the turn of the century there were seventeen classicists on the staff at school, and only two physicists! He loved words, he loved writing and he was a prolific wordsmith, and this can be seen by his letters to his Father –"Dear Old Dad"—that went from English to Latin to Greek to French to code to poetry to prose. The combination of school and parents produced an extremely elegant letter writer. He was prolific and the letters and cards were written right up to the day before he died in action in February 1917.

I think on occasions Denzil was a bit prudish, frowning on the Music Hall for example, yet his letters show a subtle reflection and a clever wit, but he hated bad manners. He was a committed Christian but not an evangelical one and he enjoyed comparative religious discussions. He did not seek death but he felt that it was God's decision as to when he did die, and this gave him a certain calmness that was so valuable in the actions he was in in the Great War.

He was rather aesthetic in his tastes but he really enjoyed good food and champagne when available!

So how to conclude? He was an extremely intelligent and bright young man, certainly of Oxbridge calibre today. The letter to his mother in early August 1914, with war breaking out, showed a realism about what would happen that puts to shame the many leading lights who said it would be over by Christmas. At this early stage, he sensed that the comfortable, confident middle class world that he knew would never be the same after what was erroneously called "the war to end all wars". Above all he worked very hard at his friendships, writing 57 letters one week, whether sitting in a dugout on the Somme or in more salubrious conditions; but these were replies to people who had written him. He adored his family and this was the centre of his life. To me, he seems to understand the advantages his family and school have given him and to realise that he could make a difference to those around him.

To the historian, he has left a treasure trove of archives, and his descriptions of the first day of the Somme and later conflicts is wonderful primary evidence, sometimes literally written in a captured German dugout with battle still raging. He did not like being shelled but he said that he would not have swapped his being part of July 1st 1916 for anywhere else at that time. To understand that rather unlikely and strange thought, read on!

Denzil Heriz-Smith's life whilst living at home and being at school, was heavily dominated by his beloved family, his sport, the School Corps, debating, a general interest in world affairs and politics that he shared with his Father and sisters, and his own ambitions. His archives are full of lists varying from German ships sunk in the early days of the War, to his own collections of birds eggs and books, of friends with whom he must correspond, his financial affairs, of those who were in the pecking order for promotion at school, and of goals he set himself to achieve that term. Some of these lists will appear verbatim later in the book.

2

The family of Denzil Heriz-Smith

Denzil's Father, Charles Mitford Heriz-Smith, was born on the 4th February 1853 at Loddon in Norfolk, and he died on the 23rd June 1938. The 1901 census describes his occupation as ex-Public Works Department Madras Presidency. He appears to have retired from India in about 1895, and it is difficult to be precise about any further employment, though letters during the Great War show that he often stayed in Ealing and presumably worked in London, perhaps on government work.

Denzil's Mother, Marion Frances Georgina Johnston, was baptised on September 28th 1862 at Howick, Northumberland, and she died September 26th 1956 aged 94. They were married in the Bristol area in the third quarter of 1885. They had four surviving children, two boys having died at a few months of age in India. The eldest child was Joan who was born in Madras, India, in 1892, and who died on the 13th November 1978. Denzil was next, being born in Filey in Yorkshire on February 21st 1894. Next was Sybil who was born on August 18 1895 at Great Cornard in Suffolk. Finally there was Lewis Gillian [Gill] born on October 19th 1899, and who died on June 29th 1987. None of the daughters married, and this has made developing precise family details difficult.

Mother was the daughter of William Henry Johnston and his wife Fanny Lewis Johnston. William Johnston was born in Wicklow in Ireland in about 1834. He was one of HM Inspectors of Factories and in 1881 the family lived in Edgbaston, near Birmingham. Eight children, 4 boys and 4 girls were then living at home, and several servants were employed. Mother was probably a member of the family that owned Ransomes, Simms and Jeffries of Ipswich. The family must have been quite well off.

Father was the third child of ten of John James Smith and his wife Agnes Maria neé Mitford. He was the Vicar of Loddon, Norfolk, for about 34 years until his death in 1883. He was also a JP for Norfolk and formerly Fellow and Tutor of Gonville and Caius Cambridge.

Both Grandparents were from eminent families of the time.

John James Smith, born October 4th 1807, was the son of Joseph Smith of

Mr Charles and Mrs Marion Heriz-Smith

Earliest portrait of Denzil and his sisters

Shortgrove Park, Newport, Essex, and his wife Margaret. Joseph Smith was the private secretary to William Pitt the Younger. In addition he held many other lucrative posts such as Agent for the Bahamas and Newfoundland, and Comptroller of Bills. When Pitt was in personal financial difficulties in the early 1800s, Joseph helped to arrange funds to meet his debts. Joseph Smith's wife Margaret Harriot neé Cocks, was a niece of Lord Somers. In the 1861 census, John

James Smith, Vicar of Lodden, had his wife's parents staying with them. Joseph Mitford was born in Mitford Castle, Northumberland, in about 1792 and was a kinsman of Lord Redesdale.

The origin of the Heriz prefix is hard to trace. John James Smith, and many earlier generations, used the surname Smith without prefix. Charles Mitford Smith married as plain Smith in 1885, but in the 1901 census he styled himself Heriz-Smith, and several parallel branches of the family were then using the prefix. It is just about possible to trace the family back to Norman times, but some of the links may be a bit tenuous. One of the names on this line of descent is John Smith, alias Heriz of Woodcote, who died in 1545. Prior to this, the name becomes De Heriz back to a Robert De Heriz [1070-1120], who was one of William Peveril's knights and who lived at Tibshelf and Oxcroft. William Peveril was an important tenant in chief in the Midlands and had custody of Nottingham Castle and the Castle of the Peak in Derbyshire. Presumably, once this link was established, the family decided en bloc to adopt the Heriz prefix to distinguish them from all other Smiths.

The family of Charles and Marion Heriz-Smith lived in Bushmead Avenue Bedford, before moving to St Georges Lodge, St Georges Road in the same town. They seem to have

Haymaking

A cold day on the Suffolk coast

An early bookworm

A favourite past time

Recently commissioned. Autumn 1914

periodically employed a French foreign subject tutor, a governess, a gardener, a cook and a nurse.

Their holiday home was on the Suffolk coast at Great Cornard before they moved to Four Winds in 1921. Two of their daughters remained living there until their own deaths.

3

Headmasters and the Growth of Bedford School

In 1552 King Edward VI granted a charter to the School, but by 1737 the future of the School must have been in doubt as there were only three boys attending.

The figure crept up to twelve by 1773, but by 1811, when John Brereton became Headmaster there were only six and boarders were first taken.

In 1827 there were 95 and by 1833 108, though this was less than the Modern [then Commercial] School with 124.

In 1849 the figure was 187, the highest number under Brereton, but this fell back to 113, in 1855, the year Frederick Fanshawe became Head.

By 1867 there were 204 in the School, and in 1875, the year J S Phillpotts became Head Master the figure was 293.

There then followed a remarkable growth with 630 in 1886 and 800 by 1888.

It was during the remarkable tenure of JS Phillpotts that the "modern" School[5] emerged and there were a series of developments

1876 1st Science Laboratory built

1881 The purchase of the present playing fields

1886 OTC started

1888 Iron Buildings erected

1889 Foundation Stone of the new buildings laid.

1899 Preparatory School built

In 1903 JE King became Head Master [until 1910]

1906 Purchase of the present Prep School field

1908 Chapel built and dedicated by the Bishop of Ely.

1910 R Carter became Head Master [until 1928]

Phillpotts, from Winchester and New College, had fantastic energy and throve on difficulties [there was some opposition to his changes]. It is impossible to outline the varied activities of this ever growing community, with its workshops and gymnasium, its games organised by houses, its societies and debates, its scarlet coated Corps of Royal Engineers, its Monitorial body and a curriculum of work widened and revitalised, even though taught less in the central block of over crowded buildings than in a heterogeneous collection of annexes and hired rooms.

More ample room was vital and in 1888 the old school was sold to the Corporation, whom it still serves as a Town Hall, and the new building was opened by the Duke of Bedford on October 28th 1891, and was ready for use at the start of the next term.5

In April 1902 the long and distinguished reign of the "Old Chief" ended, and Headmasters thereafter had a benchmark to try to attain [Philpott's Chair still sits proudly in the present School].

Phillpotts was held in awe and the entrance gates in Burnaby Road, erected in 1930 to celebrate his 90th birthday, express the devotion and admiration in which he was held.

It was during the tenure of John King that Denzil Heriz-Smith began his career at the School.

King's work was largely that of consolidation as the pace of change slowed down, and yet his short reign saw important changes. He greatly extended the School Field, improved and reorganised the boarding houses, and raised the numbers in the Corps, which he commanded in person, from 90 to 200. His crowning achievement was the building of the School Chapel, something that became a focal point of Denzil's life.

King resigned in 1910 to become Head Master of his own School, Clifton.

His successor, Reginald Carter, was an experienced Head Master when he came to Bedford from Edinburgh Academy. He was a very versatile man, gifted as an artist, an accomplished musician on several instruments, a good all round athlete, and a classical scholar. His greatest work for the School was probably his strong business strength and administrative skill.

He piloted the School through the dark days of the First World War, a job that imposed both emotional and administrative strain.

Prior to that he had revived the long defunct school library, which later housed the War Memorial Building [many think this is the most beautiful building on the School Estate].

This Chief was held in great esteem by Heriz-Smith, as we shall soon see.

4

Still at school

The beginning of the diaries in 1910 see the Heriz-Smith family living at 31 Bushmead Avenue, one of the most sought after locations in Bedford, and it was here that Denzil celebrated his 16th birthday getting 5/- in cash and a dog called "Beaver".

At school in February he had to swear that he had nothing to do with the cutting open of a Missionary Box, a suggestion that would have upset him greatly, and it was that month that Reginald Carter became Headmaster, a man whom, as early as June, was called "a ripping chap" and whom eventually would appoint Denzil Head Boy.

Meanwhile, Denzil had to take internal exams each year in March to retain his exhibition, something he was able to do, and he took the School Leaving Certificate in June

The Heriz-Smith family had strong connections with Cambridge University, and Denzil notes in March 1911 the death of his Uncle Ernest who was the Senior Fellow at Pembroke College, and whose grandfather had been private secretary to Pitt the Younger. Ernest was an Anglican minister as well as being Proctor of the University. It is about this time too that Denzil mentions one of the frequent trips to Cambridge to visit Mr J Nixon[6], a classics teacher and author, the man who reorganised the music of Kings College Chapel and the virtual founder of Kings College Choir School. Staying in Cambridge as his guest, Denzil played Croquet and Tennis, rode to tea at Grantchester, played countless games of Matador[7], and frequently dined at High Table, often with Knights and Lords, discussing society and politics. It is not surprising that a 16 year old who could cope socially and intellectually with this would himself be able to move seamlessly into the University, even though he never was able to take up his place.

If all this was the gaining of social poise then Denzil's triumphant entry in his diary on May 28th 1911 was that he had his first shave!

Life went on rather idyllically and he describes a three hour Canadian canoe trip on the Ouse with his sister Joan, the inspection of Martin's bird's egg collection – presumably politically correct then as they were all doing it! – and the gift from Uncle Ted of a long-range rifle with sights! The ten days of Higher Certificate Exams starting on July 19th must have seemed like an unwelcome intruder into his excellent world.

There were also frequent trips to Ealing to stay with his Grandad and a visit to the Zoo that he was disappointed with.

As usual, at the end of the year, Denzil reviewed his progress, mentioning 4th XV colours, and then 3rd, the retention of his exhibition, shooting for his house and for the Eaglets, being an option, a Lance Corporal, and being on the Committee of the Debating Society.

In January 1912 he became a monitor and deputy head of house and he spoke of great excitement; Merveilleux!

Things were going well, including ice skating on Longholme in January but he was away from school for three weeks shortly after with suspected measles, although he was well enough on his birthday to record the 23/- he got in presents!

At the end of the Easter Term, Denzil's best friend Piercy left school. Piercy lived in Russell Avenue and had always walked into school with him. Piercy went for successful interviews with Guinness in Dublin

Bolton was the new Head of School and moved from civil and military side to "our classical side", and in early May Denzil became Head of St Cuthberts

On May 19th he sent in an application for Civil Service exams, and he was having extra Maths with "Sharkie Fuller", another of those marvellous nicknames to go with that of the Chaplain, "Podgy Barnes".

In June there was evidence of mumps going around the school, and the Shrewsbury boat race was cancelled as four crew had it. In late June Denzil was ill with suspected mumps and was away for another three weeks, just after he had heard that he had won first prize in the Earl Cowper English prize open to all schools. The mumps only seemed to be of a mild strain!

In the end of year exams he came first in Classics and Maths and third in French. In September 1912 the family moved to St Georges Lodge, St Georges Road, Bedford and back at school Denzil was now fifth most senior monitor and had to read out in prayers, which he found to be "A rather terrifying experience but did not feel at all nervous once on platform".

He greatly valued his friendships and worked hard at them, and on October 7th 1912 he reflects that he has now lost his best friends, Piercy, Charlie Anderson and Eric Hogbin, saying my best friend and two others have gone this week. "A kind of ten little nigger boys performance." One went to Dublin and then there were none!

It was about this time when a "startling development" happened at school, which the Head says was beyond the monitors to deal with, though the senior monitors discussed it, but we are not told what it was!

He was "bucked" soon after this by the return of A Gompertz to school after five years in India. A later series of letters from Gompertz appears later in this book.

December 1912 was dominated by Civil Service Exams and he stayed at Ealing. The King arrived at St Pancras at roughly the same time as Denzil, who waited but only saw the royal carriage.

Exams were at Burlington House and lunch seemed to be at Lyons, Piccadilly. The exams went on for nine days and he did badly in Maths, quite well in Classics, well at French oral and dictation, and adequately at History and English.

Once again the year is summed up at its end

Senior Monitor	R
Form Prize	R
Good Report	R
1st Corporal	R
1st XV colours	W
Shooting prize	W
Exams	Not sure yet.

1913 began with frequent games of chess with dad [all logged], and with Joan, his sister, going to the Mayoral Ball at Ipswich where Uncle Ted was Mayor.

On Jan 16th School started again and hence the entry, "School as usual and in the evening prep, bother it! A totally unnecessary plague."

On Monday 20th Gill goes off to Ditchingham for the term and was rather cut up at leaving [She did not enjoy that school].

On Jan 23rd Monitors for the term were read out and he was now 4th in line! Part of the inexorable progress to the top.

Once again, however, he was away from school for two weeks with an ear abscess, the result of being "scragged" at rugby, and just as he was feeling better the CS exam results came out – Maths an utter failure, the rest fair but not brilliant, but with a fair score for maths "I might have got in". Greek best and Latin next. He came 84th out of 290.

The obvious questions are " How did he come top of Maths in the school exams last summer, and was he getting value for money out of Sharkie Fuller?"

Any meteorologist who wants to check the weather between 1910 and 1917 may do worse than look at these diaries as there are comments everyday, and the record for February 11th 1913 is an interesting one – a most extraordinary fog in the morning, one moment all clear, the next one could not see a yard in front. Sun came out later and it dispersed. Many OB's attest to this as being Bedford winter weather caused by the river and the brewery.

My overall feel about Bedford weather at that time is that they had hot summers and snowy winters, often into April.

In early March Denzil had to take an English exam, and he read Henry Esmond the day before, when he was sick and at home. The actual exam was about four books

Across the bridges
Henry Esmond
The Mill on the Floss
Lord Beauchamp's career

He rather wittily refers to the latter – "Hadn't read latter so can't expect too much from it!"

He had to take the Exhibition exams at this time, as every year.

The term ended with the Evening School Concert, or rather the rag concert, for seniors. It started off dull but went very well towards the end

May 1st 1913 was the first day of summer term and a list of monitors was read out, with Denzil as deputy head.

At the end of May there was a two-day charity Bazaar that raised £1000, and he was in charge of programme selling, and he records much coconut shying and of seeing the Nigger Minstrel.

Recently, Denzil had taken a keen interest in photography and was taking pictures of birds. It is somehow reassuring to know that he went to Boots with Lambert to buy frames!

In late June he received a letter from the Civil Service Commission to say it would be impossible for them to alter the date of his oral and practical exams for Bisley purposes, worse luck! I think Denzil may have been pushing his luck with this but the Chief said he would intervene!

July 3rd was Speech Day and the school broke up at 11am to watch the county match. Apparently the speeches went well and Denzil called for three cheers for the Chief and the masters at the end of proceedings, before going to the Gym with Lambert to put on a demonstration fencing match before a big crowd.

The Chief told him to take two days off before the CS exams. On Monday July 7th he went to the station with Martin and they and a friend they met on the tube had lunch in Lyons Corner House, Piccadilly, a luxurious lunch with a band playing apparently.

His last minute preparation was very different to what might be recommended now!

As before he stayed with his Grandad in Ealing and travelled in to the exams in Caxton Hall.

The exams seemed like a case of déja vu, good at classics and French, fairly good at history and uncertain in Maths. Some of the three hour classic exams he finished in 45 minutes!

He had lunch at Slater's before the practical Maths exam, and heard that his oral and practical had been postponed till Friday week so that he was able to go to Bisley after all. Headmasters in the early 20th century clearly were powerful figures.

School broke up on July 29th and he was not happy as "He was enjoying himself thoroughly"! I wonder how many other pupils felt the same. We shall never know!

On the 31st he went to the station to see off Gompertz who was returning to India and Denzil regretted that he might not see him again for several years; "not a very cheering thought."

He set off for Kessingland but stayed a few days in Cambridge on the way there, enjoying croquet, riding, playing cards and conversation with Mr Nixon and his guests. On the Sunday he went to King's College Chapel and commended the service and said that the entire choir were men because the boy's term had ended.

The Autumn Term 1913 began on September 25th and the Chief announced his appointment as Head of School. Denzil was also head of Choir but turned down the Debating Society. Part of his job as Head of Choir was to give voice trials to all new boys. Another musical talent he had was that he played piano and organ. He records in his diary of October 13th playing, or rather trying to play, Rachmaninoff's "Richard Carvell" in the evening at home.

October 15th was his Grandpa's 80th birthday and yesterday Denzil's Mother went up to Ealing for celebrations.

On the 17th he went to see the Chief and managed to get three half days out of him, writing, "satisfactory I think!"

October 24th was a cold day and fires were lit in the school for the first time. Many will remember that up to the disastrous fire in 1979 classrooms all had fireplaces, though they had not been used for many years.

The section on sport reveals that Denzil lost 2 teeth in the rugby match v St Pauls, and the wound turned septic. The pain became unbearable and after several days he had the remaining front teeth taken out; he had been sedated by gas. He was away from School for some time and gave instructions to GH Field who would be acting head in his place. Denzil said that the tooth extraction made him look more of a "guy" than ever. I'm not quite sure what that means as we do not use this phrase now, but presumably it meant rough and tough in appearance! Curiously he never mentions having the false teeth he must have had at any later time in his letters or diaries.

On Sunday November 26th he went to Chapel and then walked AC Martin home to Milton Road before he departed in the morning by SS Warwickshire to Ceylon. I presume he was a tea or coffee planter like Gompertz.

The end of term celebrations in December 1913 would be recognised by any senior boys today.

14th Founders and Commemoration Service.

17th House supper. He went down to Mr Kirkman for St Cuthbert's house supper in evening dress.

"Had a grand time, supper and speeches and then a house play well acted and staged".

19th Choir supper. Topping. Finished with "Syne" and God save the King.

22nd OB dinner in Hotel Russell, Russell Square. Very swanky do. I funked my speech like anything, but got through with some éclat. Stayed with Granddad in Ealing overnight.

All these events still take place, though not on consecutive days as then, but a monitor would be involved now as then.

Rather amusingly, on the Saturday before the end of term, he and the choir got locked in the Chapel, and Denzil entertained them on the organ!

On December 23rd he delivered lots of cards, and on Christmas Day he went to Church three times, twice to St Andrews, at 7am and 4pm, and then at 5.50pm to St Paul's for carols. Today he would have attended Chapel at school on Christmas morning.

On January 6th 1914 Denzil went to Cambridge by 5pm train and went by hansom cab to Queens where the exams were to take place. On the 7th he had an interview with Fitzpatrick, President of Queens, and an OB. He did exams in Latin, Greek, French, German, Maths, History and a General Paper.

After an interview with the Bursar he went on to Ipswich to stay with Uncle Eddie at Highwood.

School term began on January 15th and he had a long chat with the Chief and was told that the £80 scholarship had gone to Hake, and the £40 to me [at Queens], presumably as a consolation; He records "am awfully disappointed".

In June Denzil was informed that there were no rooms at Queens, and his mother went over to sort things out. He ended up with expensive rooms close to Geoff Bull, who had cheap rooms so they could be close together.

As his school career wound down there was not a great deal to record. He had many chats with Chief about the new monitors and school affairs. He started to have regular organ lessons. He sung in the Mikado. He continued to take an interest in Photography. He helped organise the rag concert. He had musical evenings at home with Lambert, Proctor, his mother and Sybil; he obviously thoroughly enjoyed these.

He managed to get an extra half day from the Head [Was this the real test of his ability as Head of School? If it was an important criteria then he must go down as one of the best Heads of School ever!]

Higher Certificate exams loomed towards the end of July and he records on the 26th as follows " after tea I met Griffiths and spent the rest of the evening with him discussing Latin and Greek authors [get a life!]. On July 1st walked with Griffiths again discussing King Lear."

He thought he did quite well in Lear but badly in "As you like it". He had to do an English essay and French recitation with Mr Le Jeune [who still endows such a prize at school.].

On July 28th he said goodbye to the Chief and to masters and fellows and became an OB at 8.45am, "an honour I greatly appreciated". Then it was goodbye to his family and off to Camp at Rugeley. Whilst he was there, war broke out.

5

Debates and lectures

In the early 19th century Bedford was a county town of little more than 2,000 inhabitants though it possessed 2 MP's! It was a rotten borough!

Several factors led to the rapid growth of the town; the coming of the rail links to London, the North and Midlands and East to Cambridge and West to Oxford. These links were in place by the end of the 1840's and Bedford became a commuter town, with the fast train to St Pancras not getting there much slower than it does today. Also, Bedford was acclaimed for it's river frontage and for the longevity of its inhabitants. To these could be added the reputation that grew for its schools. The town began to attract those of the middle class who were comfortably off, working in London and living in Bedford.

By 1901 there were about 800 pupils at School, and its growth had necessitated its move from the centre of town to the present site in 1891.

The School was a mix of day boys and boarders and Saturday school was an important part of the week [it still is]. There were lessons in the mornings, and games and other activities in the afternoon and evenings.

The diaries show that a "Heriz-Smith" Saturday when he was a senior ran something like this

→ AM Lessons
→ PM
Rugby/ Cricket, and depending on the fixture being home or away,
Library duty
Fencing
Chapel Choir rehearsal at 6.30
Lectures and Debates.

This may have been more than for the average pupil, but the school needed to occupy their boarders as well as offering a very important facet of educational development.

Denzil loved words, whether he was writing, listening or debating. Sundays after Chapel included the long walk with a friend such as Piercy or Lambert, often to Cleat Hill or Putnoe Woods. Their conversations recorded for posterity were often about books or politics as well as school.

The debates and lectures reflect some of the issues of the day

The first entry in his diary concerning debates and lectures was a lecture on the Navy by DW Carr. This was in 1910 when the Navy Race between Britain and Germany was at full tilt and when it had become a big political issue – "We want eight [Dreadnoughts], and We won't wait" was a famous slogan of these times and confronted the Liberal Government with a real clash of priorities between social reforms and defence.

In February 1911 there was a performance of "The Rivals" in the Great Hall, acted by friends and members of the School and very well received.

As Denzil matured so he began to get more involved, and his first speech was in October 1911 when he supported the motion that "a system of protection against foreign competition would be beneficial to England". The motion was carried 18-4 and Denzil described his speech as "a success!" Free Trade or Protection was one of the great issues of the day that had split the Tories in 1906, and was about to do the same to the Liberals.

A couple of weeks before this the debate was "This house considers a system of Socialism would be beneficial to the country", and although he voted for the Opposition that lost, he was elected to the Committee of the Debating Society. The rise of socialism and an organised working class was seen as a threat by the governing classes, not just of this country but also in industrial Europe, especially in Germany, where some see her active foreign policy as a way to appeal to patriotism and sideline socialism.

In December 1911 the debate was "Germany's need of expansion will necessitate her attempting to seize our colonies". This motion was carried 12-7 though Denzil did not speak. The background to this were the crises of Algeciras and Agadir.

Just before Christmas 1911 came the Mock Trial of Kier Hardie, often seen by many as the first Labour MP. He was being tried for sedition and Heriz-Smith acted as foreman of the Jury [Disappointingly no result is recorded].

In February 1912 Mr Rowland's French company put on the Molière play "Les

Precieux Ridiculés", and in the same month there was a debate on the motion that "Classical education is better than Mathematical", a motion supported by Denzil as he struggled with maths at school.

On March 2nd 1912 the motion was that "Women are not made for public life or public life for women". He spoke for the motion as seconder but lost the vote 12-11. The whole issue of women and the vote was beginning to peak, splitting the Government, and seeing action move from peaceful to militant in some places.

This was followed a week later by the motion that "A first at the Varsity is inferior in value to a Varsity Blue". Denzil remained neutral but the vote was narrowly lost.

There then followed a rapid series of debates "That the Chinaman without his pigtail is better than the Chinaman with one". The motion was lost and Denzil spoke against it.

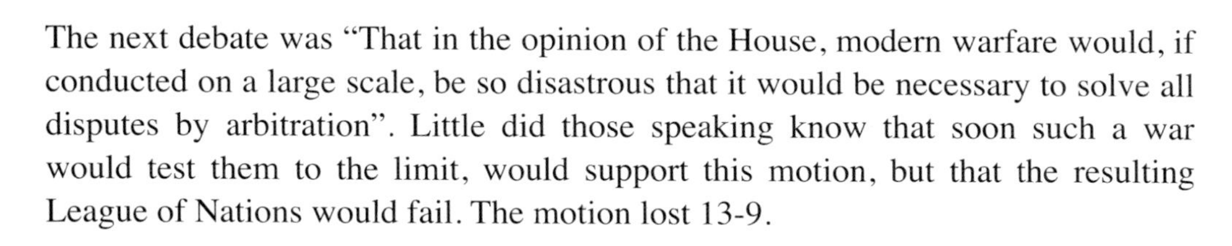

The next debate was "That in the opinion of the House, modern warfare would, if conducted on a large scale, be so disastrous that it would be necessary to solve all disputes by arbitration". Little did those speaking know that soon such a war would test them to the limit, would support this motion, but that the resulting League of Nations would fail. The motion lost 13-9.

The Debate with the High School, chaired by Mr Carter the relatively new Chief at School, was on the motion that "In the opinion of the House, selfishness is the predominate characteristic of mankind". Denzil spoke for and the motion was carried 24-23.

In May 1912 there was another debate about war, "That modern warfare would be more productive of misery than ancient warfare". Once again this motion was lost, but there was a poor attendance.

These two debates suggest certain uneasiness about international relations was beginning to grow.

There followed a debate that "This House believes that patriotism is the worse form of foolish enthusiasm that has ever appeared". This was lost 8-6.

The last debate of the year was that "Strikes are beneficial to the progress of a nation". This was defeated by the narrowest vote, and the topic reflects the greater militancy that was developing in industrial relations as our economy began to totter as Syndicalism increased and as the Labour Party began to gain in strength. The new school year began in September 1912, but the first debate, on the 28th, was on a familiar topic, "that Suffragette hunger strikers should be allowed to starve". The motion was carried by 13-9 but Denzil abstained, probably fearing female militancy in his own family!

On October 8th the motion was "That spectral phenomena do not exist". Denzil spoke at length as an opposer and the motion was lost 10-9.

On October 26th there was a Navy League lecture in the Great Hall. Denzil had to attend in evening dress as a Steward and Senior Monitor and said it was a very good lecture. The Navy League was a pressure group basically wanting more Dreadnoughts.

On November 16th the debate was on the motion that "The Turks be driven out of Europe". Once again a very contemporary subject with the Balkan Wars breaking out and one that Denzil reflected on in the Noon Star. The motion was carried by 13-4.

On January 18th 1913 Denzil chaired the first debate, motion unknown, and the following week the debate was "That cruelty is, has been, and always will be, a trait of human nature". Rather disappointingly, the motion was carried 11-7.

On February 15th the debate was the mock trial of WP Griffiths for breaking a window and being a Suffragist. This seems rather strange, as Suffragists did not believe in direct action to achieve their goals; perhaps the term was used very widely to include all those, including Suffragettes, who wished to achieve female emancipation.

On February 22nd there was what Denzil called "A glorious lecture" by Mr Dugmore on stalking big game with the camera in Africa. This was just about the worse time in the killing of wild life in Africa for trophies, so this lecture was very much a step in the right direction. It is estimated that Teddy Roosevelt killed over 500 animals in Africa, though he later came to regret this [but not as much as the animals slain].

On March 1st Denzil moved that "Science and Universities have produced greater men than warfare". He adds that this is not a good subject for debating on, but he won 13-3.

On Friday March 7th 1913 was the annual debate with the High School held in the High School Hall. The motion was that "Life in the reign of Henry VIII was preferable to life in the present day". Denzil spoke for the opposition that won 45-10, and his main opponent was Geoffrey Peel.

On March 15th He went to a lecture by Mr Atchison on "Northumberland and its birds" and described it as good and very interesting.

On May 10th Debating Society politics broke out. Quote "A violent attack was made on an action of mine as Chairman, and a vote of censure was passed on me. I resigned the Chairmanship and refused re-election. AL Martin was elected in my place." Intriguingly we do not know the reasons for the attack on his chairmanship.

On May 29th there was a performance of Sheridan's "The Critic" and Denzil presented flowers to the only girl acting.

Chapel choir, summer 1913

With his resignation from the Chair, Denzil's references in his diaries to the Debating Society become very sketchy, and it was not until December 1913 that any further reference is made, and this time for a lecture by Mr Keaton on wild life and the flying of birds compared with man's flight. "It was a topping lecture and there were three cheers at the end".

Finally for 1913 there was a School Concert on December 12th with a record attendance, with crowds in the Gallery and seats in the aisles downstairs [Health and Safety?], but it was spoilt by some recently left OB's rather rowdy behaviour. Overall though, it was a success and the Chapel Choir were splendid.

In 1914 there is only mention of one debate, though there were several lectures. The debate was at the end of January and Denzil spoke to the motion that "The tuck shop should be abolished". There is no mention of either result or reason for this. Was it on the grounds of affecting a healthy diet? Was it something he floated as Head of School? We shall never know, but it is still an issue today in schools.

On March 7th he wore evening dress for Abraham's lecture on mountain climbing. and on the 20th there was an evening of musical and dramatic entertainment including two parts of Pickwick.

There is a gap until the next mention of a lecture on May 23rd when Dr Levichs gave a splendid lecture on Captain Scott's expedition to the Antarctic. Then on June 6th he watched the rehearsal of Julius Caesar and then the actual play on June 20th. It was a great success and Leisching's Mark Anthony was "perfectly splendid".

Finally, Will Crooks, the Labour MP, lectured in the Hall, and it was "very amusing"! I assume he meant good-humoured rather than any patronising intent.

As Denzil's responsibilities grew at school so he made less contribution to debating, but this was compensated for by increasing socio/political comment in the Noon Star.

6

Games

Jeremy Paxman, in his very entertaining book "The English", states that if the French invented the Citizen, the English created the Game, and lists a number of different sports that we built up in the 19th century. He says that it had to be something to do with Empire, but also to do with the amount of safety and prosperity and the amount of leisure time. He goes on "The great boarding schools with hundreds of boys cooped up together in training for the business of Empire, made it essential to find ways of exercising the hormonally challenged". Sport came to occupy a central position in English culture

Some considered that the "Game " taught the importance of manliness, self-control and obedience to orders. Lord Northcliffe's propaganda during the Great War suggested that the German's inadequacy would be brought on by the lack of individuality because great sports like soccer had only been brought to Germany at a later date than in England. This rather overlooks the way the Germans gave much initiative to small groups of storm-troopers, who won huge early success in the March Offensive 1918 – travel light, hit hard, move on and leave the clearing up to the regulars. These were tactics that also won much success in 1940 in the Battle for France.

There are, of course, many counter arguments to this, one of which would be the collective rather than individuality needed in sports such as football, but there is no doubt that sport was a crucial part of the education offered at Bedford Grammar School, and similar schools, at the end of the 19th and the beginning of the 20th century [and now!].

There is no doubt that James Surtees Phillpotts saw the unity of the school, its bonding, to be improved by the introduction of a house system, still in existence today, where day boy and boarder are part of the same house, and that prior to this, day boys seemed to be left out in the cold. Soon after Phillpotts arrival, house games and matches in cricket, rugby and rowing were introduced, and that not only was the quality of sports in the School improved, but also spirit in both house and school rose enormously.

Denzil Heriz-Smith's letters and diaries show how important sport[8] was at school, the deference given to outstanding sportsmen, and his regard for those who played the right way, and dislike of those who cheated or displayed ill temper when losing! There was a way of playing, some would say, based on "muscular Christianity", and he is amusingly candid in his condemnation of those [often from the Modern], who failed to match the ideal of playing – this comes across in a letter he wrote to his Mother in November 1914 describing a recent rugby match.

I quote.
From Kent Gardens, Ealing, November 22nd 1914
"I played at full back for Company C v Company A and had a hard and exciting match with a good result.

"A" prided themselves on being a very good team as they had two Kent and one East Midlands three-quarters and two or three hot stuff forwards. After they scored 2 tries in the first half we woke up and finally beat them 19-12. From Geoff and my point of view it was very satisfying as their captain was an Old Modernian, the East Midland three-quarter I mentioned above, a very nasty and snide person too. Also there was another objectionable Modernian there, so we were very bucked up by the kyboshing we gave them. Then we had a grand hot bath at the place we have discovered." [There had been a near riot following a match between the two brother schools in 1911, and the resumption of fixtures occurred many decades later!].

Denzil played a number of sports, rugby, cricket, fencing, swimming, fives, hockey, athletics, shooting and some rowing. Not only did he play but he also watched, particularly during those frequent times when he was injured or ill; he does seem to have been a relatively sickly youth at times, bordering on being a "hypochondriac".

Denzil's first reference to sport in his diary of 1910 was for February 25th when he played for Bedford Harlequins against the School 3rd XV, and then in early March for the St Cuthbert's team that beat Bromham in the final of the U16 cup. St Cuthbert's won 5-3 and he played full back.

There are several entries for shooting but I will deal with those under OTC. On May 15th he watched the School play the MCC, and then, three days later, the School narrowly held on against Merchant Taylors. He records that Greirson hurt his leg and could not bowl. This could well have been the Grierson who later founded the XL Club, as there is a close connection between that Club and the School. Incidentally the match v the MCC is still played on virtually the same date as in 1910.

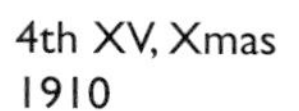

4th XV, Xmas 1910

In July Denzil was down at the river to see the 1st VIII beat Oundle in the final of the School's Regatta, and the 1st IV won the Grand Challenge Cup.

By January 1911 Denzil had been promoted to 2nd game rugby and he didn't get off to a good start, his diary entry for January 23rd says he was " jolly well sworn at for bad play"! but it was about this time that he took up fencing, describing it as "ripping", a feeling also applicable to the "lovely cold shower afterwards"! He was much keener on fencing than 2nd game rugby, and sometimes gives the impression that he was more concerned with the kudos rugby would give him in the school rather than enjoyment of the game itself.

Fencing lessons continued throughout the year, but the next entry on sport was in May when he watched the 1st XI beat St Pauls, with Maltby getting 108 not out.

The next rugby entry was on September 22nd when he played for the 3rd XV v Bedford Nomads but played very badly missing several soft tackles.

On November 28th he watched the 1st XV match v Haileybury describing it as "awfully exciting" with Bedford down at half time but coming through to win 20-14. This came just after their victory v St Paul's.

In the same month he took charge of a junior game, rather reluctantly at first but

4th XV, Easter 1911

became "frightfully interested in it and the kids", and he also watched the 2nd XV beat Oundle 50 – 0.

He also watched the East Midlands beat Kent 13-5 thus making them top of their group.

Finally for 1911, he mentions the Boarders lose 8-6 to the Dayboys, just before the end of term.

The diary entry at the start of 1912 contained his ambitions for the Easter term and a backdated comment as to whether he achieved this or not.

Gym colours	W
Robinson Cup for Fencing	W
Monitor	R
2nd Corporal	R
2nd XV colours	R
Good report	R/W
Retake exhibition	R
Win something in Athletics sprints	W
English form prize.	Postponed
Get into 1st game	R
Re-elected Chairman of the Debating Society	R

Entries for January and February 1912 show the 2nd XV beat Central Technical

College but lost to the West Yorkshire Regiment, a game in which he played poorly and dislocated a finger. At the end of that month, he played substitute full back for Cambridge Nomads against the 1st XV. He says he played much better in this match despite losing, and that this was the first time he had played in a first game. In early March he got 2nd XV colours.

The pattern of Easter Term sports remained the same until the early 1970s with rugby against men's teams as above, and including RMS Sandhurst, games that would not be allowed now on grounds of health and safety. Then at the end of term there would be the Steeplechase and Flats and Hurdles.

The entry for March 23rd, the day of the Steeplechase, described the weather as awful and the ground like a quagmire. Denzil finished the course after some stops and starts, but did not get a place, saying he got a "fit of coughing" at Putnoe Wood that "dished me up". He also describes Anderson getting cramp very badly and that he and another chap had to wheel him back to the finish on a bicycle! I suspect that he was quite pleased to have this humanitarian job to do!

Flats and Hurdles saw Denzil do well at Hurdles, but a curious entry on March 29th said there was a mysterious accident of Walker, Captain of Running, who was **SHOT** through the leg and no-one knew where the shot came from! Annoyingly there is no further discussion about this strange incident that seems on a par with being attacked by the school leopard in the spoof *Ripping Yarns* episode "Tomkinson's Schooldays" that was on TV in the 1970s. Was it a common practice in inter-house events at the school? Was there a "grassy knoll"?

On April 1st he fought in an exhibition sabre bout against Shaw the school sabre representative, and though he lost 3-2 "everyone said I won the last bout!"

On May 1st Denzil went to swim at the Newnham baths, opened for the first day in the summer [these open air baths were closed down in the 1970s].

The 25th July saw him at the Town Regatta accompanied by Piercy, and they watched the School 1st IV win two "terrific races" before losing to Bedford Rowing Club in the final.

The new Autumn Term saw Denzil in top game rugby and he records that he played badly in the first trial session. Nonetheless, on September 25th he played for the 1st XV against a strong Old Bedfordian team brought by C Atkinson who had been vice captain four years ago and who played for the East Midlands. The result was a 19-19 draw and Denzil was yet again disappointed with his performance.

Old Bedfordians RFC 1912

This is reflected by his comment on 30th September where he said, "I'm getting rather sick of making a fool of myself again," though the game was more enjoyable.

On October 2nd he played as substitute for Rosslyn Park against the XV, evidently getting the boot and "no wonder " as he missed the wing man two or three times.

On October 7th he played another 1st game, playing moderately and saying that "he would soon have to take up bumble puppy rather than footer if this goes on. There were very uncomplimentary comments about me in the Ousel about my play against the OB's."

Later in October he was touch judge for the 1st's v Oxford Edinburgh Academicals and "by no mean keen on it."

On October 19th there were matches v Haileybury and he went down with 250 others by special train to Hertford, had a sumptuous lunch with Yarde, Martin, Lambert, and Gompertz in a hotel and then set out for the two mile walk to Haileybury, just arriving as the match was starting. "Our team went to pieces and lost 22-16 but Haileybury played very well. It is a very fine school, buildings, chapel, grounds and organisation."

On October 30th he captained the 2nd XV in a 47-0 romp over Elstow, rather coyly saying that he had a shandy after the game, before returning by brake.

On November 20th the 1st XV beat St Paul's 20-6 away, but the matches against

Oundle were cancelled because a scarlet fever outbreak at the School

1913 began with some games of Hockey in Bedford Park. One of which was against Tisdall's XI [hockey was played quite a lot at School before the War, with the School producing both Blues and Internationals. The game seems to have died out after 1918 before being successfully revived in the 1970s].

He also played tennis at Priory Courts with Lambert, Martin and Tancock.

Towards the end of January 1913 he was in the first game Rugby and played in the three-quarters getting one try. After this, he rushed home got changed and went to the Gym for fencing, practising both sabre and foil with Lambert.

On January 25th he played full back for the 1st XV against the Central Technical College, played on a sticky morass, winning 18-12, acquitting himself quite well but being glad when it was over.

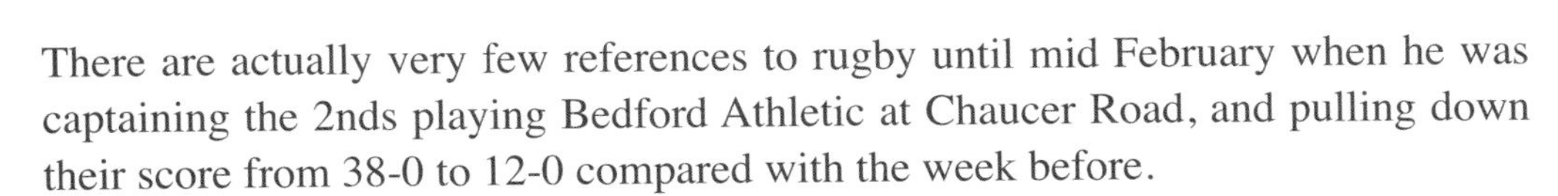

There are actually very few references to rugby until mid February when he was captaining the 2nds playing Bedford Athletic at Chaucer Road, and pulling down their score from 38-0 to 12-0 compared with the week before.

The end of February saw him in the 1st XV v Harlequins A with the School winning 52-0 and him getting two tries. He "quite enjoyed the match for once in a way", though "he dislikes being moved about positionally" – so it is not just an affliction of players today after all!

On March 1st though, he was not in the 1st XV team that lost to London Scottish A 21-22, hence losing their unbeaten record so far that term.

Gym VIII, 1913

March 4th saw him going to a fencing fight off to see who was going to Aldershot, and on the 6th he was awarded his Gym VIII colours.

His leapfrog into and then out of the 1st XV continued and on the 8th he played against a strong OB team including two old Internationals, three Blues and many other players of note. The School won an exciting game 18-14. The seconds lost 53-0 and the 3rds won 13-11. The six teams were photographed together before the match, and there was a pleasant reunion of many generations.

On March 13th the fencing team left for Aldershot and Denzil walked to the station with Lambert and Mr Atchison who was going up to the Boat Race [Oxford won after a splendid struggle by less than one length].

Denzil and Lambert went to Waterloo Station and then onto Aldershot, arriving at 3pm. They watched the boxing preliminaries and "all our men won their bouts well." There was a splendid dinner afterwards and then they had a topping sing. "The rest of our team raided our room next morning but found us fit and ready" [This still goes on!].

We watched boxing and fencing all morning. Morse dislocated his elbow but put up a good fight, before being beaten on points. I was beaten in the 2nd round of the sabres after an 'unsatisfactory fight'. [There is no explanation of this. It may be

Old Bedfordians, March 1913

that he just did badly, though he later told his mother that Bedford's kit was nowhere near as good as other schools].

We had tea with Oundle and then returned to Bedford having had a memorable time.

March 22nd was the day of the Steeplechase. The course was about 5 and half miles. " I had not had a single run this term and couldn't expect to do much". As it was, he failed to get round, the pace being too hot at the start.

The end of term saw the Flats and Hurdles. And Denzil was in 5 events.

- Throwing the cricket ball where he threw 80 yards and came fourth.
- Long Jump where he came 4th at 18ft.
- Sack race open where he was beaten in the final.
- High Jump where he came 4th at about 5ft.
- Putting the weight where he managed 6 yards.

These events were spread over three days. On the last day there was the Assault at Arms and he beat Lambert in the final of the Robinson Cup 5-4.

During the spring holidays, Denzil went to the final of the Amateur Fencing

Championship at Caxton Hall and also went to a Fencing Soirée at Queens Gate Hall. All the best fencers were there and he found it extremely interesting and instructive to watch.

On May 9th Denzil went down to the gym to fence with Parkin. There was some hard exercise there, doing some skipping, sabres and foils, running, vaulting and exercise of sorts, all, of course rounded off with a topping cold shower!

May 9th was described as an utterly wretched day, but the 1st XI played Mr Kendall's XI in steady rain, the pitch becoming an utter and hopeless quagmire. He sat in the pavilion all afternoon with Yarde, Hope, Geddes, Lee, Tisdall and others, with Mr Battenbury and there was a pretty hilarious party. In the cricket, the School got 189 and their opponents 164.

On May 21st Denzil played cricket for the Second XI and had a successful day getting 6 wickets though only 3 runs.

On the afternoon of June 2nd he watched the house match between St Cuthbert's and Ashburnham in which St Cuthbert's were 360-6 at close with Weir getting 173. The match carried on the next day but the result is never mentioned. He would be disappointed to know that there are no longer house matches at cricket, let alone two day ones!

On June 7th cricket was cancelled by an outbreak of scarlet fever at school. He would be interested to know that several sports fixtures in 2006 were cancelled due to a very virulent tummy bug [it briefly closed some boarding schools down.]

On June 30th the 1st VIII left for Henley Regatta but had the bad luck to draw with Trinity Cambridge in the first heat. [In fact on July 3rd Trinity easily beat them]. But! "Yarde, Captain of Boats, was away and so I was acting Head of School for 6 days!"

July 2nd was the starting date for a county match between Beds and Suffolk, and Weir was in the home side.

On July 19th Lambert came round to say that he had just been awarded his cricket colours after the win over the Leys, and on the 21st Denzil got his 1st VIII Shooting colours. On the same day the School beat the OB's by 5 wickets.

The next day saw the house swimming finals and he took part in the 100 yards race in the river by the Boat House. He did badly due to the frightful crush at the start and came in very low. It is hard to imagine the same event be putting on at the

Bedford Regatta, 1913

same venue today. I think Social Services might complain, not to mention the odd parent or two!

On July 28th Denzil was elected Captain of Gym by 7-1 for next year at the Games Committee. He says, "This was rather rough luck on Lambert."

On September 17th the Heriz-Smith family returned from Kessingland and it was back to school on the 19th. Denzil presided over a meeting of the 1st and 2nd XV's to elect the Captain and Hon Sec. Weir was made Captain and Leisching Vice Captain with Bull as Hon Sec.

Games proper began on Saturday September 20th in very hot weather on very hard ground. Denzil wrote that "he was more or less damaged with a sprained wrist," but he was there on Monday playing at full back, a position he preferred to the centre or wing. He kicked six goals out of seven in the trial match. He played there the following Wednesday against Mr Powell's OB team but an injury to Baker meant that he switched to the wing. A hard game was won 22-14 and he got a try and kicked two goals.

Denzil missed the next game with a strained shoulder but was at full back on October 11th against Oxford Scottish and the game was won 13-10. He had a lot to do, especially tackling and kicking [2 out of 2], and was given his "blue bags" after the match; he remarked that this was the first time he had got colours on the field.

The St Paul's match was on the 25th and it was a hard game that Bedford just won. Denzil lost two teeth tackling the St Paul's winger with both coming out at the root. However, he got his colours after the match!

Denzil made his come back on Wednesday October 23rd against Keble College and had a lot to do in an 11-8 win. Keble hit the upright with the last kick of the match and it was cleared with some difficulty.

The injury led to frequent toothache and this meant that he had to sit out the match v Haileybury in which the School won 5-3 in what Denzil describes as "one of the stormiest and most exciting matches I have ever seen." There was a huge roar from the crowd when Geddes got the winning try right at the death, as up to that point the School were losing.

On November 15th Denzil went by train to Cambridge for the match v the Leys. He was met at the station by Pullen [St Johns], and walked to the King's Head. He had dinner with Capel Cure in Hodges rooms. Incidentally the School won the match 30-8.

On November 22nd there were the match's v Dulwich. The 1st XV were out of school at 10.00am and went to Dulwich by the 10.40 train. We bussed from St Pancras to Holborn and then on to Dulwich by train, changing at Herne Hill. "On arriving at the school we were taken to lunch with the rest of school in the Great Hall, and it was very nice."

It was a very close and exciting match between two teams who had not lost to any other schools. We beat them forward but they were better than us behind. Eventually after the fiercest struggle I have ever played in they beat us 16-15. We had very bad luck, one drop only missing by inches, and in the end we got over three times, only to be called back for some infringement, and we were swarming all over their line.

After changing and a hot bath we had a splendid dinner in their Great Hall, about 8 courses!

We got home at 10pm. [I wonder what the modern generation would have thought of it all!].

On November 24th there were house match finals, and Denzil had to play in the centre v St Peters due to injuries to Baker and Hailstone. He comments, " I had a thoroughly rotten time. A collision in the first half left me winded and then another one and my nose bled for ages, and I swallowed some that made me feel sick. I was a passenger for the rest of the game and we lost 18-9. Due to the workings of the league we have to play again."

He was on the Games Committee, and the meeting in late November discussed the reflooring of the Fives Courts.

1st XV, 1913/14

On the 29th there was a match v Richmond and the Captain and Vice Captain, the Secretary and several forwards were missing being at Army examinations. Consequently we were well beaten and I had my usual bad luck with a blow in each eye, a strained shoulder and slight concussion! [Was he just unlucky, were they softer, were games rougher or weren't they taught how to tackle properly!?].

By the way, on December 3rd he dislocated his toe, and that was the end of his season and he had to watch the victory over the OB's and the replayed house match final watched by the whole school. St Peters won 6-3.

The final rugby of term was the annual match between day boys and boarders with the latter winning 13-9.

The first sport mentioned in the New Year 1914 was on Saturday January 3rd and a visit to Goldington Road to see Bedford draw with Edwardians in a poor game. [The Blues still play at the same venue].

The diary then jumps to the 21st and the cancellation of the fixture with Downing College owing to a hard frost, and then a week later Denzil missed the match v the Royal School of Mines due to a headache.

He was OK for the fixture on the 31st when he played full back for the 1st XV in the win over the West Yorkshire Regiment 31-10.

He continued to go to the Gym to practice fencing and to do punch-bag work, and he also watched the junior house final when his house came from behind to beat St Peters 6-3 in a rousing match. He comments, "well done our team, who played with any amount of grit."

But disaster struck on February 14th when the 1st XV lost to Merchant Taylors, something he believed had never happened before; even in a bad year you beat them!

This defeat led to team changes in the next game v London Scottish A, and he played in the centre and set up a try for Sturgeon, but in the process sprained his ankle and was a passenger after that! Still, a win is a win!

He was fit for the match v Downing on February 28th, and played well at full back, and for a change injured one of their men rather than himself!

Denzil continued to chair the Senior Games Committee that was looking at the

School versus Royal School of Mines, Easter 1914

School versus Merchant Taylors

rescheduling of the junior championship scheme, and later he was asked to codify all existing rules re-games, adding the comment "a pretty job too!"

March saw practicing of place kicking, fencing practice and then watching the run v Polytechnic Harriers in which both Lambert and Bull collapsed due to lack of preparation. He also practiced the long and high jump for the impending Flats and Hurdles.

School versus Downing College Cambridge, Easter 1914

He records that Shaw of Cuthbert's, his "dark horse", won the junior steeplechase, with Brereton winning the senior.

Denzil won the Robinson Cup for foils beating Lambert 5-3, but lost to him in a sabre exhibition bout. He also participated in wrestling.

March 31st was the beginning of School sports, and Lambert won the throwing of the cricket ball with a throw of 87yds 4inches.

Denzil came second in the high jump at 5ft 1 and three quarter inches. also running in the relay in 3minutes 35 seconds [presumably 400 yards, but even that seems very fast for the time!]

I don't think Denzil was anything more than an enthusiastic cricketer. In early May he went to town to buy some cricket boots and then played in second game trial. He got 19 but then "he started to slog, did not succeed, and in doing so, lost my wicket." Beautifully put and a maxim all aspiring cricketers should follow.

In mid May he went to the LNW station and met the Oxford University Fencing team and walked up to the School with them. He records a splendid afternoon, though very hot, with a good audience. Oxford won the Foils 5-4 but the School won the Sabres 3-1. They then had tea with the Chief and Denzil walked them back to the station. Later in his diaries he records the tragic fate of several of the Oxford team in the War.

Denzil watched several of the 1st XI matches, including ones v Keble, St Johns, and Christ Church. It seems to me that more seemed to watch School events then than now, I assume because of lack of other distractions and because it was more understood that one did that.

In early June Denzil records that he had to take 4 junior games at the same time. He got Garroway to do one. I don't think this would be allowed now.

He also acted as Steward in the "Incubator" sports and really enjoyed himself.

On June 17th he managed to get a half-day holiday out of the Chief, to watch the 1st XI game v The Leys. Lambert and Field both got centuries and the School declared at 307-7 to which the Leys replied with 170-3 – a pretty dull draw to set before the crowd! Perhaps they should have been playinglimited overs matches!

On Tuesday July 21st, Thomson, Wheatly, Lambert and Denzil went to the Priory

"Not so much a high flyer as it might seem!"

Tennis Courts for one and a half hours and then went to the Bonbon for some lemonade. Hardly worth a mention except that immediately afterwards they went to take an exam on Thucydides – a very long and wearying one too! How cool can you get!

It was now OB cricket week which always featured an OB concert on the Wednesday with singing and the putting on of the play "a Double Conspiracy" – he records acting as Steward and that the concert was very good and enjoyable.

He also reveals his Cricket averages for the term taking 32 wickets and getting 212 runs at an average of 19 – a veritable all-rounder!

On Friday 24th he was meant to have rowed for the footer and cricket[9] but he got horrible pains in the head during the Higher Certificate Exams and didn't turn out though he was at the OB Dance night.

This was the end of his School Sports, though he continued to come and watch at the School if he was off duty at the weekend during Army training; for example he watched a game between two Scottish Regiments based in Bedford on October 24th, and on December 5th the 1stXV v Canadians

Denzil continued to play rugby and cricket in the Army when this was possible as seen later on, and he was organising platoon cricket leagues on the Somme virtually up to July 1st 1916.

He was obviously a better than average sportsman, a 1st team player at Rugby [though he was very injury prone!], a cricketer who didn't take his performance too seriously, and an excellent fencer and shot. He did understand the importance of "bonding" at sport, decades before that word was used, and undoubtedly sporting prowess at School did wonders for ones standing there.

7

Aims and objects 1913

Denzil listed these in the front of his 1913 diary. They show how extensive his interests were, but also how he was driven and anxious for success. They are an impressive list, but also there was no way that one boy would achieve all these things at a School as large as Bedford, and, indeed, there would be no way that a Head Master would allow one person to dominate in this sort of way.

I suspect that Denzil's father was determined that he would work hard for success. Later on when Denzil got in to Queen's College Cambridge, Father reflected that he thought this was OK, as if he had another college in mind for him.

Having said this there was genuine affection between PPF and son, an affection that allowed plenty of ribbing with no harm done.

Easter Term

Sergeant in Corps	R
Deputy Head of School	W
1st XV Colours	W
Represent the School at Aldershot	R
1st in house race	W
Pass standard test	W
Win sabres at Aldershot	W
Good report	R
1st in form	W
Gym colours	R
Shooting prize	W
Speech at High School Debate	R
Win Robinson Cup	R

[6-7]

Summer Term

Deputy Head of School	R
Good Report	F

1st in form	W
Shooting VIII Colours	R
Pass Standard Test	R
Form prize	W
Represent the School at Bisley	R
House Shooting colours	R
High in Swimming races	W
Pass Exam	W
Retain Chairmanship of Debating Society	W
[5-5]	

Autumn Term

Head of School	R
1st XV Colours	R
Company Sergeant Major in Corps	W
Good report	F
1st in form	R
Head of Choir	W
Chairman Debating Society	W
President Games Committee	R
1st XV Cap	R
[5 – 3 – 1]	

R = Right W = No F = Fair

8

Aeroplane at Bedford School

July 24th 1913

In the evening Graham White [OB] who was giving an exhibition at Biddenham soared gracefully overhead in his aeroplane and alighted unexpectedly on the school field at 7.30pm.

Great excitement ensued and in less than 15 minutes 2,000 people were on the grounds and the crush was so great that it looked as if the aeroplane would be damaged, but "by dint of forming a ring and shoving hard the school chaps managed to clear everyone off the field."

"On the 25th School finished at 11am to see Graham White give an exhibition flight. The field was cleared so that he could get a clear run, but no one but the school chaps were allowed inside. Huge crowds watched outside. I have never seen an aeroplane up close before, and have never seen one rise from the ground, so the exhibition was pretty interesting. He left for Hendon by aeroplane amidst great enthusiasm at 5.30pm."

I wonder how many boys were inspired to join the RFC in the war by this event, and almost certainly Jamie Thornton was. [A contemporary of Denzils who joined the RFC in the war, and who was later killed in a flying accident].

9

Three letters from India

Letter from Gompertz to Denzil, probably 1913, written on board boat taking him back to India.

Oh! Denzil, I wish I were back. Every Sunday I think of the choir and every Saturday and Wednesday too. I pray for it every night and for all the kids for whom there is still an aching void in my heart, which it seems can never be filled up again. I miss every thing and most of all my friends – you in particular. Charter on board is a nice chap but I can't talk to him about things closest to my heart. You don't know how I miss some of those chats we used to have. If God wills it we will meet again, but it is all in his hands.

It is very hard to be plucked from those you love

There then follows a chat about relationships.

Please don't show any of my letters to Lambert as I don't want him to see them. Let the sallow one, Perry, Yarde or Griffiths see them by all means if you think best but not Lambert!

Letter from India from Arthur Gompertz 21-1-14

Tescaud
Shevaroy Hills
S India

My dear Denzil

Thank you so much for your nice long letter of the 26th inst. You ask for more detail about life out here. This is rather difficult by letter, as the fire of your question does not stimulate my information, as it would be if we were talking together. However I'll do my best.

At 6am punctually every morning, I hear "BoySirBath-

ReadySirChotaReadySirGoodMorning-Sir", delivered all in one breath and in a dull monotonous tone like a bee in a bottle. "Chota" means little, the full term being "Chota harizze", or little breakfast. This consists of 5 native-made cakes or pancakes of coconut milk, eggs, etc, and a cup of coffee.

I get up and have my bath [each bedroom has a separate bathroom] and go across to the stores, 400 yards away, used for keeping coffee before sale, implements etc, at 7am. Roll call takes place, each coolie answering to his or her name. We have only 30 women and 16 men. At present as the coffee berries are ripening it is a very busy time, and all the women are picking. The men have to go to the pulping house and pulp the coffee, wash it etc. It is then carried to the stores where it is dried on a flat open space, made of bricks and cement.

The native merchants or "Chetties" are beginning to come round now, offering to buy the planter's crops. Of course, the Shevaroy Hills is nothing but coffee estates- covered with them, most of them much bigger than ours. The coffee is priced by the bushel, but generally sold by the crop. E.g. we are asking Rs 11 a bushel [14/- 8d], but we hope to have 1,500 bushels to sell. Which will realise £1'100 gross. Of course on the big estates the owner clears a net profit of, say, £1,000 on his crops. But that would be on an estate of 200 acres whereas ours is only 45. You see, we have got nearly 300 acres of land in Tescaud, but only 45 acres is under coffee cultivation and the rest is jungle, and will be valuable virgin soil when any one cares to open it up. I hope later to plant a lot of fruit trees over this jungle. If I had only a camera I should take a lot of views of our estate, and they would be worth pages of description.

Being at the top of the hills [4,000ft up], of course we have magnificent views. In one part of our estate, we've got a very nice precipice 50 or 60 ft high, formed out of the rocks. A lot of monkeys live at the top, and when they are surprised by the visit, it is thrilling to see them jump off onto the tops of the trees below.

I haven't been able to shoot one yet, as they are so wily, and make off when they see I've got a gun.

We have no dangerous wild animals permanently living up here nowadays, but there is usually a panther [leopard] or hyena on the prowl.

Two people have reported seeing packs of wild dogs here lately, which is a very rare occurrence. Of course, they are very nasty animals to meet in a lonely place, though one would be safe from attack with a lantern, as all wild animals hate fire.

We have a goodly collection of snakes here, some of them deadly poisonous, from the cobra downwards.

In India one has many more servants than is usual in England. Thus, we have a Boy [Butler], a chokra [a youth about 15 to help the boy]. A tailor [whom we've had for 30 years], a cook, a waterman, a housekeeper, a sweeper, a cook's help, and a grass cutter. The last three only are women. Of course, when my sister was here and we lived in better style and entertained a lot, we had more servants, and, of course, gardeners. But I'm afraid everything is going to rack and to ruin in the garden now, as my father has been too old to look after things; and now I've come I am not too keen, and know nothing about gardening! So we only keep it weeded.

Natives are like children and one has to be more peremptory with them than with English servants. If you say, "Do this please" he will try and get out of it. If you say, "Do this" he will do it and respect you for it all the more.

It is very funny, even out here that there are class-distinctions, and our Club is very exclusive. There are some people up here who are not admitted to the club because they are not "not-not-not quite don'tcherknow"! And they are by far the wealthiest people here; so it shows we haven't been tainted by filthy lucre yet!

It is a great luxury playing badminton and tennis with an adequate number of scouts to pick up the balls. In fact their parrot-cry of "Barl, Sar!" is almost overpowering.

I am learning the language as fast as I can. Isn't it funny; I used to be able to speak Tamil perfectly as a kid of 10, and now I've forgotten every word of it. It's a great handicap in dealing with the coollies, not being able to swear at them in their own tongue, "understanded of the people."

In the hot weather, the plains are too hot for people, particularly ladies and children, so they will migrate to the nearest hills. This is what we call the "Season". There is no work to do on the estates, as the coffee is in blossom; the coolies [who like the heat] all go down to the low country; and there are parties and picnics and dancing and everybody is very jolly until the crop begins to ripen. Then comes the busiest time of the year [Now].

I ought by rights to be on the estate now, 9.30am, but the excuse of mail letters is keeping me in.

As I said to Griffiths "for heaven's sake write yourself and get other people to write to."

Well, I must stop now.

Yours affectionately

Arthur Gompertz.

PS Please give my respects to your mother.

I love this letter with it's gentle humour and irony. The relationship between boss and native labour should not shock and it is typical for the time, but most bosses had native welfare as a consideration, perhaps more so than the new types that he turns up his nose about, in such droll fashion!

Another letter 26-2-1914

How is the School getting on, and how do you like swaying the balance of nations in your capacity of Head of School?

I hear you have returned at last like the prodigal son, to your alma mater, the Sixth. Lucky brute you are! Think of the company and sights in the 6th. Only don't get under Liesching's[10] *thumb. A ripping chap to know superficially, but he has a nasty knack of ensnaring everybody.*

10

Politics and World Affairs

The 1910 election

The period in which Heriz-Smith kept his diaries and wrote his letters was a particularly turbulent one that ultimately would lead to the collapse of the Liberal Party and the rise of Labour as the opposition to the Conservatives.

The key issues in 1910 were the People's Budget and it's blocking by the House of Lords, the Irish question, the rise of female militancy, the size of the navy, the growing stumbling of Europe towards political crisis, and the welfare plans of the radical Liberals under the pressure of Lloyd George. There were also economic crises as the domination of Britain in world markets was both challenged and then surpassed by the USA and Germany. There was the growth of unemployment in the old industries such as coal, shipbuilding and textiles.

Both Denzil and his Father had a keen interest in the political issues of the day, and even wrote about some of them in the family magazine, Noon Star, that was compiled between 1909 and 1916. This will be shown later in the book.

They both seem to be to the right of the political spectrum, and we should not be surprised at that given the growth of new taxes to be paid by the rich and middle classes to help pay for schemes of Old Age Pension, National Insurance and Educational reforms.

Denzil heard Mr Balfour, the leader of the Conservatives, speak at the Corn Exchange, Ipswich, on January 6th 1910 and described it as "splendid", stating there was great excitement about the forthcoming election

Quite clearly the Diary entry in January 1910 suggests disappointment about the election results in which though the Liberals lost seats won in 1906, they were still able to form a Government with the support of Labour and some Irish. Attenborough, Conservative, won in Bedford, but the "Radicals" did better than expected, winning two seats in Ipswich, and also winning North Bedfordshire.

Denzil and his Father attended the counts both in Bedford and Ipswich; obviously electoral arrangements were different then.

Denzil was delighted to record some details of an election in 1912. On September 11th a Unionist won the Midlothian election and it was a crashing blow for the Radicals!

Death of Edward VII

On May 6th the diary states that the King was very ill with bronchitis, and that Denzil went several times to look at bulletins [presumably in Bedford].

On May 7th King Edward VII died, and George V came to the throne. All flags were at half- mast, and on May 8th the Dead March in Saul was played in Chapel. For the record, Halley's comet was visible as well, often seen as a harbinger of great events.

On May 19th he got permission from the Chief to see the funeral of the King. He went, together his father and Piercy, getting up at 3am, catching the train at 4.28 am. There was a terrific squash, but they got to the Mall and then Hyde Park though Denzil nearly fainted. He saw the King, the Kaiser, heads of various European states, Kitchener, Queen Alexandra and Edward Roosevelt.

On June 22nd 1911 Coronation Day was celebrated and he went to a service in St Paul's.

St George's Lodge was decorated with red and white ensigns, smaller flags, bunting and crowns.

In the afternoon there were aquatic sports and illuminations in the evening.

Domestic politics and industrial unrest

Denzil reflected on August 17th that he was glad he was at home because a rail strike had broken out and there was dislocation of transport.

Also there was a collision at Liverpool Street and two were killed.

By the 18th the price of food had risen and there was a military guard on every station

August 19th there was a great riot in Llanelli[11] with seven killed and several bayoneted by the military [not borne out by recent research].

There were scenes of distress throughout the country and much of the striking was political in motive and connected to Syndicalism. A political antidote to this was

Denzil's attendance on January 9th 1912 at a great Unionist meeting with FE Smith as the main speaker and with Lord Ampthill and the Marquess of Tavistock present.

The Titanic

On April 12th 1912 Denzil heard of the Titanic disaster – 45,000 tons he records. There are many more references to this and on Sunday 22nd at Matins as usual collections were taken for the victims.

The sea

Whilst at Kessingland in the holidays he makes several references to maritime events or sightings, on May 27th seeing a large cruiser and flotilla of 12 destroyers, and on June 8th recording that a French submarine collided with a battleship with the loss of 24 men.

On the 26th August the Royal Yacht, Queen Victoria and Prince Albert, with Queen Mary, Prince Christopher of Greece and Princess Mary on board, and a large cruiser escort, passed close by on it's way to Denmark.

Local

On the 29th of that month he records that Norwich had dreadful floods with 10,000 homeless. "The bottom of our garden is knee deep in water".

Allies

On September 14th General Nag, the Japanese General who captured Port Arthur in the Russo-Japanese War, committed suicide on the late Emperor of Japan's grave, to show his devotion, and his wife followed.

"What a shame. He seems to have been a fine man. That suicide custom among the Japanese seems to be a very foolish one and has robbed Japan of a fine man."

Vague rumblings in the Balkans

Balkan troubles were one of the causes of the Great War and Denzil reflects on some events leading up to this

October 5th Montenegro declared war on Turkey. The other states not decided.

October 18th War at last declared by Serbia, Greece, and Turkey.

October 31st Turkey at last wins a big success with it's field army near Adrianople, repulsing the Bulgarian attack

America

Oct 16th Mr Roosevelt was shot and badly injured yesterday by a mad alien, and at a few yards distance

Scott

Feb 11th 1913. The death of Captain Scott and his Antarctic exploration party after reaching the South Pole is announced. They died in March 1912 in a blizzard of 10 days duration during his return journey from the pole, when only 11 miles from a depot. A tale of great devotion

On Sunday 26th the Dead March was played for Captain Scott in Chapel

Miscellaneous

June 4th Derby Day – entered for form sweepstakes, but did not have the same luck as last year [won by Cragamour but disqualified].

August 16th 1913. 1st day of the Great Water Plane race around England [he never uses Britain!].

An aeroplane passed flying beautifully over the sea at 3.30pm.

A flotilla of destroyers, about 30, with a cruiser steamed fairly close in morning going north

On January 20th 1914 the Chief made reference at prayers to the sinking two days ago of Submarine A7 with loss of crew including the OB Commander Welman. The submarine had been on an exercise near Plymouth but never surfaced. All 11 crew died.

On Monday 25th May 1914 there were Empire day celebrations, with saluting the flag and a march past.

11

The School Chapel

The building of the Chapel was the principal event of the Headship of JE King. For many years the boarders and a fair proportion of the day boys had attended a School Service on Sunday afternoons at St Paul's Church. Soon after his appointment as Headmaster notice was given that, owing to parochial needs, the school afternoon service must be discontinued. It was decided in December 1903 that the only satisfactory course was to build a chapel for the corporate worship of the school, such as was possessed by the large majority of English Public Schools.

The funds necessary had to be raised by voluntary subscription and no money came from the Harpur Trust or the Governors. Mr GF Bodley RA was invited to submit a design in keeping with the preset school buildings, the money was raised and the foundation stone was laid on May 18th 1907, and the Chapel was dedicated by the Bishop of Ely on July 11th 1908, two years before Denzil's diaries begin.

The Anglican Church and the School Chapel played an important part in Denzil's life and that of his family.

It was his norm to attend church twice on Sunday and occasionally more on important dates in the church year.

Whilst at School there was regularity about how he spent Sundays, with the services interspersed with walks with either his family or his close friends such as Lambert or Piercy. He sang in the Chapel Choir and frequently read lessons, though it seemed to get him in a "funk".

His Father obviously was an important layman in St Andrews and the diary entry for February 1st 1913 has him meeting the curate Mr Howe and discussing future plans for the church.

Denzil also attended St Paul's quite frequently, particularly out of term time, and the entry for February 10th has him being present at the presentation to Canon Woodward in the Town Hall on his resignation from St Paul's

School Chapel interior

Denzil was not afraid of early starts and on Easter Sunday 1910 he attended the 5am celebration.

As a senior boy he took a large interest in the Confirmation services and seems to have been delighted in the confirmation of his young friends especially noting this on March 27th 1914.

One of the last Diary entries concerning the Chapel was that of Sunday July 5th "Chapel and then for a walk with Yarde and Lambert and then had tea with the Camerons." All these were killed in the war.

It is fitting that regimental crests from the wars and memorials to those who fell now fill the oak panels in the Chapel, as well as the rough cross that marked Denzil's grave before the laying of the Regina Trench cemetery.

12

OTC and Shooting

In the first year of the Head Mastership of JE King in 1903 there were not more than 90 boys in the Cadet Corps, and Colonel Glunicke, the Commanding Officer, was also in charge of the Town Corps. Owing to various difficulties about this arrangement, the Head Master was advised to take the command of the School Cadet Corps himself, which he did in the next year. This step helped smooth away difficulties and as a result more boys joined the Corps. King had to spend some of his time in training at Chatham, but in 1910 the cadets were transformed into the OTC. In 1910 there were 200 boys in it, and, of course, out of this came young officers for the Great War at a cost that is all too clear when looking at the boards in the Memorial Hall. Indeed, in June 1918 the King, George V visited the School and paid tribute to the splendid record of the school in the war, and encouraged those who were about to join the Army at a time of great gravity in the history of this country. He was very popular when he said that he had asked the Head Master to give the school an extra weeks holiday at the end of term to celebrate the royal visit.

Denzil had been in the OTC for some time before his first mention of it in February 1910, and it was a very important part of his school life.

In February 1910 he was promoted to the 1st section of the Rifle Company, but seemed to escape a row in the Corps about dirty accoutrements. He frequently shot on the school range – which was behind the area containing the school library today—and at Millbrook, near Ampthill.

On March 28th there was a miniature "Bisley" at Cleat Hill and he came third in the boys U17.

In early May he went to Millbrook with the 1st Musketry Squad and shot lying at 500 yards for the first time getting 51 out of 85, and he received his marksman badge in June 1910

On July 1st 1910 in Corps drill Denzil had to fix bayonet for the first time with 10 minutes skirmishing afterwards. This was exactly six years before he took his company over the top on the morning of the first day of the Somme! He also had become a bayonet instructor in the Army. He undoubtedly used the bayonet in the war.

July 7th was the Inspection, carried out by Major Ashmore and the Corps was praised for everything and did drill with fixed bayonets as well as a sham attack.

The summer camp was at the end of July at Tidworth, with Reveille at 5.30am, parade at 6.30am, drill between 9.30 and 12.30, and Battalion drill at 3.30. The Duke of Connaught carried out the inspection on August 3rd and Denzil described the fine sight of a forest of bayonets.

The School was 1st Company in the 1st Battalion, and marched six miles to attack a hill held by 3rd and 4th Battalions but were sadly put out of action!

On the 5th August there was a big field day with regulars and territorials. The School units had to defend against Territorials and the Yeomanry, and were just at close quarters when the "ceasefire" was announced; generally the regulars smashed the Territorials.

On the 6th there was a night attack that was "jolly fine"; why Generals in the War were so loathe to use night attacks is one of the abiding questions, particularly concerning the Somme.

At the conclusion of training there was a big singsong that Denzil thought was fun, actually the word he used was "ripping!"

In January 1911 there was a field day near Cambridge, and Denzil had to scout the enemy right flank, but there was no firing.

At the end of the month the Corps marched down the High Street with bugles and a horse and private carriage bolted, crashing in to another cab, overturning and throwing the coachman into the road. There is no further mention of this incident, but there would be hell to pay if it happened now!

Frequent corps drills took place in Park Avenue and the Kimbolton Road.

There was a review of the OTC's at Windsor on July 3rd, with 18,000 being inspected by the King. The School Corps set out at 7.15am, and Denzil makes reference to the sighting of three monoplanes flying near Hendon and several on the ground. They arrived at Windsor Park at 11.00, and the review was at 3pm. He mentions the fine sight of Coldstreams and Lifeguards, and the splendid view of the King, Queen and the Prince of Wales.

On October 22nd 1911 Sergeant Major Simms died suddenly and unexpectedly. Denzil describes this as a great loss to the School and town, and a "link cut off from the School as I know it."

His funeral was on the 25th and there was a service in Chapel, with the Corps in uniform and after the service marching to the Cemetery for the last part of the service. Simms was buried with semi-military honours and Denzil thought the whole thing impressive.

On November 3rd Denzil was made Lance Corporal in the Corps, and he was promoted to 2nd Corporal in February 1912, being 2nd Corporal in the 1st section of the 1st Company.

On May 8th at Millbrook he had his first shoot with his own rifle, and on the 24th there was the Empire Day parade. There was a march past saluting the flag with the Mayor and Corporation in their robes and the rest of the school being lined up at the Pavilion behind the Saluting Dais.

Less impressive was the Inspection of the 5th Battalion of Bedfordshires and the presentation of their colours by Field Marshall Lord Methuen, on June 20th.

The Corps went in their uniform and Denzil didn't think much of the aforesaid Battalion—" men fainted in droves, whereas none of the Corps did." He said they were a "scruffy lot" and didn't march well. [I wonder if this was one reason why he didn't join the Bedfordshires in the autumn of 1914?]

Denzil was ill for the School Inspection on July 4th and someone from the Bellroom came to his house to see if they could borrow his belt, as there weren't enough to go round!

It was about this time that he started shooting competitively for the School—for example there was a match with Marlborough and Glenalmond at the end of May in which he shot his best round of the season so far, 31 at 200 yards and 28 at 500. If he had got a bull with his last shot he would have won 1st prize but he hit an outer!

On October 3rd promotions were read out and he was promoted to 1st Corporal after 6 years. He says that more people were promoted over his head. "The Band of course! I might be a Brigadier-General if I joined it, in next to no time!" He says that he served about the longest of anyone in the Corps and was only a 1st Corporal. This was the same beef as he later had during the war, that he got overlooked and others were promoted above him. I cannot explain this but wonder if he was too outspoken and individualistic at times – he doesn't seemed to have suffered fools gladly very well. Did he have a tinge of arrogance about him that put some off?

On November 3rd there was a field day at Ampthill with Cambridge University OTC, Berkhamsted, The Leys, The Perse, Haileybury, Elstow, the Modern, Dulwich and Harrow plus others. It was pretty stiff work but we "walked into the enemy!"

In early January 1913 Denzil went with a detachment of the Corps to the opening by Field Marshall Lord Methuen of the new Territorial building in Ashburnham Road. The Corps lined the Midland Road.

In February Denzil became a Sergeant in command of 3rd section A Company, just in time for a field day near Cambridge. The Corps fell in at 8.30 and marched to the station arriving in Cambridge at 10.30. After reforming they marched nearly nine miles to Fulbourn where operations took place. Denzil started the march with a big blister due to the size of his army boots, and the rest of the day was torture. However they returned by 7.30 having won the battle.

In early May there were "furious deluges of rain" whilst at Millbrook and he got soaked through. "The weather was very detrimental to good shooting, for besides being very wet and uncomfortable lying in puddles the rain got into my eyes and aperture sight, and pattered up and down on the barrel. At times the target was a mere blur."

There were shooting matches in mid May with the School beating Wellingborough, Denston and Rossall, and then Lancing in early June. But in House matches he berated himself for carelessness with his final shot that would have won the cup!

On June 11 he went to Millbrook for "Standard Tests" and he was in good form creating a range record, by getting 92 out of 97, including 30 out of 32 at rapid shooting [8 shots a minute at 200 yards]. It might have been two better but for a mistake made by the marker.

On the 12th the whole CCF was photographed line up in 3 companies.

There were a remarkable series of shooting matches, often involving long distance travel [or it would seem like that today, and it is very doubtful whether a modern Head Master would sanction so many fixtures.]

On June 22nd they were at Runnymede shooting v St Paul's and Dulwich after a journey that took them to St Pancras, Praed Street and West Drayton in a journey lasting 2 hours 40 minutes. It is not surprising that they lost!

Two days later they shot against Clifton, Winchester and University College School this time with better results, with both 1st VIII and Denzil getting their best scores of the year.

July 17 and 18th he was at Bisley but the School shot badly at this prestigious tournament, nonetheless Denzil was awarded his 1st VIII colours.

There is barely a mention about the Corps or shooting again until February 1914 when he records going to the clothing store after school to get a new tunic and stripes, and that he stayed for an hour jawing with the Sergeant Major.

The next day he went to school in uniform and field day started at 12.45. He marched to Goldington with 1st and 2nd Company, had lunch, and then attacked a position on the Kimbolton Road, held by 3 Company. He records that "We were theoretically successful but there was a sad lack of ammunition!"

On March 3rd he reports another field day at the Old North Road near Cambridge. "We did a lot of marching and counter-marching through ground resembling a quagmire, but only got into action at the very end when we were charged by the enemy's cavalry."

On March 3rd "Beefy" Columbine lectured the Corps on shooting and the rifle.

In May 1914 the Companies were arranged according to a new system obtaining in the regular Army [Into platoons]. Denzil was now a platoon commander, the position he was in for a lot of active service on the Somme.

Towards the end of May he was back at Millbrook shooting against Denstone College, score not recorded but he shot badly. Later he returned to School and watched some of the 1st XI v the MCC.

On the 27th he took the Standard Test at Millbrook. He got 16 out of 20 at 200 yards snap shooting, 31 out of 32 rapid fire from 200 yards, but he failed badly at 500 yards, as his rifle "fouled up badly." He had to take this last practice again.

On the 29th there was a match v Marlborough, the Leys, Lancing and others in which he shot much better.

I am tempted to ask if he ever did any work!

On June 4th his platoon did engineering and bridge building

The 18th was a blazing hot day, and in Corps he spent practically the whole afternoon on fixing bayonets and "pretty awesome it was too!"

On the 25th he went to Colchester to shoot for the Eastern District Trophy; the school came 2nd and he won £2.

The weather was hot and sultry, with thunder on the 1st day of July but the match with Eton went ahead, despite frequent heavy showers and Denzil shot like a "parylitic popinjay" and returned a "vile score."

Annual Inspection Day was on July 9th and it was hot and dry. The parade was at 2pm and then salute and march past in close formation, and then advance in review order. Then there was company drill. The Inspection Officer was called a "jolly decent chap."

Bisley started on the 14th and the School came 16th out of the competing teams. Denzil had tea with Uncle Ted in the ARA hut, and then listened to the band afterwards provided by the Sussex Regiment, a "topping band."

On the day of the Ashburton Shield he discovered that he was too old to shoot for the School. He was "frightfully fed!"

His spirit, though, returned in the match v the OB's on July 22nd. He had the satisfaction of making the highest possible at 500 yards and this was an excellent finish to the season.

Speech day was on Monday July 27th. Denzil went round to Mrs Carter's at 1.30 and was introduced to Mr Geoffrey Howard, Mr Norman Craig KC. MP. [An OB], Major Campbell and General Layard. There was much conversation before the arrival of Lord Roberts.[12]

The School Guard of Honour drew up outside the house, with the rest of the Corps in De Parys Avenue. He arrived at 2pm and he was introduced to me and he said a few words. Then I went to lunch, invited by Mrs Carter, but found there were too many to get into the room comfortably, so "I cleared off" and acted as Steward in the Great Hall [do I note a tone of relief about this?]. Lord Roberts presented the prizes. He got the Tarbutt prize [still awarded to those who have taken an active part in encouraging others to participate in sport, and not necessarily given to those who were best at sport]. He also received a special prize [presumably like the Head Master's prize today]. Lord Roberts was described as "very kind". Denzil's speech went off well.

13

Summer 1914 in photos

Monitors at School Summer Term 1914

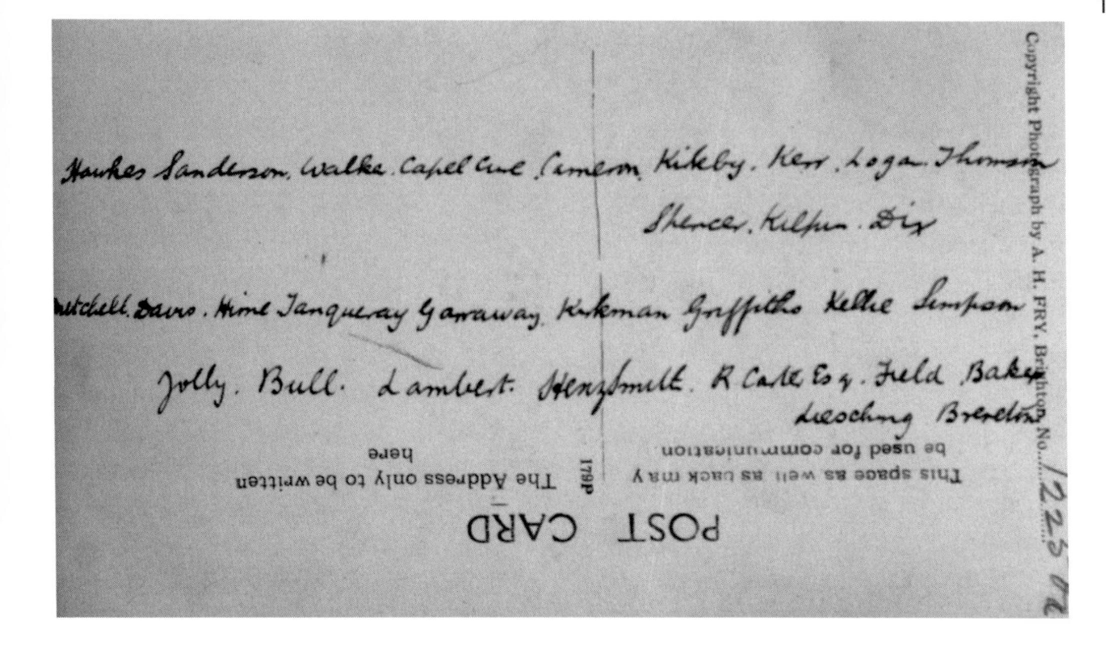

Hawkes Sanderson. Walke. Capel Cure. Cameron. Kikby. Kerr. Loga. Thomson

Spencer. Kilpin. Dix

Mitchell. Davis. Hine. Tanqueray. Garaway. Kirkman. Griffiths. Kellie. Simpson

Jolly. Bull. Lambert. Henzsmith. R Cade Esq. Field. Baker

Lessching Brereton

POST CARD

This space as well as back may be used for communication

The Address only to be written here

Copyright Photograph by A. H. FRY, Brighton No. 1223

Visit Of Lord "Bobs" Roberts to School Speech Day 1914

Bisley 1914

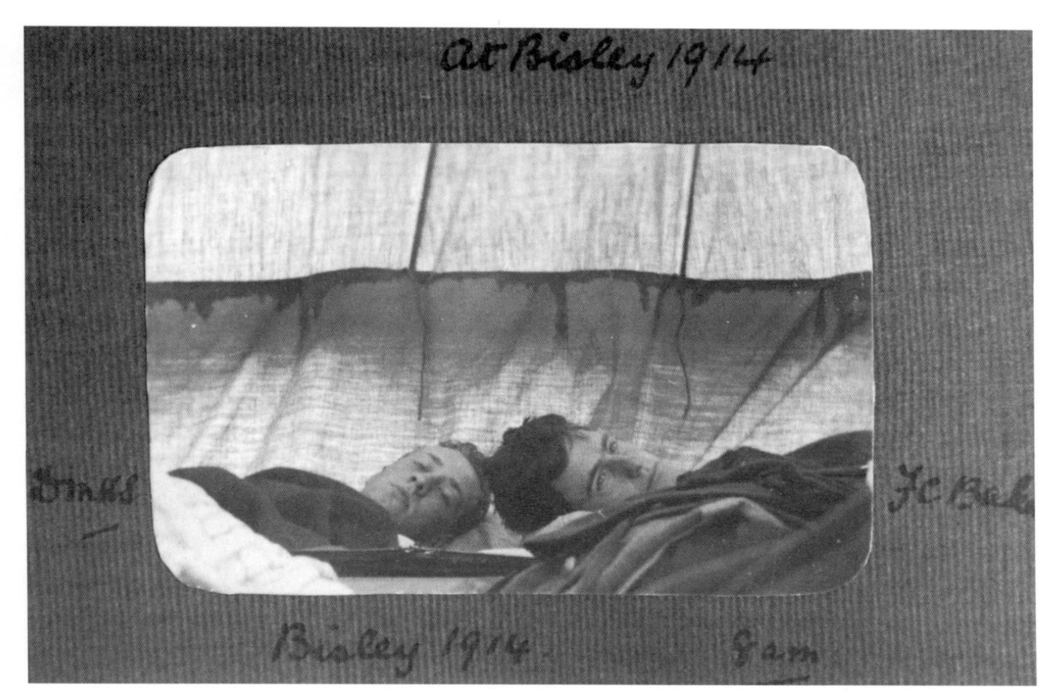
At Bisley 1914
J C Baker
Bisley 1914
8 am

Bisley 1914

J. C. Baker
At Bisley 1914

The Choir 1914

End of School!

1st XI cricketers
Summer 1914

Corps camp at Rugeley

This was Denzil's last event of his long school career travelling up by train on Tuesday July 28th. It was a "ripping journey" to Rugeley, in Staffordshire, in which everyone got put under the train seat and was ragged in the carriage in turn. They arrived at 5pm and marched to Camp – the photo accompanying this text is my favourite out of the whole archive, wonderfully capturing the spirit there was amongst friends at the end of their school careers, and not aware that war was to break out whilst they were at camp.

Camp began with a parade for prayers at 7am, followed by rifle inspection. Denzil was orderly Sergeant for the day and had to get up before Reveille at 5.30 and the work was hard in a hilly area on a hot day

The routine carried on with out post practice on

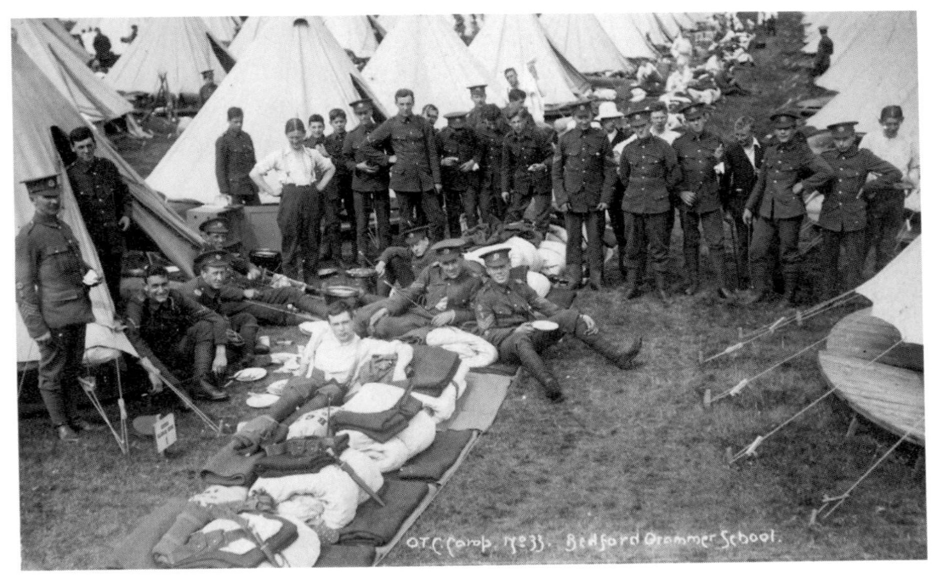

Friday July 31st. Alf Jolly had to return home leaving 7 in the hut; Kellie, the two Simpsons, Griffiths, Mudford, Lambert and Denzil.

On Saturday August 1st war was declared between Russia and Austria and there was considerable excitement in the Camp, as it was expected that England would join in. Denzil also heard that he had won the Railway Cup at Bisley.

On August 2nd war was declared between Germany and France. It poured with rain all day and in the afternoon there was a photograph of the whole corps.

On Monday August 3rd a "riot" took place in the camp, begun by Felsted and Lancing, and it was only quelled by officers appearing from the mess and then fall-in, when the CO cursed the Battalion. "We, of course, being in Church, were out of the row."

There were two small field days in which Bedford did well. On arrival at camp we found that the cook had gone, and so we had to supply our own, a job undertaken very well by Sanderson and Chappel.

England mobilised on the 3rd and the camp broke up the next day.

On Tuesday August 4th there was Reveille at 4am, tents were struck, stores and blankets handed in and the party entrained from Rugeley at 10am. They arrived back at Bedford at 4pm.

Denzil went home, showered, went down to the Station and set out for Lowestoft and then onto Kessingland.

War was declared by England on Germany at 11pm, because of "Germany's failure to comply with the ultimatum sent by England concerning Belgium neutrality."

Denzil was aware of considerable naval activity, and already soldiers with fixed bayonets were guarding the cable, boathouse, and the beach.

The world had changed forever.

Predictions of what the war will be like

Camp
Rugeley
August 1st 1914

Dear Mother.

I write in great haste. We are having a ripping time; march past for the whole battalion this afternoon, and inspection by some General. There is a report that all those over 17 may be asked to stop in camp for further training but this is entirely unofficial. If it is true I will do so.

This war will be a terrific and terrible business, but it will clear the air and it is a very favourable moment to settle with Germany if it is to be done at all. They may even offer commissions to the senior NCOs of the OTC but of course this is only barely likely, but the cost will go up like fun now and if necessary I will volunteer. It seems very funny to think that what we have so long dreaded is now almost on top of us. ***It is likely to be Armageddon now with a vengeance****. They will keep the volunteer officers at home I suppose though. All the officers of the camp are to be ready to break up the camp at a moment's notice and go on active service, so I may be home any time and then nous verrons, Monday is possible if war breaks out. A foolish and as it turns out unfounded rumour went about today, that it was to be half rations for the next week or so for us. I hear coal in Bedford has gone up to 8/- a ton.*

Well, well these are stirring times. I do hope this will wake up the Government about the need for training! So much for the Pacifists. I suppose the Expeditionary force will go to Belgium and Indian troops to Egypt. Germany will have an exciting time with England in Belgium, the English fleet at her doors, France in the west, Russia to the east and Japan in the Pacific to fight, especially if Italy remains neutral.

No more now except to say that I am very fit and having just drawn my pay, which necessitates a visit to the canteen.

I miss you all very much. This is the battalion Sgt Major just outside now drilling the guard.

Fix Bainets! As he puts it in a falsetto shriek.

Yr loving

D

14

The Chief's verdict on his Head of School

August 2nd 1914
Grammar School
Bedford

Dear Mr Heriz-Smith

I have been very much occupied in the present time, other wise I would have written to you earlier to congratulate on Denzil's School record. He has been an excellent Head of the School, and I attribute the satisfactory behaviour of the School, and the high standards maintained by Monitors, in a very large measure to his influence. I sincerely hope that he has learnt many valuable lessons from his experience. To me this has been a very pleasant year and it is with greatest regret that I say goodbye to

REGINALD CARTER, M.A.

Friends

Denzil. He will be sorely missed. I wish him every happiness at Cambridge and in his after life, and I trust we shall often see him at Bedford.

With kindest regards

Reginald Carter

The Ousel

December 17th 1914

With feelings only reassured by the dignity of my subject, I take up a long since rusted pen to compose a biography without the assistance of any register or description. DENZIL MITFORD HERIZ-SMITH, to plunge "into the middle things", as Flaccus have it, was born on the 21st February 1894, and entered the School, small in stature, but great on destiny, in September 1904. With steady progress he clomb the treadmill of our curriculum, shining like a good deed in a naughty world, I presume [for when I first met him he adorned the Sixth]. After a year or so in that atmosphere of erudition, during which, I believe, he gained his 3rd XV and 1st XV colours, and commenced his cursus honorum with an optionship, he dwelt in the Tents of Khedar ["which they say signifies "blackness""], or IC VI, for a period of circa two solar years. But as for this, as the Ousel's learned contemporary poet put it [and as Francis—Shakespeare had put it some years previously],

Esteem it as the foil wherein to set

The precious jewel of his home return,

Which consummation befell in the fateful year of 1914.

He became Head of School in the Christmas term 1913, and fulfilled the arduous duties of that post [which is that of Sergeant Major, Quartermaster Sergeant, and Prevot Sergeant combined], with the same vigour and skill which distinguished his lusty singing in the School and Chapel Choirs, and his fine play at the back for the XV. I was going to add, "quorum pars magna fuit", but that phrase is true of every department of School life. That was the best-earned prize on the whole list when the late Earl Roberts presented to him last Speech day, "For the best all round boy". He represented the School in the Gymnasium and on the shooting range. His fencing, particularly with the foils, was peculiarly excellent and elegant. He gained his 2nd XI colours for cricket. There was no branch of activities that he left untried, including fives and hockey.

His powers of organisation were displayed at every concert, in the Games Committee, at the Sports. In the Debating Society he was always the one on whose lips we hung. His eloquence had a mystic flavour, with a trend towards the personal, showing a vague hankering after puns, and as high a detestation of split infinitives. As a Sergeant at Corps he proved himself worthy of His Majesty's Commission, which he now holds.

He left the School after the Camp of 1914, long to be remembered, ostensibly for Cambridge really, we trust,

"To ride in triumph through Kaiserpolis."

15

The "Noon Star"

In 1885 Charles Heriz-Smith married Marion Johnston and their first years together were in India where Charles, an engineer, was involved in railway construction. They lived in India for 17 years and two sons were born to them, Philip and Selby, but both died very young.

They returned to England in 1900 and lived at Great Cornard in Suffolk where Charles became interested in market gardening.

During this period they had four other children, Joan, Denzil, Sybil and Gillian. All the children were talented, artistic and lovers of nature. Their summers were spent by the sea at Kessingland where Charles acquired a piece of land by the sea, at the end of Holly Grange Road. Eventually the house, "Four Winds" would be built there in 1921.

All existing archives suggest that the summers spent by the sea with friends and relatives were idyllic, until the war shattered everything.

When the children were old enough, the family shifted to Bedford for their schooling, though there is no evidence to suggest why. Was it to do with John Bunyan that appealed to their religiosity? There are some who believe Bunyan went to Bedford School [This is not something that the school archives have ever confirmed].

Charles's father was rector of Loddon in Norfolk as well as being a Fellow and Tutor of Caius College, Cambridge, and a close friend of the Archbishop of Canterbury, though Marion was the more religious of the two parents, having been brought up as a high Anglican at Clifton. Prayer was more important to her than art.

All of the children were artistically gifted. Joan was to become a writer and gymnast, Sybil a speaker and writer of verse who later had a close professional friendship with John Masefield, Gillian was a "dancer of spirit", whilst Denzil was a man of many parts.

From this well of talents there emerged a family magazine, Noon Star that came out twice a year from 1909 to 1917.

Noon Star was a remarkable journal of family observations in which they expressed themselves in comment, essays, nature notes, stories, poems, drawings, paintings and photographs, and competitions. The magazine has interested others as a primary account of aspects of pre-war England. The magazine was hand written and hand bound and involved all members of a very close family. Archival evidence suggests that in Denzil's short life his main passions were his family, his school and his country.

The idea for the journal may well have come from Sir Charles, who was a keen poet, who kept an album of his poems, and who frequently read from his book to his favourite daughter Sybil; her love of poetry and her future role emanated from the inspiration of her father.

Each member of the family took a pseudonym, or more than one!

Charles and Marion appeared as Sir Charles and Lady Mooring, Joan, the editor and who wrote the magazine, became G Bernard. She later became a PE teacher.

Denzil came under three pen names, R O'Neill, B Smithson and D Wilkinson.

Gillian was G Smith, and Sybil, who succeeded her sister as editor, wrote and painted as Mr Murray and M Lyttelton, M.A. She later taught elocution and did poetry readings at Oxford for Masefield, Yeats, Eliot and Fry, having been a nun for a short time at Malvern. She cared for her parents at Four Winds and died there in 1980 aged 90.

Gillian was a revolutionary character who hated her schooling at Ditchingham Convent, and who became a gifted dancer and a horticulturalist. She died at her own house, Marans, Kessingland Beach in 1987, aged 87. She was well known in the village and with affection, for her certain eccentricity.

Father was elected President of the Noon Star in April 1909

Friends and relatives are mentioned quite often in the Noon Star and some of these had pseudonyms. They were mainly from three families, the Stauntons, Schofields and the Ransomes of Ipswich.

The Noon Star provides a vivid glimpse into the local life of Kessingland, and the national life and opinions in England just before the War began in 1914. Journeys by road and rail and bicycle are described – a plane takes off from Benacre even, and flies to Corton; warships steam across on the horizon.

An entirely new line of family interest appears through friendships with Welsh, Scottish, Sussex and Yorkshire troops who were "billeted" with the Heriz-Smiths at Bedford on the outbreak of war; curiously this is never mentioned in Denzil's letters home.

The very last contribution is in a letter home from the Western Front for "R O'Neill" dated July 4th 1916.

Volumes 1 to 4 are bound separately in green cloth and run from 1909-13.

Volumes 5 and 6 consist of 10 pamphlets of stitched paper.

There is a large amount of poetry in *Noon Star*, and also in the exercise book belonging to Denzil, which accompanies the magazine.

This is his first poem.

June 1911

The moon is shining peacefully,
No cloud rack dims the sky;
And ripples lapping 'gainst green banks
Breathe a sweet lullaby.
The river dankling rolls it's course
In stately majesty

Upon its bosom dark and drear
A gentle breeze doth play;
It's swaying rushes seem to weep
For the departed day.
And God hath sent his restful sleep
Man's troubles to allay.

Hushed is the breeze, the ripples still;
A death like silence falls
And now with dismal croak nearby
The house night raven calls—
That harbinger of mighty woes
Whose dreadful cry appals.

And hark! A threatening murmur shrill
Answers the raven's cry
The wind with soughing breath awakes
And whistles down the sky.
Those sombre clouds that hide the moon
Denote a tempest nigh.

A vivid blinding glare bursts forth
From out yon riven cloud
The heavens tremble with a crash
Of thunder, deep and loud.
And peel on peel succeeding roars
With greater power endowed.

And so when life a placid course
And even way pursues
Look thou for storms, nor deem thou'st safe
For all it's brilliant hues.

And in the summer of 1912 he publishes another on the same theme

The Storm

With mighty crash Jove's thunder roll,
Resounds the heaven from pole to pole,
The Levin brand with blinding glare
Resistless stabs the quivering air
And mark! How on yon distant shore
The thunderous surges ceaseless roar
The shrieking storm wind sweeps the strand
Upraising blinding clouds of sand
Till Pluvius Jove o'er hill and plain
Pours forth a sheet of hissing rain
Appolo's beams can find no way
Through scudding racks of dreary grey.

Hushed is the roar, the wind is still;
The storm fiend now has worked his will
Vain hope! For lo! With matchless might
A livid streak of dazzling light
Speeds forth from out yon riven cloud
Followed by mutterings long and loud.

Another flash! The shattered oak
Long rues the lightning's deadly stroke
For scorched and blackened by it's side
Lie branches that have long defied
The utmost power of wind and rain

Which oft to wreck them strove a main
Anon the wind from soft repose
With added strength once more arose
And drove the clouds athwart the sky
Apace, till far away did die
The growling thunder; and again
Was heard the ceaseless pattering rain.

And a comic and rather dark attempt

The Eerie Wiggle – about superstition

"Why was it", earwig you will say
"You did not kill me yesterday,
when round me lay companions slain?"
I did not shrink from giving pain;
"Twas not because my mood was kind;
Twas not that I felt so inclined;
Tis safe to say that of your tribe
Each earwig I have caught has died.
"What then – perhaps you'll say to me
has caused such wondrous clemency?"
to such a query I'll reply
"No superstitious fool am I
for yesterday 'twix dawn and e'er
I slew what earwigs could be seen
Twelve were they – you'd have made 13"

On to a weightier and contempory

August 25th 1912

Ad Turcos
The Turko-Balkan War 1912

Where is now that pomp and splendour
And that pride with which of late
Into battle's turmoil entered,
O ye Turks, ye bearded fate.

Through your camps in livid vesture
With a slow funereal tread
Stalks a wan and ghostly spectre
Glorying in his heaps of dead.

Better far were sword or lance thrust
Bursting shrapnel, screaming shell
Than in agonies to perish
By a death so grim and fell.

In your midst are plague and famine
Death by shot or shell before,
In the near inglorious safety
And respite from grievous war

Now show forth that dauntless courage
To your father's hearts so dear
Might that, e'en in distant peril
Mocked at death and knew not fear

Pride and honour both now bid you
Bravely win or fighting die
As your fathers fought at Plevna
Under Osman Pasha's eye.

So fight on, ye gallant warriors,
Rise superior to your woes;
Fight; and from your country's borders
Back in triumph hurl your foes.

I have selected a number of articles written by Denzil on topics that were of importance at that time, and which appeared in the Noon Star.

Some views on women's suffrage

By R O'N Volume 4 number 1

I have entered, I know, perhaps somewhat rashly upon a subject of a decidedly, or even fiercely controversial nature, but I will make no apologies for a very simple reason that the relentless editor has driven me into a corner out of which I may not escape till I have written something for the edification, or the reverse, of the readers of Noon Star.

My views on the subject are of a very decided character, and I care not who knows it. I will therefore do my best to unfold a few of those that I feel to be most important. In order not to leave the reader in doubt any longer, I will at once say that my camp is that of the anti-female suffrage party.

Upon careful consideration of the whole question I have come to the conclusion that there is but one redeeming feature about the attempt to gain the suffrage for women, and even that is a purely extraneous one. It is that this particular movement does not owe it's existence to the efforts of a zealous party politician engaged in an attempt to strengthen his position by cramming rare and refreshing fruit into the mouths of classes and persons already near choking in their efforts to masticate the last dose. That, I say, is, in my opinion, the only redeeming feature of the movement, and even so, great as it is, it fails utterly to convince me of the equity, reasonableness or the feasibility of the scheme.

I shall only review one or two of the numerous arguments against the movement, not only from the fear of engaging too much space in this magazine, but also for my time is very limited.

The most obvious objection to the conferring of the suffrage on women is that such a measure would vastly increase an already "overcrowded" suffrage. The franchise is far too broad now without the introduction of a large number of women to make things worse [I am leaving out for the moment the question of the fitness and ability of women generally to exercise the power of voting]. There are in the present electorate thousands of men who know nothing about, and care less for, the person or object for which they vote. There is yet another class comprised of those who only vote for or against a measure that concerns themselves, taking no thought of their responsibility to the nation and empire, and I hold that the introduction of many thousands of women voters will increase this class of voters, already sufficiently large, to a positively dangerous extent.

The present Radical government is pledged to bring in a measure conferring the vote to all men of over a fixed age. In such a case, and granted that their demands are acceded to and that women who possess the property qualification, are admitted to the suffrage, the government of the time can hardly help bringing in a measure of universal women's suffrage. To a Conservative and Unionist, the very idea of Universal Suffrage must be abhorrent, as one that reeks of Socialism,

There seems to be hardly a doubt that the government took this measure as a way out of the almost inevitable disaster that would occur to themselves if they gave the suffrage to women who possessed the property qualification. It is almost certain that the mass of these women would vote Unionist, and the Radicals probably think that by conferring the suffrage on all men, they will be able to counterbalance this gain to the Unionists, on the assumption that the majority of men of the lower classes would vote for them if enfranchised.

I am unfortunately precluded from approaching the question of the ability or otherwise of women, both physically and in temperament, to exercise the power of voting, by lack of space and time, much as I should like to do., but I will refer the readers of Noon Star, if their interest in this subject is sufficient, to the pages of an esteemed contemporary "The Standard". They will gain from the perusal of the Women's Column [if only they have the patience], a fact or two, here and there, a knowledge of the way in which English should not be written, and incidentally, much diversion and enjoyment, not to mention a splendid view of human nature and it's crochets. To do this however they will have to delve into a great conglomeration of utter and unadulterated humbug, to wade through seas, or rather oceans, of nonsense, and probably to endure all the discomforts of a sea voyage in the process.

Before I conclude I should like to record a protest against the actions of the Suffragists and "Antis" in dragging such a subject such as a subject like the Titanic disaster, into the turmoil of their war. Many of the Suffragists indeed have gone utterly beyond the bounds of decency and good feeling in their letters on the subject.

My readers have almost certainly heard of the maniacal outbursts, recently, on the part played by the Suffragettes in smashing windows of unoffending shopkeepers and doing damage to the value of several thousand pounds. It is idle to assert that only a few Suffragists do this, and that no condemnation of the movement should be found in their account.

I say most emphatically that the militant suffragettes have, in many ways, more of my respect than the others, for they have, at any rate, the courage of their convictions, and they are certainly the leaders of the movement.

To conclude; putting all the questions on one side [and amongst others that burning question, so long and eagerly disputed in the Standard, as to whether St Paul was a suffragist or not!], I give it as my opinion that it will be a disastrous day for England when any measure of female suffrage whatsoever is passed by Parliament.

Home rule for Ireland

By R O'N Volume 4 number 3

My digression last week was too long so that I should go straight to the point without further loss of time.

Different opinions are, of course, held on the amount of public behaviour bestowed on the Home Rule Bill.

The more advanced radicals welcome a measure of Home Rule for Ireland merely as a step forward in a general policy of decentralisation. They would like eventually to grant a measure of autocracy to Scotland and Wales as well.

The Unionists are horrified by the mere thought of separation and prophesy oppression for the Ulstermen, misgovernment, anarchy and all sorts of evil as a result of it. *[A view still held by the Reverend Ian Paisley almost 100 years later!].*

A few of the more shallow minded of both parties favour it only as a welcome relief from the present domination at present exercised over the government by the Irish Party in Parliament.

There is little doubt in the writer's opinion that the majority of English voters are opposed to the measure, and still less that the major position of the Irish electorate are enthusiastic supporters of it.

The Ulster Protestants [who form a very strong and vigorous minority] are certainly bitterly opposed to the Bill, and are even at present aiming to prevent it being passed. Their leaders go as far as to use the threat of civil war but how far they are justified in taking such a strong line seems to the writer to be very doubtful. Even as a threat it seems to be a very violent form of intimidation, and as a fact it is almost unthinkable. It also gives the Suffragists and all advocates of violent methods a very good excuse for using them, when the leader of a great political party gives his full approbation and support for these threats, and this cannot be too strongly deprecated.

In spite of these views the writer finds it very difficult to see what else the Ulsterman could do owing to the fact, as was said above, the Government, which clings to power at all costs like a limpet to a rock, is not in this case supported by the majority of English public opinion.

This policy of clinging onto office necessarily entails some pandering to the desires of the Nationalists, in order to retain that support which renders their precarious position just tenable and no more. The half hearted method in which the government is proceeding in this case show up the bill, not as a "sop to Cerberus" but as a foretaste of the said sop which is not to be given till Cerberus shows signs of restlessness, when it may be dolled out to him – always with reservations and piece by piece.

It is, in fact, very difficult to steer a middle course between two such extremes, or to avoid bigotry, and the writer confesses to an utter inability to do so. He abominates the very thought of separation, and equally detests any measures which will give a handle to advocates of violent methods, whether Suffragettes, Ulstermen or anyone else.

But worse than this hate of violent and unlawful methods and attempts on the King's peace, is his loathing for that corrupt, tottering and effete administration that gives cause for these and other bitter grievances to be aired in such a fashion as Home Rule.

The only remedy, in fact, that the writer can suggest is that the Government should forthwith appeal to the country making Home Rule the chief plank in their platform, and then that question at last could be satisfactorily settled.

Whether, if Home Rule was granted, fair presentation and adequate consideration would be granted to Ulster, seems to be the case for the conscience of Mr John Redmond, though the writer has his own thoughts on the subject. Or what would happen if the positions of the Nationalists and Ulstermen were reversed? He also has his opinions, and they do not tend to better his views on human nature.

The Turco-Italian War
Vol4 4

The war in Tripoli, if it can be called such, is a very curious affair. There was, indeed, some sharp fighting on a small scale shortly after the declaration of war, but since then, save for a few spasmodic efforts on both sides, there has been no action worth speaking of. In fact, hostilities on the Italian side seem to be confined to a little bomb dropping by aeroplanes, some shell firing at intervals, and a few sudden descents on islands in the Aegean Sea.

The warlike operations of the Turks are perhaps even less energetic, and they are confined to the hasty "sauve qui peut" on the part of the Turkish Governor and troops, which ensues on the occupation of each paltry island by the Italians. The Turks, however, may be excused for their inaction, as besides their everlasting troubles with the dwellers in the Yemen, they are always on the verge of war with one or other of the Balkan States; just now it is Bulgaria, a short while ago it was Montenegro as well. Albania too is always ready to take advantage of any trouble that may be floating about, and there is always the pleasant possibility of a "scrimmage" with all the states put together. In that case Austria, Russia, France, Germany and England will all want fingers in the pie, which will probably be very hot indeed and each or all will burn their fingers in it.

Then again, there is no possibility of doing much in Tripoli as the Turkish troops there are isolated, owing to the fact that Italy commands the sea. They can get no reinforcements and very little help from anywhere, and have to rely on the Arabs, who, though decent enough fighters, are not always quite amenable to discipline and have, in all likelihood, other irons in the fire. However, they do help the Turks in their own fashion, [the Turkish commander, by all accounts a very fine man, is an Arab by descent], but the latter are hopelessly outnumbered and have no resources to fall back on like their opponents. Given anything like equal numbers and resources I believe there would be very few Italians in Tripoli, and they would be prisoners. The Turkish fleet cannot and will not fight, not only because they have no ships worth mentioning to oppose the fine Italian vessels, but also because the Turks have always made very poor sailors, just as they have made very good soldiers. The battle of Navarino, and the easy Russian victory at Sinope in the Crimean War are sufficient proofs of the wretched state of the Turkish fleet, just as the defence of Plevna and other feats form sufficient testimony to the excellence of the Turks as soldiers. Furthermore their English organising admiral has, of course, been ordered home so they are not likely to do anything at all.

All the little pic-nics [sic], however, which the Italians indulge in cost money and the result is that whereas the Turks appear to have spent very little money on the war, the Italians have already spent millions of pounds and are not much nearer to their object, the possession of the Tripolitain region, than before.

There are, every now and then, rumours of approaching peace, but nothing ever comes of them, and the war drags on and will probably drag on some time longer.

The Italian national honour will not rest satisfied till Tripoli is added to the Italian dominions. In other words, Italian national honour is pledged to a gross theft and Turkish national honour with more reason, refuses to allow the Italian burglar to carry off the spoils in peace.

*Personally the writer is all in favour of the Turks, first for the above mentioned reason, and secondly because, although the Turks have, again and again, proved themselves to be incompetent as administrators, he has no wish to see the Turkish Empire, or rather what is left of it, dismembered; lastly because he has not much admiration for the Italians [en passant he never could by any chance admire Garibaldi!].*Despite Garibaldi being given a hero's welcome when he came to Bedford in the 1860's!

Were it not that England is, and had always been, a friend of Italy, I should think it would be to her advantage to go in and attack Italy, if only to remove, at least for the time being, an element of danger in the Mediterranean. Only nowadays one cannot have a good "mill" without the immediate congregation of crowds of vultures to the spot, to snap up anything they can get, or [an even more likely cause] to pick a quarrel with the victor. I shall end this article with pious wish that Turkey may obtain peace with honour, and that Italy may get her deserts, which is certainly not Tripoli.

It must be remembered that a sixteen-year-old boy wrote these articles, and they reveal a conservative outlook but one tinged by pragmatism. His article about the Turks and the possible break up of their Empire and the effect this would have on the great powers, is not that far off the mark in the immediate run-up to WW1.

Eventually the theme of the war intrudes on the journal, beginning a little before it's outset and continuing up to Denzil's death in 1917. However, Volume 5, number 3, the last to appear before the war, has an item of literary interest with the news that *"Those eminent authors H Rider Haggard and Rudyard Kipling were seen strolling arm in arm "along the briny beach"*, and that this was a cause of excitement in Kessingland on Sunday April 13th 1913.

Sybil contributed a colourful account of her travels in Belgium where she fell in love with Bruges, not knowing that in a few months it would be under German occupation.

Generally speaking the family's view of the Great War was one of fierce patriotism to the mother country, and support of the war effort, whatever their misgivings about the causes of the conflict and their fears and doubt about it. Generally it was seen as a fight between right and wrong.

Denzil's frustrations about not getting out to the front quickly enough reveal this family zeal.

Extract from Noon Star Vol VI No II

December 31st 1914 Christmas 1914 Special Number.

A titanic struggle, in which nearly every nation of the civilised world is engaged, and by which certainly all are affected, has converted Europe into one vast battlefield; it is draining Britain, France, Russia, Serbia, Germany and Austria of gold and supplies, and of that which is more precious than either, of the best and bravest of their sons; and it has left one nation, with devastated fields, and smoking homesteads from which the inhabitants have fled or under the ruins they lie buried, martyred by the invading German hoard; but it has left that nation with an imperishable name and has revealed her to the eyes of the world as endowed with the qualities which go to form, whether in a country or in individual man, an heroic soul. That the virtues, which have established the greatness of Belgium for all time, are personified in her ruler has often been repeated. We feel as if we know him – Albert the Brave — as if he belonged in some subtle way to us a little as well as to his own subjects; for his courage, his self-sacrifice, his simple dignity, and the care and sympathy he shows for his people in this terrible hour of their need, and his devotion for the very soil of his country, we salute him, and not the man only, but the Spirit of Patriotism which animates alike both King and people.

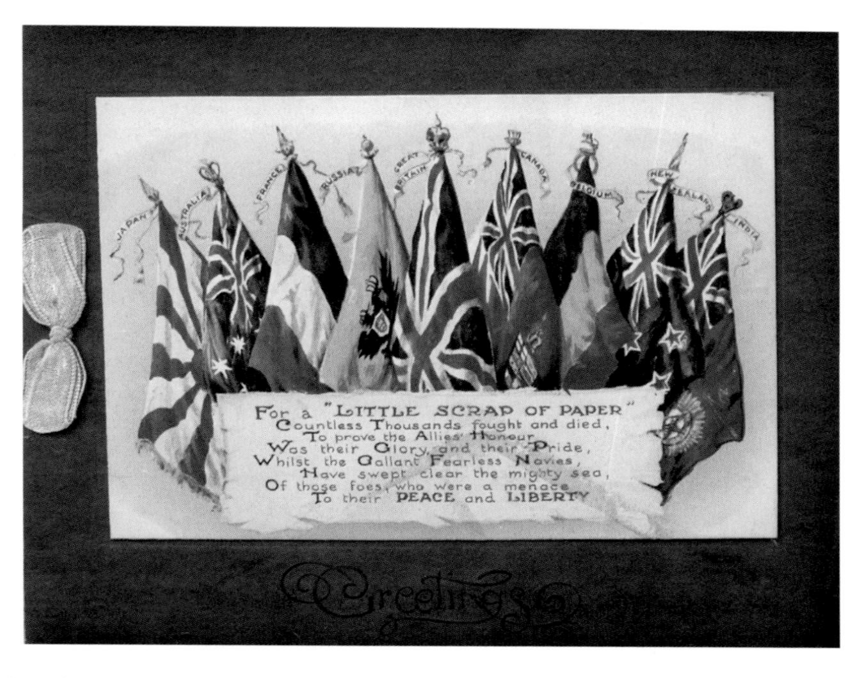

There has lately been published a book in which the manly virtues and nobility of "le bon petit roi" have received no more than their due need of praise; it was neither my intent nor my business to speak of military matters on this page, but that I have done so serves to illustrate the fact that war permeates, if it does not constitute, the atmosphere of our very life at this crisis of the world's affairs.

It seems strange that one continues still to do the same little insignificant things that were done before war broke out; it seems strange that one does not cease to do things that seem not to matter now, when the whole horizon is filled by the fearful

spectre of the Great War — but perhaps it is as well sometimes to take our eyes from the horizon and to fix them, if only for a moment, upon matters nearer home. This is the "raison d'être" of our little paper.
Editorial by G Bernard.

The Noon Star continued spasmodically during the first years of the war and featured photographs of Scottish soldiers from Highland Regiments who had been billeted at Bedford.

Under the pseudonym of Mr Murray or M Lyttelton, Sybil often contributed in verse or prose.

Always triumphant in spring, obsessed with the re-awakening of nature and new life, she invariably turned to verse to express her deeper feelings and forebodings.

Vol VI Number 1
I cannot hope for summer; these alien skies are grey
That hurl the frozen snowflakes along each frost bound way;
In rows, like stiffened corpses, the trees are staring stark
And in the common darkness my world within is dark.
1914

Mass conscription led to troops from many parts of Britain being sent south by rail to train and prepare for shipment overseas.

Bedford became a sea of Tartan colours as Highland regiments arrived there, and the Heriz-Smiths, with rooms to spare, billeted some of the kilted clans.

The Noon Star reflects some of the experiences of this and their attitude to the soldiers from the North.

Extract from Noon Star Vol. VI No. III
March 1915

When the Army arrived on our doorstep, it was an army of civilians and some time elapsed before five Highlanders were tramping the Bedford roads, each swinging a Seaforth kilt in time. With the skirl of the pipes, each with a rifle over his shoulder and a stag with wide spreading antlers decking the ribbon on his Glengarry; they fancied themselves no little the first time they donned their skirts; it was a proud day for us, by sympathy, when our Londoners became Scotchmen. [The guest book kept by the family shows that many of the Highland regiment came from the London area, though we do not know if they were of Scottish origin.]

During the actual advent of the invading army there seemed to be scant time even to draw a breath. Nevertheless, five spring cots and five palliasses had gained entrance and found standing room within the third floor back and front ere the sound of heavy footsteps and a clinkety-clank, clinkety-clank – not of spurs, gentle reader, but of tin plates and mugs of the same musical metal containing knives, forks and spoons — gave us a formal intimation that our soldier quintet was on the way to take possession of the billet.

From that time to this, the army and its doings have been a source of great and continuous interest and a well-nigh inexhaustible topic of conversation. The full strength of out of our "fighting force" is eighteen effectives – or more justly, seventeen effectives and one sick soldier, for one always seems to be on the sick list – which number includes one lance corporal and two sergeants and excludes a few isolated units supernumerary to the establishment.

The first "section" had not been beneath our sheltering rooftree before they became known to us as

[Robert] Dixon
[Frederick] Robinson
[Leslie] Marshall
[Frederick] Watt
and [Sidney] Dix

and a short while longer before they were spoken of as

Weekend Bob
Rob [Night Commander of the Bath]
Makershallalbashbaz
What Ho!
And Pixie.

Though it is true that they did not, in every case, answer to these names and would probably have been not a little surprised if one had so addressed them.

One incident of their sojourn shall be recorded here. One day, one fine sunless rainy day in late autumn [but the little birds sing, or at least whisper, even in the moist and miserable months of the year], the Colonel, the Major, and the Billeting Officer went forth a-visiting. There seems a magic in the very name of inspection, and when they came to call they found a house in order, and all was pure and tidy; nay, uncannily so.

The supernumeraries must not be forgotten. Two are folk billeted at one time in the adjoining house and who, when Dixon and Dix were with us, formed a curious quartet, their names being Dixon and Dickinson [Robin]. There remaineth yet one other, another Stewart, and another Geordie Stewart at that, who is the brother of Rab.

Here ends the chronicle of the Home Army. One said that they were given something every time they coughed or sneezed, but there is one thing we shall give them, well or ill, in England, Scotland, France or Flanders, in Egypt or Berlin, or wherever they may find themselves, and that is"Good Luck".

That is so. Yes, that is so.

In February 1915 Denzil was still in Colchester and hating it.

In the same month Sybil penned verses to spring that seemed appropriate with the departure of the Bedford Highlanders to Flanders.

> *They told me spring was here, the lads that swung*
> *a-down an English road, their purpose true*
> *faring in fancy with the friends who flung*
> *the fold's of Britain's banner to the blue*
> *Spring dwelled within their heart, glance from their eyes*
> *And none might say them nay*
> *That watched the dusty column breast the rise*
> *Then dip into the day,*
> *And hear the bugles calling to the skies*
> *The wordless things they say*
> Lyttleton

Sybil missed Denzil awfully when he was away, and theirs was the closest relationship between the children. They wrote frequently, and not always in solemn fashion.

Extract of a letter from Denzil in the spring of 1915

8th Northants
Colchester.
Private, Confidential, secret not to be divulged, O.H.M.S. etc

My darling Tobbins

Here we are again, as Oberleutnant von Falkenmoltkemackensen said, when he looked down for the fourth time on the dark lights of Colchester. In other words, I shall gabble for a space on topics general and then proceed to a thrilling account with three Zeps, a Taube and a German sausage.

By now you will have seen that there was a raid by Zepps on east coast towns. Well this information is not to go further than the family **on any account** *d'ye see. They raided London, I hear, Walthamstow and Leytonstone way, and Blackfriars. They had a shot that failed at Chelmsford's big wireless station, but did a fair amount of private property damage, and killed one or two new owners. They dropped bombs, I hear, on Ardleigh, not far from here, and some other places and they came over Colchester dropping one bomb.*

Don't *say you have a brother in Colchester and he heard a Zep and knows a bomb was dropped there. It is against regulations to tell you what I have told you, so don't leave the letter lying about either.*

Well, no more now, my Tobbins. Good night and tons of love. Also my usual heaps of love to the darling wee tit and to our Gill.

Yr loving brother Tadger.

Printed in *Noon Star.*

April 1915
Extract from a letter from Mrs Smith

Of course you have seen in the papers all about the Zeppelin coming to Lowestoft. You would never forget it if you had heard it. I though there were half a dozen airships the noise was so dreadful. About one o'clock the fire alarm sounded, and it was not long before bang went a bomb, and very soon two more went off. I just peeped out of the window and I could see the lights of the Zeppelin – it was quite close to the house. Very soon we could see a tremendous blaze and we thought all Lowestoft was on fire. I thought certainly the station was blown up. I was thankful when the old thing went buzzing off – it was hovering around for a quarter of an hour. I can tell you I wish Mr Smith was at home with us. Denmark Road houses were shattered to pieces, but no one was hurt. Of course, you heard they killed a chicken or frightened it to death.

In the same month Sybil had written a poem about the departure of the Scotties. It was called England's Eyes.

England called to her sons, and they are gone
The soil that loved them kissed their marching feet,
Breathed a long blessing, ere they slipped across
The narrow strait, to triumph or to loss;
And weary eyes that waited, leapt to greet
Eyes new with hope, where lamps of purpose shone.

The editorial for Noon-Star in April 1915, Vol. VI No. IV, was as follows.

The war proceeds with its usual slowness and with more than usual horror. The Germans have out-Hunned Attila, and by their use of noxious and asphyxiating gases they have added one more outrage to the long and ever accumulating list they seem to take daily delight in augmenting. But are we down-hearted? No. At least, if we are, any of us, we would do well to go and watch the outward bound armies marching away

Yes. The summoning bugle has blown through Bedford Town at last, and our brave boys, out "Heeland ladies" have left us lamenting their loss deeply, but loving their courage, their high spirits, and their devotion to the country we are so proud to call Mother. The streets lie deserted, mute and bare in the strengthening sunlight. The mocking voice of the bugle no longer calls "you can be a defaulter as long as you like, so long as you answer your name." No more Last Post thrills to the night sky and the listening hearts; the bagpipes and the drums are silent, and there is something wrong about the house, which was never apparent before May 1st. The Home Army has left home, and has now gone forth to fight for it; whither as yet we "dinnae kin". But we shall not forget "our boys."

The Editorial for Vol. VI No.V in July 1916 virtually coincides with Denzil's letter from the trenches sent on July 4th and after the beginnings of the Big Push. It is a remarkable civilian view of a highly complex world map.

It is more than a year since our Magazine was last issued, and in consequence there is much news to chronicle. The War, which some had hoped would have run it's course before the beginning of 1916, is still raging fiercely on all fronts; indeed since I last addressed my readers in these pages, a new Front has been created at Salonika, where the Allies landed an expeditionary force to oppose the Bulgars; for Bulgaria, under her ruler Ferdinand – King Fox, has definitely thrown in her lot with the Central Powers. Greece herself remains neutral, but we hope the day is not far off when, by an overwhelming majority in the elections, which are actually taking place at the time of writing, she will proclaim herself for "Venizelos", and so enter the struggle as our ally.

The Dardanelles Expedition was given up some six months ago, but the troubles of the Turk have augmented of late by a serious uprising of the Arabs, who have seized and continue to hold, Mecca and Medina – the Holy Cities.

The British Government, too, had it's taste of an armed Rising, in the outbreak of the Sinn Feiners. For a week things looked ugly and Dublin was practically in the hands of the rebels; but by good fortune Sir Roger Casement,[13] *the leader and originator of the movement, fell into our hands [under most romantic circumstances] at the very outset of the affair, and soon the immediate danger was overcome. There seem, however, to be rocks ahead over the Irish question, which is as yet unsettled.*

Referring in a figurative way to rocks, one is reminded of that cruel, stormswept coast off the Orkneys where HMS Hampshire met her fate, being sunk by a mine – two or three days after having done her part nobly in the great and glorious battle of Jutland. With her went down, as all sons of Britain know to their sorrow, the man with the eyes of steel – the silent man- K of K [Kitchener of Khartoum]—one of the greatest of those sons, we may say the greatest of our time.

The joy of our enemies that he is no longer at the helm, serves only to show how much they feared that Englishman, and in no way disturbs us, for we know that his spirit is still with his country –still fights for her in the armies he created. His boys will carry on his work to a successful issue, and so will raise an everlasting monument to the name of Kitchener.

Everyone is eagerly following the course of events in Russia, where our allies have taken the initiative, and are making good progress. In Italy where, after a temporary setback, General Cadorna is pressing on with his gallant army. In France where, under Sir Douglas Haig, we are, in the words of Thomas Atkins, "Pushing" at last.

The *Noon Star* July 1916 contains the letter from Denzil after the big push of July 1st. It is included in that section of the book.

John Gregory in his excellent book, *Sybil, The Poet and the Speaker of Verse*, says that the family were fortified by "the nobility of patriotism", by the "warmth of comradeship", and that they had little conception of the carnage that was destroying a generation of young men.

The full horror of the war could not be really told by the ever-increasing lists of the fallen but that a cloud of fear and dread numbed them.

When news of Denzil's death hit them it was as if the heavens had fallen and the world had collapsed about them.

"For Charles, the loss of his treasured son was annihilation of the spirit. Marion was inconsolable, and the sisters stunned. For Sybil it was the loss of her dearest playmate."

Post war, the Heriz-Smiths moved from Bedford to Suffolk and a permanent home at the House of Four Winds on Kessingland Beach. The girls followed their various course, Joan in Physical Education, Sybil in verse speaking and teaching, and Gillian in dancing.

The Noon Stars are full of paintings, and contain two short stories spread over several editions. They also contain a large number of nature notes. It is not the purpose of this book to contain details of these, but I include the etching of a ketch off the Suffolk coast (see page 108).

Joan

Sybil

Gillian

"Four Winds". The house at Kessingland the Heriz-Smiths designed and moved into in 1921

16
War

Signing up to the Public Schools and Universities Brigade, Royal Fusiliers

When war broke out on August 4th Denzil and his family were on the Suffolk coast at Kessingland.[14]

Almost immediately his diary reflected the news he had heard and also the way the war affected the small community.

6th German minelayer, Koenegin Louise, sunk off Harwich by destroyer, but British cruiser Amplion, struck a German mine of Harwich and sunk with 130 lives.

8th A destroyer and two submarines went by. Aeroplanes and destroyers a common sight.

12th Hear from Piercy that the East Anglian Engineers are quartered in the school gym and that billeting is in full swing in Bedford.

13th Saw a destroyer and then a cargo ship; both swing round and go off.

18th Great excitement caused by the passing of a large fleet of destroyers [1 cruiser and 16 light destroyers] going along at a fair pace, followed by a sub, while a cruiser and more destroyers passed it going north

Friday August 21st 1914
Partial eclipse of the sun visible at 12.20pm

Bathed with Mother from Staunton's Bathing Hut and swam down to the Caledonia. Could not get back because of the tide and walked back.

22nd A big dreadnought passed going north today.

24th Great excitement caused by a foreign looking man who planted himself

From a sketch from "Noon Star"

with a bicycle in front of the bathing shed, and asked various questions, while I was dressing. Some soldiers and scouts were watching him. He was stopped and interrogated but allowed to go on; but it was said he was arrested in the evening.

25th British army in action at Mons.

26th The army did well against superior numbers at Mons. There are reported victories of the French and British in Belgium, and a heavy defeat of a German Army by Russia on the East Prussian frontier.

Austria declares war on Japan

28th During the morning an extraordinary mist came down and thickened every instant. Suddenly we heard an aeroplane, which suddenly plunged from the mist very near to the top of the houses. Evidently the officer could not see the earth and had to come down quickly 400 yards away.

29th Austria declares war on Belgium
British naval victory at Heligoland;[15] a German patrolling squadron intercepted and a fight between the two flotillas – two light cruisers sunk, another escaped in flames and in a sinking condition. Two destroyers sunk, many damaged. British casualties light, no ships sunk.

September 7th Heavy firing out at sea all morning. All light ships, harbour lights and the lighthouse extinguished in the evening.

The family returned to Bedford on September 9th and found the town full of Highlanders.

On the 12th Griffiths, Yarde and Martin all left to take up commissions, and on the 16th, a wet and pouring day, Denzil went to town to sign forms of enrolment. He was medically examined by a Major of the RAMC at the Headquarters of the Argyle and Sutherland Highlanders in Goldington Avenue.

477 2944

Army Form B. 111.

SHORT SERVICE.

(Three Years with the Colours).

ATTESTATION OF

No. Name Heriz-Smith Denzil Milford Corps Royal Fusiliers

Questions to be put to the Recruit before Enlistment.

1. What is your name? — 1. Denzil Milford Heriz-Smith
2. In or near what Parish or Town were you born? — 2. In the Parish of ... in or near the Town of Filey in the County of Yorks
3. Are you a British Subject? — 3. Yes
4. What is your Age? — 4. 20 Years 9 Months
5. What is your Trade or Calling? — 5. Gentleman
6. Have you resided out of your Father's house for three years continuously in the same place, or occupied a house or land of the yearly value of £10 for one year, and paid rates for the same, and, in either case, if so, state where? — 6. No

You are hereby warned that if after enlistment it is found that you have given a wilfully false answer to any of the following seven questions, you will be liable to a punishment of two years' imprisonment with hard labour.

7. Are you, or have you been, an Apprentice? if so, where? to whom? for what period? and, when did, or will, the period of your apprenticeship expire? — 7. No
8. Are you Married? — 8. No
9. Have you ever been sentenced to Imprisonment by the Civil Power? — 9. No
10. Do you now belong to the Royal Navy, the Army, the Royal Marines, the Militia, the Special Reserve, the Territorial Force, the Army Reserve, the Militia Reserve, or any Naval Reserve Force? If so, to what unit and Corps? — 10. No
*11. Have you ever served in the Royal Navy, the Army, the Royal Marines, the Militia, the Special Reserve, the Territorial Force, the Imperial Yeomanry, the Volunteers, the Army Reserve, the Militia Reserve, or any Naval Reserve Force? If so, state which unit, and cause of discharge — 11. Bedford Gram. S. O.T.C. Left School
12. Have you truly stated the whole, if any, of your previous Service? — 12. Yes
13. Have you ever been rejected as unfit for the Military or Naval Forces of the Crown? If so, on what grounds? — 13. No
14. Are you willing to be vaccinated or re-vaccinated? — 14. Yes
15. Are you willing to be enlisted for General Service? — 15. Yes
16. Did you receive a Notice, and do you understand its meaning, and who gave it to you? — 16. No Name W. J. Thing Corps R. S.
17. Are you willing to serve upon the following conditions provided His Majesty should so long require your services?
(a) For a term of three years unless the War lasts longer than three years, in which case you will be retained until the War is over. If employed with Hospitals, depots of Mounted Units, and as Clerks, etc., you may be retained after the termination of hostilities until your services can be spared, but such retention shall in no case exceed six months. If however, the war is over in less than three years, you will be discharged with all convenient speed. — 17. Yes

I, Denzil Milford Heriz-Smith do solemnly declare that the above answers made by me to the above questions are true, and that I am willing to fulfil the engagements made.

D M Heriz-Smith SIGNATURE OF RECRUIT.

J. W. Wilkinson Signature of Witness.

OATH TO BE TAKEN BY RECRUIT ON ATTESTATION.

I, Denzil Milford Heriz-Smith do make Oath, that I will be faithful and bear true Allegiance to His Majesty King George the Fifth, His Heirs, and Successors and that I will, as in duty bound, honestly and faithfully defend His Majesty His Heirs and Successors, in Person, Crown, and Dignity against all enemies, and will observe and obey all orders of His Majesty, His Heirs, and Successors, and of the Generals and Officers set over me. So help me God.

CERTIFICATE OF MAGISTRATE OR ATTESTING OFFICER.

The Recruit above-named was cautioned by me that if he made any false answer to any of the above questions he would be liable to be punished as provided in the Army Act.

The above questions were then read to the recruit in my presence.

I have taken care that he understands each question, and that his answer to each question has been duly entered as replied to, and the said recruit has made and signed the declaration and taken the oath before me at Bedford on this 16th day of Sept. 1914.

Signature of the Justice Harry Brereton [illegible] of Bedford

If any alteration is required on this page of the Attestation, a Justice of the Peace should be requested to make it [illegible] alteration under Section 8 (f), Army Act.

The Recruit should, if he require it, receive a copy of the Declaration on Army Form B. 111.

Friday 18th September 1914

Maurice Simpson and Mudford came round just before departure time from Bedford, to say goodbye. Down to station in cab with Jolly, Mrs and Miss Jolly, picking up Geoff Peele en route. Quite a crowd at the station to see us off. Arrived at St Pancras about 11.30am and went by bus to Westminster. Our bags were deposited at Central Hall, and then we rushed off [against orders] to get some lunch [party consisting of Elliot-Smith, self, AJ and GP].

Ate lunch in record time and made bolt for Hall again. Briefly saw Aunt Flossy. Then came an interminable wait in the Hall getting labels etc, and on top of that we had to sit on two rows of kerbstones in Tothill St waiting for the word to march. At last we got started under a peppery old fellow, who must have been a retired Major or something of the sort, and arrived at Victoria in fine style, entraining with very little delay and on arriving at Epsom we marched to the market place, and then we were marched off with our bags to be billeted. Our quarters, the Cooperative Hall, are at all events clean, with a very hard floor. 50 of us are billeted here.

Each man has a chair to put his clothes on and 3 blankets for the bed. On this night no food was provided so we had tea and supper combined in a restaurant in town. It was jolly welcome too Then we went to a cinema and were bored by the impossible adventures of Sexton Blake, standing all the time as the theatre was packed with our fellows.

Have met a number of OB's today. Some are billeted in fine private houses with beds [and very few in a room], sitting rooms, meals etc, some, like us in public institooshuns and others in shops, while the worst off are in those more or less dirty houses with kids in them.

I saw Geoff Bull on Victoria Street marching past and then again in Epsom market place, but not near enough to talk too.

September 19th

Food didn't seem to be provided at this stage and we had to get supper and lunch in town at our own expense, as we have been paid nothing yet. But in the morning we were arranged in companies [a company is 250 strong], which is one step forwards. All men having previous experience of training as officers were ordered to fall out of the parade, and then the Company Commander asked our ranks etc. No less than six men in this Company alone have already held commissions, and one has seen active service. These men and all old non-coms who hold certificate A were made platoon sergeants temporarily. The rest of us had to fall in again, but have pretty good chances, I would think, of being made Corporals later on.

In the afternoon, suddenly, all billets changed and we were marched off to a road called Miles Road, in the suburbs, and billeted there. We fetched our traps from the Co-op and nous, voila, Geoff Bull and I at 19 Miles Road, Alf Jolly and Elliot-Smith at 21, and Geoffrey Peele and Coperman at 23, all these houses being next to one another. Not so bad!

September 22nd
I was offered a Commission through Chief, I think. But there are multifarious considerations to be taken into account

1 *What is the Bedford regiment?*
2 *Is it worth joining as an ossifer when one is having a good time here and all my friends are here?*
3 *What about the ossifer's expenses*

We are at last in our companies. My place is No 5 section, of No 10 platoon, of C Coy, in the 2nd Battalion. We have a very nice commander, one Captain Hammond, and the 2nd in command, one Lt Skee is also a very nice chap. Our platoon commander, one sub-Lt AJ Jolly is a nice fellah, our section commander, one Corporal D Heriz-Smith is a ____ yes! I was made section commander for conspicuous gallantry on parade ground one or two days ago

One of the ex-commissioned ossifers who had joined with other ranks was made Platoon commander on the strength of this, having been an ossifer before [I may say that the platoon commander is an ossifer, usually a 2nd Lt. [but he turned out to know so little that he was demoted].

The Brigade Commander hardly considered my claims at all when they fell us out, because I "looked too young".

Well I got the telegram at about 2pm just as I was going on afternoon parade, and it put me in a bit of a stew, I can tell you. I was thinking what to do for some time and finally went up to the Captain, and asked his advice. He said "Well, it is simply a matter for yourself. If you want the commission take it, but we would be sorry to lose you, and you have an excellent chance of starting here with three stripes [i.e. of being made a Sgt and apparently a very fair one of doing the Jolly touch and getting a commission in this corps]

Goes on to describe the digs
Please send the Ousels as they come out until further orders, carefully please as I will send them back to be stowed away.

If you see anyone I know get them to write to me and let me know how things are at the school. ***That school is part of my nature now, I believe!***

Card to Mother Sept 24 1914
Have wired Adjutant 6th Bedford's to refuse commission. Quite bucked with this at

present. If we get fed soon, Geoff and I shall apply for one regiment together.

Address of all letters to be
Sgt D M Heriz-Smith
C Company
2nd battalion
U and PS forces
Epsom

You may also put Royal Fusiliers but it is optional.

Card to Mother
September 29th 1914
Expected to be summoned to Aldershot any time now to interview with the CO. Lambert is second in command of a Company Northants Regiment. Liesching [Percivale] is in France

19 Miles Road
Epsom
October 2nd 1914

My Darling Mum

I'm afraid I have some bad news for you in this letter. Yesterday Geoff and I went down to Aldershot to see the Adjutant of the 6th Beds, a Lt Leyborne Popham. He was a nice fellow. Well I filled in a form giving all the normal details, such as have you been medically examined before, what is your length of service etc, and then went off to the medical officer to be examined while Geoff waited his turn. The man started examining me and sounded me out all about the place carefully. Then he made me swing my arms round and around several times and then sounded me out again. Then he asked me if I could run long distance races, and whether I felt breathless after short sprints and finally said he could not pass me fit for service. I asked why. He said that my heart palpitated hard after swinging my arms and that it was not quite right. He said that if I had continuous long marches every day and woke up at night I should probably break down completely.

I told him this was rot, because I had been for a considerable number of marches and walks over 20 miles without feeling anything. He said he couldn't help it but it was so and he wondered if I had had heart palpitations before. Well of course I have but I simply put it down to lack of training after sprints etc, and then I said that I had been sounded several times before by the Medical Officer of the A and S Highlanders at the Depot in Bedford, and they had not found anything wrong. He said he sympathised with me but he could not take me as an officer, with a heavy pack and long marches that would probably strain my heart badly. He would pass me as fit only for the ranks, but as an officer he would not.

Well of course that was a bit of a blow for me, especially as I had heard the examination for officers was not half as rigorous as that for men. You see an officer doesn't carry as much as men by any means. I suppose the reason why he would be willing to pass me as a man not as an officer is that they couldn't afford to lose their officers like that, but that a man wouldn't matter so much. Anyway after asking me whether I had had rheumatic fever or scarlet fever, he said he had to be careful what he did and could not pass me. Of course that dished the Commission. Geoff refused his and we went down to the station again and talked it over. I managed to persuade Geoff not to be a fool enough to refuse his commission to stop with me, so we went up and saw Popham again. He was very nice about me and said the Doctor would have passed me as fit to join the ranks, and that he was sorry that he couldn't have me. Geoff then filled in a form and as we had an hour to kill we went up to the Officers Mess to have drinks, and then we had to wait another 2 hours for the Medical Officer again, and as he turned up at 7.30 rather than 6.00, and then Geoff was examined, we bolted for the station. We missed our connections and only got back to Epsom at 11, after the most fedding day I have had for years.

Meanwhile, as Captain Hammond thought it was certain that I was going to get a commission, he reduced me to the ranks, since he wanted to test someone else as section leader. In the morning, the officers, especially Captain Hammond, were very decent about me and Hammond said he would be very glad to have me back, and would make me a sergeant at once. Lt Skee advised me to have another medical you see, as I can't get a commission anywhere else as they will ask me whether you have been examined before for any of HM's Armed forces. So I suppose I'm a fixture here. It will be very dull when Geoff leaves, since Alf is an officer and can't speak to me.

Oct 5h 1914
Writes to Mum and says he will consult the Chief [his former Head Master] to help him get a commission.

Oct 12th
There was a reply from Felixstowe re the Head's move on this.

The Headmaster
Bedford School

Dear Sir

In answer to your letter of the 9th inst, I do not know what establishment the War Office has fixed for the new battalions. If they [H-S and Bull] are anxious to get Commissions I think the best thing would be for then to apply to their orderly room for army form 423. I have none here. Failing that they should apply to War Office for the form, fill it in and post it to me here. If I forward the applications for these two gentlemen, of course it will be altogether on your recommendation as I have to sign that I know them and can recommend them.

Yours Sincerely
Lt Col Hammond

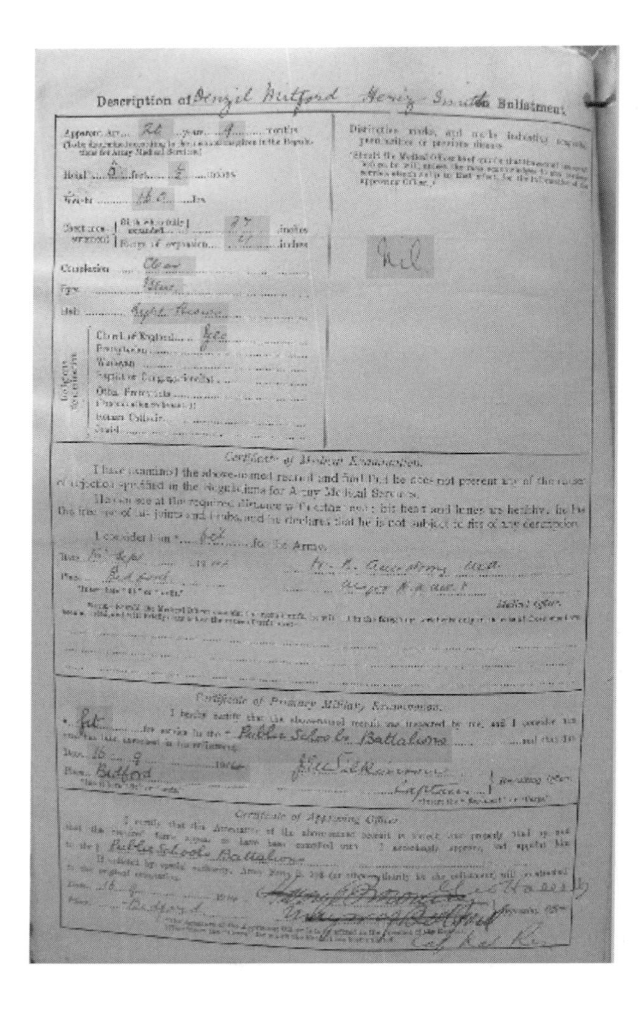

Description of Denzil Mitford Heriz-Smith on Enlistment.

Certificate of Medical Examination.

Certificate of Primary Military Examination.

Fit for service in the Public Schools Battalions

Place Bedford

Certificate of Approving Officer.

Public Schools Battalion

At the time of his medical examination in September 1914, Denzil Heriz-Smith was 6' 1/2" tall, 160lbs, 37" chest with 4" expansion, and had brown hair and blue eyes. His profession/ trade was "gentleman".

But there remained some doubt about his heart according to an army doctor seen in September, but these fears, that Denzil always said were wrong, were scotched by the successful examination on November 1st.

18 Charles Street
Berkeley Square, W

Nov 1st 1914

Mr D M Heriz-Smith is in perfect physical health and has no lesions of his heart or lungs.

SB Lamb

Shoreham
Thursday November 12

Dear Sir

I have duly received your letter of the 10th inst, and I note your excellent report on Mr G R Bull. Should this gentleman ask me to assist him in obtaining a temp commission, I will, on your recommendation, do my best to assist him

8th J Battalion Beds

Letter to Mother
From Kent Gardens Ealing. November 20 1914

This letter appears in the earlier section on Games and describes an inter company rugger match where they came up against some Old Modernians. Fortunately the match was won.

This letter throws up two points. Firstly that the rivalry with the Modern School was healthy even in 1914, and there are references to this later in the book. Anecdotal evidence suggest that there was a near riot in 1911 concerning parents watching the local derby, and that this was the reason why two brother schools, so close to one another, did not play matches against each over until the last 25 years or so!

The second point is that throughout his army career he mentions when a bath is available! This was a real problem in the trenches, of course, and it was a cause deemed worthy of noting in diary or letter when a bath was found!

28th Weekend leave for half company stopped owing to fears of a German raid. All to be in Epsom to turn out on any alarm.

Footer match v D Cy on Epsom College grounds after lunch in drenching rain; won 18-0

Tuesday Dec 1st Marched up to Headley, about 5 miles, and did an attack which the Brigadier said was very good as an exhibition of open order drill but was lamentable as an attack. The CO's of the 1st and 2nd Batts, Col Lord Scott and W Gordon, had mistaken the General order!

2nd Demoted to private today because of my application for a commission. All NCO's in this position are demoted to the ranks

Sent for at 5pm and CO said an order for my discharge had come from the WO and told me to give in my equipment etc

Back to Bedford

6th Sang in Choir in Matins and evensong [[can't keep away from the place]

11th Down town with Syb and a rumour that the Argyles were starting for the front.

12th Heard that 1st XV had beaten Haileybury 21-11

Sunday Chapel 11am

St Andrews early service at 8am

Founders and Commemoration service at 4.15pm

17

6th Northamptonshire Regiment

On December 14th he was posted to the **6th BATTALION NORTHANTS REGIMENT**, but ordered to report to the Gordon Highlanders for training on Wednesday

Went to London to order my uniform

The 6th Northamptonshire's

Although the War Diary for the 6th Battalion, Northamptonshire Regiment starts a day before embarkation to France in July 1915, they had moved to Shorncliffe on the 4th September 1914, and on to Colchester shortly after, and the revered Lt. Colonel Ripley[16] took command on the 13th October 1914. On the 21st February 1915 a German aeroplane dropped a bomb just outside the camp causing a bit of a stir.

The battalion marched a three-day trek to Hertford in May 1915 and then onto Codford on Salisbury Plain by train. Most of the training referred to is rather vague apart from a lot of stiff-upper lip and better men for it stuff. Although Denzil seems to be with the 8th Battalion at times, he was probably never fully transferred to them. It is likely that "technically" he remained with the 6th Battalion he joined in December 1914 and with whom he joined in France in December 1915. He was "left behind" by the Battalion when it went out to France, something he bitterly regretted, as one reason for him joining was because of his great friendship with James Lambert who did go to France in July.

Each Battalion had a detachment at its Base Depot, which did not take the field when the Battalion was on active service. The Base Detachment consisted – in theory – of a subaltern, two Sergeants and 91 Privates to form a first reinforcement (to make good Battalion casualties or other losses); four Storemen, the Band Sergeant and the Sergeant Master Tailor. When the Battalion went on active service, it left behind the Bandmaster and the Sergeant-Instructor of Musketry, for service with the Reserve Battalion. It is entirely possible that the subaltern left at the Base Depot for the 6th Northampton's was Denzil Heriz-Smith. The fact that he is in the photographic line up of officers from pre-France, a photo later in the book, does seem to suggest that he was part of the Battalion before they went to France, and the photo was published in the Northants Independent on July 24th just before the Battalion moved to France.

Colchester

This letter from Piercy of the Middlesex Regiment sent in early 1915 reveals the burden that troops had to bear when "yomping"! Piercy left school a year before Denzil and had been his best friend.

We are very well equipped now, each man having a very warm vest, two shirts, two pairs of pants, a cardigan, tunic, trousers, great coat, and best of all a short leather coat without sleeves, it is well lined and very warm. In addition we have a pair of ordinary gloves and a pair of fingerless ones for the trenches. Socks seem to be the things which are most needed, and here we have to wear two pairs all the time and of course they need frequently changing. I think that these are the best things "Sister Susie" can make. Of course all our kit is most useful and indispensable but it is a great weight to carry around and we don't like marching with it at all even though we did a lot of route marching with packs in England. Most of us have some private kit as well, personally I have two additional cardigans, some books, a Tommie cooker, two towels [one bath towel!], writing things, two sets of shaving tackle etc; in addition we have iron rations, respiratory and field dressings. Fortunately our blankets [three between two men] are carried on the transport.

Our food has been fairly plentiful although of course we get a lot of biscuits often

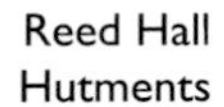

Reed Hall Hutments

in place of bread. A ration of 1oz tobacco and 40 cigarettes are issued once a week.

For the most part Denzil did not like his time at Colchester with the long patches of boredom when others seemed to be going to the Front. Tensions broke out even concerning Lambert who had become his best friend.

Letter to Mother. Before 20th Jan 1915
From Reed Hall Hutments[17]
Colchester

I arrived after a good break at home. There was no taxi at the station, so I had to phone town for one.

The taxi would only go as far as 11th Fusilier Huts, so there was a large area of muddy ground to be crossed. There was no man in sight for bags, so I left them with the sentry and told him to bring them when his duty finished.

The Huts are 120ft long divided into three sections, and my room is about 12 by 8 separated by matchwood from rest areas.

The rooms are bare of furniture, and I had no bed, sleeping bag, blankets or anything. Also my bags had not arrived. One fellow was away due to illness, and I was able to take his bed and I had a fairly comfortable first night, but if he turns up I am in the soup.

I had a bad fit of blues last night and was as miserable as it is possible to be. Things are a bit better this morning, but am still worried due to the following circumstances. This Battalion is 12 officers over strength now, and they are going to the front with only 4 supernumerary officers. So 8 have to go eventually and I may still squeeze in as a proper platoon officer, but 'tis unlikely, and even to get in as a supernumerary will be a struggle. As for the 8 unlucky ones, goodness knows what they will do. I presume they will be either discharged or transferred to another Battalion of the Regiment, probably the 6th as the 7th is full, but whether I can effect a transfer I don't know.

Personally I am fed up with the whole show and am in the unenviable position of having no servant, no light, no coal, no bed, blankets or anything, and what I'm going to do tonight I don't know. Lambert is too occupied on his own affairs to give the slightest help, so my position at present is very nasty. The station is 3 miles away and the post office 15 minutes walk, and the time I have to spare is nil.

Well my little darling, I'm sorry to give you such an account, but it will probably improve later. At this rate at all events I would ten times rather be at Epsom!

20th Jan

Things are brightening up and I know some of the chaps, and find them more to my liking than before.

However my camp kit has not turned up yet, and luckily neither has the chap whose bed I have. When he does I will be sans bed just as I am at present sans washing kit!

I have not got a platoon nor have I any chance of one. There are far too many supernumeraries.

Of course my luck has it that having made firm friends with the Batt. Sgt Man, he has, I suppose, been blowing my trumpet for me, and yesterday gave me a private hint that I was to be one of those to be kept in the Battalion. This, of course, means the "super" job, and I don't quite know what to think of it. One thing though I have been lucky in. I have procured an A1 servant, a middle aged man who has done the servant for a Major for several years and served in an Officers Mess. So I am all right as far as that goes.

As musketry practice was prevented by the downpour, and the Major said do something to break the monotony, I read to my platoon. They are quite decent lads. If one gets the rough in this war it will be rather a good experience for them and me.

Colonel Ripley is a nice old chap, and I have put Lambert into a more amenable frame of mind.

Colonel Ripley thinks we will be soldiering quite a year longer, and already talks of our serving on courts-martial.

25th Jan

To Joan

I am only a supernumerary as Mum has perhaps told you and am a bit bored but the ossifers are quite a decent lot. It is now said "on reliable authority" that we are going out to France about the middle of February to complete training and then to be in the firing line about the middle of March, as other battalions are to come here. Whether this is true or not I don't of course know.

All my company is down with vaccinations – only 20 out of 250 were on parade this morning, so they have 4 days slack, and so of course do we. [This had happened too at Epsom when Denzil became a "victim" as well. What could the Germans have done if they knew when men were about to be jabbed!]?

I was nutting about with binoculars and maps, and white badges as an umpire in D Coy manoeuvres [My Coy being C], putting a man or two or half a section here and a squad there out of action. In fact doing "the heavy nut" with complete success.

It was grand about the Blucher wasn't it?

It is now I am in a Positively Painful Funk of going on writing as it is lights out soon.

[This latter phrase PPF was used a lot and I think it comes from the Latin Pater Pater Familia, second father in the family. Father, Son, and four daughters]

To Mother same day and much the same news
Good news about the Blücher[18] *isn't it, but pity it wasn't the Derrflinger instead.*

Jan 27th to Mum
On Sunday morning at 9am I went with the battalion on church parade. Each Coy has 2 officers on parade each Sunday, and my turn came last Sunday. It was rather funny sitting in the seats of the mighty at the top of the Garrison church wherein two battalions were seated with 13 other officers, and clanking out first from the service. This was quite a decent one and taken by our little padre, a man named Bennett, who is the only man I have met who remind me of Perry. He has not got Henry's black hair but bears a distinct resemblance and I like him for it.

He is a great friend of Betteridge's and sits in our room occasionally gassing. Lambert often comes in and bags my writing paper and turns everything upside down and inside out so that I have to spend 30 minutes getting my things in order after he has gone. I sometimes think that I will not suffer any longer him using my room at all except as a favour, but I don't want to ruin a friendship. It is however just this lack of consideration that he and Perry really split up about with great bitterness even now.

As soon as the battalion had got back from parade, and I had squelched through the mud to my quarters, I found orders awaiting me to parade at once and march 120 men down to the Brigade orderly room to change their old rifles for new Short rifles.

Well, I went to see Captain Wace for instructions but he didn't have the slightest idea where to go to, as there were no specific instructions, but he thought it was at the Suffolk's and that we might get them near the Hospital, but that the Sergeant of Musketry would know. So I took over command of our party and demanded from the Sergeant where we had to go to. He didn't know, but thought it was in Wimpole Street but didn't know where that was. No one knew where we had to go! Well I thought I would try Wimpole Street though I hadn't the faintest where it was. So I marched my men and when we got near the Hospital I met our Coy Sgt Maj returning from town and I summoned him to see if he knew where to go. Well, he knew it would be from the Brigade Orderly Room and that it was in Wimpole Road and that that was near the Garrison Church. After many experiences and directions we at last arrived, having gone about 2 miles out of course in our wanderings. I beaded the Quarter Master, marched the men about changing rifles, signed various receipts, and formed the men up again in the street and did some more "nut" don'tcha know!

Party—— pay attention there on the right, pull that rifle barrel in! What is that man doing there moving about? Party – tchun. Slooope arms as you were!! Move smartly now men or there shall be some drills going about soon. Slooooope Arms!!! Party will move to the right in fours. Form fours!! I'm waiting for that man in the second section now. Right!!! And off we went at last with her main self strutting 3 paces in front. It was a sight for the blind and has to impress the nuts and the Colonel who was watching. Much impressed he was! Well we went back a considerably shorter route.

Since then we have been firing on our musketry course which is a very slack job for supernumerary officers, as there is little to do until it is your turn to fire, though you must look busy! I'm not shooting very well at present and certainly nothing like last July.

Uncle Ted has got me a nice Webley Fosbery revolver, and also a pair of ear protectors, and Auntie Flossie has got me a pair of binoculars with my name engraved on them. These are birthday presents and they are coming to see me tomorrow. Isn't it grand!

To mother Feb 2nd
Chides her for telling me that she had told half the world to call on him! You know how I hate at the best of times getting to know people and going to see them for the first time [I wonder if an innate shyness sometimes made him seem aloof or haughty?].

I looked forward to the visit of A M-T with horror and apprehension and when she did arrive, I'm glad to say that she was under convoy of Auntie Flossie, which softened matters a lot. Aunty looks very well and quite handsome. It was a pleasure to see her. A M-T is a funny old thing and she sat there like a sideshow while Flossie talked.

Tells his mother, for goodness, goodness sake don't invite anyone else to see me, as it is an honour I don't appreciate and sends my temperature up at once.

Lambert is going home this weekend, lucky dog! As for me, this illness [sore throat and tonsillitis] will put off the day of my leave, I'm afraid, as I haven't the face to apply after being absent from duty for so long

I hear the list of transfers is made out and I'm not therein, which is a compliment, as all the ones who came later than me, and most of those before, have been given the order of the boot. Still it doesn't mean a platoon, which is what I'm after.

Feb 6th to Mother
I have just been putting my gettable in order and scanning the lists of those to whom I have written or mean to write. Just shows how the times alter. On the list when I reckoned up for a short period I found 40 names excluding JSG and Dad and yourself. Six months ago the army would have been represented by 1 Gentleman Cadet at RMA Woolwich, and an officer in the Terriers, the Navy by 1 Midshipman. Now the army is represented by 1 major and 13 2nd Lts, Cadet RMA Woolwich, 2 officers on the unattached list Territorial force, 2 privates in the regulars, 2 Sergeants and 11 cadets of the OTC, and the Navy by 1 Midshipman. Of the remaining 7, 3 are too old to serve, 2 are ladies and 2 are too young and abroad. Pretty good isn't it but that doesn't mean the list is exhausted, and these are only my more intimate friends.

NB He is always asking mother to send out photos, Ousels etc that will be sent back with instructions to put in his drawer or photo album.

There is a discussion about the military photos of Denzil. He does not like any of them but particularly the side profile one. He thinks it is an unmitigated failure. It has a distinct post-pre-futurist-cubist- impressionist Raphaelite look about it, if you understand what I mean!

From Dad. Date unclear but in early 1915
Bedford

We had a Zepp alarm the other night, and it was quite weird to hear the dozens of rifles from all directions suddenly ring out at around midnight. At the time there was an air of unreality about it, but I heard afterwards that it was real.

Feb 28th Letter to Mother
It starts "Here's a howdy-do, here's a pretty state of things" Mikado!

7th Bedford's have arrived and now occupy the barracks. Originally heard it was going to be the 6th's and that I might be able to meet Geoff Bull, but no such luck.

Yesterday I went out entrenching and I was, for once, in sole charge of the platoon, and we had to construct one section of a long line of fire trenches and part of a communication trench and I was awfully bucked with the work when we had finished. We covered up the freshly turned earth with sods, brushwood etc and when I ordered the men to man the trenches, I went out front to see what it looked like, and all that was visible was a grassy mound with numbers of rifles and blue caps appearing above ground. It was nice and all dug in 6 hours too.

Well, the howdy-do is as follows. Captain Willows and Lieutenants Woulfe, Heriz-Smith, Fawkes, Simpson and Stokes are detailed for a month's course of training at the Staff College, Camberley commencing tomorrow when we all leave Colchester.

The syllabus of the course of instruction is for senior subalterns of the new armies before promotion to company commanders. I am not a senior subaltern and the senior subalterns here are not allowed to go on it by the Divisional General. Also it is perfect folly to think of being a CO Coy at this stage of the proceedings so everyone is wondering what on earth the meaning of this is. However the essential point is that we are going to take the course, and we are to be worked each day from 7am to 7pm, though it looks like I might be able to come home on Sundays.

Staff College Camberley
March 1915 to Mum.
Writing from the Staff College Camberley

We arrived at 5.30 and cabbed up to the College in time to report at 6pm. Camberley is a quite decent little town in the middle of beautiful hilly thickly wooded country. The Staff College itself stands in very wide grounds and RMC Sandhurst is 3/4 mile away in same grounds.

The College was, of course, in peacetime a training college for the staff to which entrance is obtained only after the toughest exams that exists in the whole army and only a few selected ones get in. They then go through a very advanced and arduous course in the college, and when they finally leave, if they are Majors they become brigade majors, if captains, staff captains etc. All the Generals or almost all come from this college. On the walls and panels are all sorts of interesting records. Thus there is one giving the names of all graduates of the College since 1887, and one sees Captain Smith-Dorrien, Captain DC Haig, Major Allenby etc etc

Back to Colchester

April 7th to Mother

General chit chat and then

It appears old Maxse[19]*, the Divisional general, wants reports on all the officers in our Division who went to Camberley. The Major of our Coy at Camberley, sent up individual reports to the War Office, and Maxse applied that the War Office should send them off to him. Now an individual report was quite an impossibility really because we did our work in groups of five, and never doing individual work. So we were rather keen on knowing how they were going to produce these reports, not to say a little pessimistic, since we knew that Major Fiennes was very savage indeed that Maxse should have sent "supers" to undergo a Coy Commanders course. So it appears that this course, far from helping us in our rank is going to be a very anxious thing for us. We met some men of the Bedford's and others who had been at Camberley and they informed us that they had one and all, been thoroughly "ticked off" in this report. One man, quite one of the most efficient in the Coy at Camberley had had his platoon taken away by the CO of this Batt. on the strength of this report, and only the Captain of that lot got a good report.*

The CO turned up today and showed us the reports. All of us if you believe, except Capt Willows, got this report "Could not recommend him as Coy Commander without much more experience". We were fed up particularly as at Camberley our schemes had met with tons of approval, and we had very flattering things written about our schemes, which we have still got luckily.

So we explained our views at great length to Colonel Ripley, explaining that reports coming from there could not be very good, as at the end of the course the Major did not know all our names! He also seemed angry at having supers sent out. Captain Willows knew least and perhaps worked least of all but one of us, and yet he, like all the other captains, gets a good report while all the subs we have met got trashed off. Now one of our lot was Simpson who I have talked about [and the originator of Poortaag! [This rather affected phrase was used a lot by Denzil, in one spelling or another and presumably means "bad Show" or "bad day".] Well he is a very much older man than us being about 32 and a master at

Wellingborough. He is not a super but a 1st Lieutenant and is the trainer of our Battalion scouts. He is generally looked upon as a good officer. So the Colonel rather opened his eyes when he saw that he also got a bad report. Colonel Ripley is a very nice fellow, though, and said that he never had much opinion of that sort of report and that it was a waste of paper as far as he was concerned. He only asked us whither we had worked, and whether we knew any more than before. He would also rather trust his own judgement and that this report would make no difference, so all would be right, but that Maxse had seen the reports with a view to transfer if unfit, not that it will make much difference if we do fairly well. What annoyed me though was that he said in the report that I was the youngest. Why will people think me so young when as a matter of fact that is far from the case?

A lot of the Supers, but not yours truly are being transferred to, I think, the 54th Bde.

April 22nd 1915 to Mum from Woodbridge Suffolk
Yesterday we started for Ipswich very early. Reveille was at 4.45am, so we did not do much the day before so we had time to pack our things and get all straight.

Well we started with reveille at 4.45, brekkers at 5.30, and parade at 7am. All the battalion were in full marching order, with transport, water carts and everything. My pack weighed 60 pounds and this was in addition to my haversack, water bottle, and pouches stuffed with stones in lieu of ammunition, and revolver in holster and field glasses. So you will imagine we were fairly well laden. We joined the rest of the Bde at a rendezvous outside Colchester and started off with our guns, transport and cavalry etc. When we had marched 3 miles we were met by the 53rd Bde coming in from their treck. They had started at Ipswich at 3am that morning and the 2 Brigades marched past one another with General Maxse looking on. They had had a very hard time and owing to inexperience had suffered many hardships. A great many had fallen out, and no wonder, for what with the inattention of platoon commanders for their men, and disorganisation and delay in getting food they hadn't had much fun. Yet they looked, at times, better and healthier for the trek.

Our first long halt was at Stratford St Mary 8 miles out where we stopped for lunch at 11am. After lunch we marched till 3pm when we arrived in the outskirts of Ipswich. By this time the men were very tired and the leading battalion the 7th Beds were falling out in shoals, so were the Fusiliers and Middlesex, but the Northants only had one man out all the way and he hadn't been on parade for some time before. The Colonel made it a point of honour that we should keep up our reputation as the best marching battalion in the Bde. So the platoon commanders made a great point of encouraging the men who just at the critical time caught the infection, and went along jeering at the Bedford's who fell out and shouting "Come on the old firm". After aggravating the rest of the Bde like this they couldn't really fall out themselves. Platoon commanders carried the rifles of the younger men who were feeling bad, and these were encouraged by the men so that all resolutely refused to fall out. At one stage I marched a mile myself with all my kit, and 2 rifles. So it fell out that we marched onto Ipswich in high spirits, some limping, but all very bucked with themselves and lording it over the other battalions like anything. Whenever the march got sloppy or dejected, there was at once a shout from one of the Sergeants "Come on the Cobblers", or, "Stick it Steelbacks"; these of course being the nicknames of the Northants [These nicknames are in common parlance being the nicknames for Northampton football club, and the county cricket side known as the Steelbacks]. All became like clockwork again. Also whenever a milepost was reached there was a yell "One, two, three, four, five SIX" all along the line and at the next milepost "one, two, three, four, FIVE". Thus the battalion had only one man fall out and they wouldn't have but he fainted. Maxse praised us for fine marching. An hour after that those who were not lame and some very bad were wandering about Ipswich as lively as crickets, and a good few were, I'm afraid, very "wide" before they went to bed. One man by the way had to be supported into Switchip by two men on each side, and his pack and rifles carried by others, but he didn't fall out. What ho' for the Steelbacks!

Well, owing to the necessity of seeing the men comfortable, I had to tea and dine at my billet. My billet was with another officer; name Laughlin, who was a radical dissenter in business and a jolly fine old fellow too, except he was a strict teetotaller and so we were confined to water. Well, I saw Aunt Flossie right away down on the borders of Ipswich where she had come to see the Bde, but she didn't see me. However at 8pm I found my way to Highwood and had a topping time, including a ripping bath, for 2 and half hours.

This morning we started for Woodbridge at 9am and we said goodbye to the other billets and set forth. At a cross roads I saw Aunt Flossie and Uncle waiting as I had phoned them with the time of departure, and as luck would have it the battalion stopped for 2 minutes at the corner and so I had a minute or so converse with them. It was topping seeing them. We marched for 2 hours and then did a big attack across 2 and a half miles of country, and I arrived here at 4pm, having done 11 miles today, a light job, but enough on top of yesterday's 19 with 60lbs on ones back.

I'm going next door now to have a chat and a drink with my Coy CO Captain Clark, since the battalion has kindly provided us with a bottle of cherry brandy, one of sloe gin, one of whiskey, one of light tawny port, and one of Vermouth. No I shan't get tight even if you think so!

By the way, when we get back to Colchester on the 28th the 55th Bde follow us in the march returning about April 5th, then, I believe, the whole division moves out of Colchester to Salisbury Plain or Borden for Divisional training. This will not take long, and I believe the end of May will find us, either at the front, or more likely, perhaps, at the Dardanelles.

May 4th
Colchester

Now we are all packed ready to go for an early move tomorrow. I'm going to try to get some sleep this afternoon before tomorrow. Tomorrow's stage is to Braintree 15 miles. On Thursday we go to Bishops Stortford, 18 miles, on Friday to Hertford 13 miles, billeting each night. We entrain for Codford on Saturday morning.

Codford

Codford[20]
Codford St Mary
Wiltshire

May 8th 1915

Our march from Bishop's Stortford to Hertford was very hot but through some lovely countryside up to Ware and the first 6 miles was rather cool, as the hedges were tall and decent. At Hertford, to our disgust, we found it was so full of troops that 40 officers were to be billeted in the Corn Exchange on the first floor. However that sport Captain Willows directed me and another to a billet that was jolly comfortable indeed. The family consisted of a lady and 3 daughters. I should call them superior tradesmen as it was in the High Street, and over a shop, but it was very luxurious and they were very decent people. Also I got indirectly the offer of hospitality at Haileybury from a master there called Anderson, but it was too far.

We trained from Hertford at 4am and arrived here at 1pm This is the 3rd night running that I have been to bed at 11.30 and up at 4am. Our camp is quite near the village here, and the village has 2 churches, 3 or 4 shops, a pub and dozens of booths erected by Salisbury tradesmen. I procured a table, some oil and a brush from the ironmongers where you seem to be able to get almost everything.

Salisbury is 14 miles off, and Bath quite near with Bristol further, but I wish I had a bike here.

We are in the midst of rolling downs and within easy reach of the rifle ranges.

May 10th
He is in a bad mood.
I have just mysteriously lost my purse therein having £2 10/- in notes and silver

I have lost a book of stamps
I have lost a key

Am I fed up? Oh no, of course not. I have never known anything to disappear so quickly. I think it was pick pocketed.

We have just been informed unofficially that it is unlikely we shall get out before 2 or 3 months! Reason that the policy of the War Office is to have at least 100,000 men fully armed and equipped constantly in England to repel raids. Kitchener's first army is ready to go but they will not be allowed to go till the 2nd army [ours] is fully equipped with artillery and machine guns, which we have not got as yet. When we are equipped we will have to wait till the 3rd army is fully equipped i.e. about 3 months.

They say that men are not particularly wanted at the front at present, but artillery and shells, shells, shells, also they console us [all this is of course unofficial] with the report that the war will take a good two years or more and we shall all have quite enough and too much of it before we have finished.

We are going to do big divisional days with the 27th as well as our own. We are also going to attend an 11 days firing practice with live shells, and do another musketry course.

There are dozens of camps now and according to rumours Salisbury Plain contains 500,000 in training.

The men are awfully fed up at the moment what with the latest about going out and there is talk of applying for transfers in shoals. They may apply till they are blue in the face but it won't do any good.

May 20th to Mum
The day before yesterday we were, as has happened quite a few days ago, confined

to barracks by the terrific and continuous downpour of rain. It is one of the most tiresome things on earth to be confined to barracks as both officers and men get weary and fed up with Swedish drill[21]*, arm drill, manual exercises, care of arms, visual training, lectures and a thousand and one totally uninteresting items of the sort, only varied by bayonet fighting that is some sport for the men. At one o'clock it cleared up of course and the battalion went for a route march of 11 miles.*

My goodness when I think of the days when I considered 4 miles in light shoes and comfortable clothes a jolly old sweat, whereas we consider it a mere fleabite now to do 11 miles with full packs and jolly lucky to get off with anything up to 15 merely as a little after dinner exercise, together with morning drill and night operations. My sainted aunt!

Well that same evening we did a hot night attack involving another 6 miles and a charge, returning at 12am. The consolation for us was that the Divisional route march next day didn't start as far as we were concerned till the lady like hour of 9.50. Consequently your humble didn't have to get up till 8.45, but reveille for the poor beggars of men was at 6am.

The march was very interesting, units were moving out of Codford on the 14 mile march at unearthly hours, or rather I should say the first unit went out about 7am and got in again at 12, the last unit went out at 12 and got in at 5pm. As a matter of fact the last unit marched past the Brigade Officer of our Bde, as the first unit entered the other side of the village on the home journey. I found it very amusing when we ourselves had done 6 miles to think that a lot of units were just on the point of starting out, and yet the whole road between me and the camp was covered with men, horse, guns, brass hats, bicycles, generals, flags, transport and heaven knows what else all forging along while the same thing was going on up front the whole way up to the camp on return! We ourselves got back at 1.30 pm and had a nice slack afternoon, most of which I spent reading the newspapers and then throwing the cricket ball with a lot of other fellows and ending up by kicking a rugby ball over the posts before dinner with Lambert, Beasley, Schreiner and the padre.

We are lucky to have all the papers here; Bystander, Illustrated London, Sporting and Dramatic, Tattler, Sketch and all the other dailies except Standard and Daily News and Telegraph, Punch and the Northampton and Bath papers. Captain Willows being on the mess committee and the fact that the President, Major Wyndowe, who at Colchester lived with his wife in town, and never turned up to mess, and didn't care a brass button what happened to it, now has to dine at mess and has made a revolution in the conduct of the mess. We are, thanks to Willow, now quite comfortable, having paper serviettes, a table cloth every night, liqueurs and a bigger range of wines and cider as a common drink, better cooking and more cleanliness, and that's not all, at the same price as before. He's a good man is old Willows. By the way our mess charge is 2/3 per day but in a great many down here it is much worse and sums no less than 10/- per day in some messes [the whole of one's day pay and field allowance].

The jolly old Colonel has got a touch of sun, owing to his having, as he put it, during a long halt outside Hertford on one of those scorching days, laid on his stomach and got his backbone roasted. He has gone home on a weeks leave. I hope to goodness he doesn't get ill, because he is the regiment and that we are so good is largely due to him and all the men love him.

Talking of leave, no leave is to be given to officers and men, except for urgent private or business reasons [to be explained in the Brigadier's office]. I wouldn't face the old Brigadier with insufficient reasons. He is as bad as Maxse. Our Coy Commander turned his men about on the road the other day to go the shortest way home instead of by the road, which is perfectly allowable. Unfortunately Maxse came up just at that moment with his staff and without waiting to enquire why asks " Why the ———- was he marching his company up and down the road." So you see what we get. Maxse's bark is worse than his bite, but the Brigadier's is worse than his bark though that's bad enough. Maxse is quite unnecessarily rude and uses "some" language, but he is probably the best trainer of men in the army and nothing escapes him, even the minutest point. The Brigadier gets into a temper now and then and if you can get behind a bush or hide yourself somewhere [only don't let him see you do it], so much the better for you when he is taken that way. The jolly old Colonel can do a good job of telling a man off, but he doesn't make himself so disagreeable as the others.

I am paying the Coy today so I didn't go out on Bde manoeuvres, which accounts for this letter. Half an hour ago I staggered into camp with £100 odd in my haversack.

I am glad Asquith, Grey, Lloyd George and Harcourt are staying on, and I favour Winston getting another job in the Government, Balfour being 1st Lord of the Admiralty with Fisher and Curzon, Milner, Bonar Law, Austen Chamberlain Landsdowne and Long, but I hope to goodness they give FE Smith anything or Carson. The idea of appointing Kitchener Viceroy of India or Commander in Chief, which is an empty post with George at the War Office, is abhorrent. By all means let Lloyd George, who is quite the right sort of man for it, take up the job of organising munition supply. I see the Rads still hang on to McKenna and Haldane, who is only a stage better than FE Smith to my mind. Some suggest Beresford at the Admiralty but I prefer Fisher.

I must say I fank the German chemists. I thought the beggars would not stop at gas and see that they have poisoned a river now with arsenic. They'll do more too before their finished. It is nasty to think of our using stinks, but I suppose it is inevitable.

May 24th to Mum

On Friday our platoon commander, Wilcox, went off to Bedford on special leave. His uncle was killed at the front and he went to Bedford where his relations live. So I got the platoon at last and as luck would have it we had a very long and interesting day, marched 18 miles and did a lot of wood fighting and were highly complimented by the General for keenness and dash shown. Well we had to wade through a very boggy road, as well as along the Roman road, an absolutely straight road going as straight as a dye through a wood for 2 miles, awfully nice. On the way home we halted on the edge of the wood for the usual short halt – we march for 50 minutes and then rest for 10. Well we halted as I say of the men they were done and looked it. I was in great form myself but couldn't have done more with the men than keep them going without falling out when by good luck "D" Coy passed us and their men gibed at us and said "Come along C. Done already" etc. Our fellows got annoyed and shouted "We'll catch you up next halt". Sure enough the fellows marched like mad, and we caught the other Coy just getting their packs on again after their rest 2 miles down the road. They swung past cheering the others ironically and these got annoyed in their turn and were going to pass us next halt they said. By Jove, you should have seen our fellows marching, yelling "Hard up, hard up always jolly well broke", and "Yes Kitchener loves us because he told us so," and "Oh tomorrow morning just before the break of day, I shall be miles and miles away," and other such melodies, shouting, swinging along all in step and all in great spirits as if they hadn't done a mile. The Coy Commander saw this and thought it would be a good thing to get back without the regulation halt. However he asked them "Did they want to halt?" and they yelled "No." You see the D Coy was 50 yards behind, so we finally swung into camp fresh as a fiddle yelling with joy and 400 yards ahead of D Coy. I never saw such a change in all my life.

Saturday we had a Battalion field day in which I again had the platoon. This time they didn't distinguish themselves, as my particular platoon was dropped on for doubling down hill by sections in a straggling way which annoyed me particularly because I had given special instructions to the section commanders about that very thing and while doubling myself at the head of the men had cursed the sections on my right and left all the way down the hill for it.

In the evening we had a Bde concert whereof I send the programme. I nearly died of laughter several times, the songs were topping and I particularly liked "Till the boys come home". You might get it for me if and when I come back next time.

June 1st to Mother

On Saturday last the run came off. It was rather a fine sight. Some had proper running clothes, others had long trousers and grey army shirts and others had brilliant colours. Consequently 2,000 men streaming up the hill at the start in such a variety of colour made a very fine sight. Everyone who started i.e. 500 from each battalion in the Bde. was meant to do the 6 miles course in 50 minutes. Anyone who didn't counted 2,000 points while every one who did counted the number of his place in points i.e. the 31st counted as 31 points. The Battalion with the lowest score wins after the all the penalty marks for those who didn't finish were added.

The 7th Bedford's won it and we were second, 73 of ours not finishing compared to 48 of them. They had trained more than us and had been made to go on drill runs. We hadn't and we should have won had some of our men not just wandered off before they were counted. Also the Beds all had shorts while most of our men had to run in Khaki trousers, with shirts and brown canvas shoes, though some were enterprising enough to wear pyjamas tucked in at the knees. I really ran this time and came 200th out of the 2000. The winner's time was 33 minutes and he was a professional runner before the war. I did it in about 38 1/2 minutes pretty good for me! Lambert came in 18th in about 351/2 minutes. My servant apparently raced me round making desperate efforts all the way to overtake me with a pal of his. I never saw them at all but apparently they just got past me in the last 20 yards. They wouldn't have done it if I had seen them, the beggars!

No less than 1,650 out of the 2,000 finished in under 50 minutes, pretty good seeing that a lot of them were old soldiers of 40 and over.

On Sunday I decide to go on Church parade so that I should be free afterwards to go to Bristol. When I got there I found I was in command of the company — "some nut what"!

Yesterday we had a scheme set by the Brigade and I had a platoon for a change and got on quite well. Not long ago we had a night trench digging and got back about 12.30.

Today we had an inter-brigade scheme, which turned in to a ridiculous farce for several reasons too long to begin here. Suffice it to say that an idiotic commander of the Bedford's calmly went to sleep, allowed the enemy to surprise and rout them, thus getting on the flanks of the Bedford's and Fusiliers and rolling them up. We had to retreat and we did it in a very bad way owing to the stupid instructions of the Bde that overrode our own ideas. Consequently two of our companies were caught by 8 machine guns all together no less, as they emerged in fours from a track running through the woods and were swept away.

Maxse was pretty averagely blasphemous about this and I don't wonder at it. You see, half the officers were men new to their jobs since the proper Coy Commanders were attending a course while the commanding officers of the Brigade had gone to the front for four days.

Our new rifles have just come together with new boots etc, and one brand new Lewis Machine Gun has also turned up, so we are getting on. The first army of Kitchener of Khartoum is composed of the 9th, 10th, 11th, 12th, 13th and 14th Divisions. I hear definitely today that the 9th, 12th, 14th, or the 9th, 10th and 14th have gone already, so it's getting on. The 2nd army is the 15th, 16th, 17th, 18th, 19th and 20th divisions. I expect the 18th will go away the first of K2.

I suppose you saw that Basil Maclean has just been killed at the front. He was still in command of the Coy of Gentleman Cadets at Sandhurst when I was at Camberley. Also I saw that DH Sewell, nephew of a friend EHD of mine at school, had a marvellous escape. The Evening News called it the most marvellous of the war. He was knocked senseless by the explosion of a shell and lay stunned for two days, and is now in hospital.

You remember the three men who came down last summer to fence against the school for Oxford University, one of them, a man called Sprint. was killed. He was in the Bedfordshire's. Now I see a second, the sabre 1st string of the Varsity, whom Lambert beat, called Taylor, is killed also. Two out of 3 men I met quite by chance, both gone.

June 10th to Mother

I got no less than 5 letters in the post yesterday, including one from home, Cyril Mudford, Evan Jones, Jamie Thornton, Titch Smith. Yesterday I got a parcel from Aunt Flossie containing a respirator!!! What ho! For the water chute sang Waggles. [If you don't understand this last remark, ask the Cabbage Bug]. [His Dad!]

We have had some strenuous times lately. It was fearful hot on Monday and Tuesday, when we did trench digging in thick chalk, and musketry. We had such a day yesterday. Started at 7.50am for a divisional day. Marched 8 miles and then had excursions, marches, counter-marches, attacks, defences, high jinks up hill down dale. No food, curses and heat till 8.30pm at which time we came back to camp. The atmosphere, apart from the heat, was somewhat electric. And became overcharged later owing to an unfortunate event, which led Maxse into certain lingual indiscretions, and thereafter the air was, well, redolent with curses, swear words, ill temper and bad language of all sorts all round. During a particular brilliant charge on the enemy's position by the Northants and Beds, the Norfolk's {the enemy} complained that a round of ball had been fired and had whizzed over their heads, and this was said to be from the Northants. Considering the other Battalions had been firing on the range with ball and we hadn't even seen a ball cartridge since Colchester it isn't likely it was us.

However, Maxse dashed up on his horse and had all the officers of the Northants out and told them it was d———d disgraceful, and swore like a second hand trooper. He appears even to have gone to the Colonel and hinted that he would get the push if it happened again. The Colonel hinted as much to the Battalion and I tell you the language he used was unprintable. He would hardly dare do it, however, even if it did occur again, as the officers would transfer as a body and the men would mutiny on the spot if the Colonel were to go. You see, whereas the men love the Colonel, the second in command is loathed and hated like poison by officers and men. He is never at work himself but sees that everyone else works full hours and much more if possible. The men hate him and I hope for his sake that he won't go too near the firing line!

The Colonel returned safely from the tour of the trenches, he had an interesting time and says that a shell burst 20 yards ahead of him on one occasion. One other of the party of Colonels had a much narrower escape, when talking to a Terrier he was taken off to see something by another man, when a shell burst, killing the Terrier Colonel and took the right hand off the other man who was standing by.

He announced that this time definitely WE are for the front in about 5 weeks time. The latest rumour is that the 17th was going to the Dardanelles, but got measles and we are going instead. Anyhow things are coming in fast now with new rifles short and long bayonets issued on Monday. Field Kitchens arrived, all guns came except 4. So we look like business. Another rumour is that Maxse is not going to the front with us. He is, of course, in very ill odour with most of the other generals, particularly French. He doesn't get on with anyone, but I don't think at the 11th hour they will change but it makes the Dardanelles more likely.

So much for military affairs, except that like the men and a good few officers I am completely fed up with the army and most things appertaining. They work us like nothing on earth. Even after 13 hours on end yesterday and no food, reveille went at 6am this morning and there was a parade at 7. This did not concern me of course because I had in the ordinary course as Orderly officer to be at the issue of rations at 6.30 am, but it was "thick" for the men. The general feeling is completely and absolutely fed up, and at the present moment I very much doubt with my experience whether horses and traction engines, much less patriotism, would drag me into the army. I'd go shell making.

My orderly Sergeant to date has done 9 years in the regular army and 1 in reserve and says that in all that time he has never done as much work as we have done in 9 months. But enough of this. It has got to be stuck!

Later H-S refers to a visit he paid to this aunts and cousins in Clifton. He was taken to a reception at Clifton College, and was taken on a tour of the school.

He said, *"I admired it greatly. The Chapel is splendid and the organ — !!!!!. I felt quite in my element I tell you.* **There is the same sort of atmosphere in public schools and it suits me.** *I felt as "at home" after a very short time there as in the School Chapel at home. In the afternoon I went to Chapel again. The singing was topping, 10 or 11 times better than at Bedford, in fact a revelation. Dr David was the preacher and he is a perfectly splendid man, and to crown all, that organ!! When I say that the organist was a perfect artist he was at least 4 or 5 times better than any I have ever heard, and to cap all the piece he played was from Wagner [my favourite as you know] and from "Lohengrin" at that and finally when I say that I sat with my mouth, eyes, ears and senses wide open and could have sat for hours on end, you will get some sort of idea of what it was like. The organ cost about £2000 and was beaten only by the Rugby one."*

Letter to Mother June 28th 1915
My own darling Tittie

"No word from home for it seems such a long time. Dad's last letter was not altogether cheering to hear that the family was almost all suffering from various ailments. So it is additionally alarminating to hear no news from home. I hope, you naughty little Tittie, you have not got up too soon as you always do. Please don't do anything foolish.

I'm rather pessimistic tonight to put it mildly as we have just heard that all the supernumeraries are going to be transferred to the 8th Battalion of this Regiment when this Batt. goes to the front!! Then they will go out with the drafts. Isn't it pleasant to be back at Colchester, a place I never wanted to see again, to be under Coy Commanders who have got the push from this Battalion for incompetence,

An OB called Loughlin digging trenches at Codford in 1915

wherein I don't care for it at all, and in a Battalion that is doing elementary work when I am practically a fully trained officer.

It was seen in a letter from the WO in the orderly room, and though not officially given out, is what we have to look forward to. I am fed up to the teeth, and I know it will not take too much to make me chuck the Army and transfer to the Royal Naval Division, which is at least certain to go to the Dardanelles. Meanwhile we are all working like plantation niggers here.

Day before yesterday we had a Divisional day. Start out from camp at 6.30am. Back to camp tired and nearly melted 8pm. One would have thought a bit of slack advisable. No! Reveille next morning at 5.30am. Proceed to Yarnbury Castle 6 miles from here for trench digging. Dig away in a blazing sun for hours and return at 5pm."

Notice how narrow the trench was going to be, and compare it with some German trenches of this time.

Up at 7.15 next morning and on the ranges all day until 8pm. Tomorrow all subalterns for a course of bayonet fighting at 7am. Moses, you should here the men swearing about it. It has become almost part of the training to call the men idiots for being so discontented and that they are not ready for the front, when all the while the said subs are raving just as much inwardly. Well, I have been a private for 3 months, and a subaltern for 7 and the only end result is the 8th Batt. Sooner or later.

I believe my temper will become a very evil one.

We did some bayonet training this morning. All of us have to go through a bomb and hand grenade course soon. The Division got their 3 field ambulances yesterday and the officers thereof having no mess are the guests of our mess at present. There are 600 men in the ambulances, and on the march they occupy 3/4s mile of road with their motor ambulance wagons and transport etc.

We began our 2nd Musketry course and I did fairly well, getting 45 out of 60 and coming 2nd of the officers. One was a grouping practice, then 5 shots at a disappearing figure which I hit every time, and then at 8pm when the light was very bad I only managed 10 out of 20 at 400 yards which though better than all but a few did not please me because owing to carelessness in setting my sights I had a "miss"."

July 15th 1915
Mayfield
Northwich

Dear Heriz-Smith

Just a note to ask you how you are getting on. I have no news but I only wanted to write for the sake of the past. Those old days of School, Chapel and the games. Doesn't it shake you to think it has all gone? Doesn't gone sound so awful? I suppose I shall have to wait for the re-creation of man and then —. One feels proud that one lived at such a time!

I always feel sorry for a chap who says that School was rotten; it shows he didn't take enough interest in it. I'm going to join the OB's Club when I've got enough money, and I wrote for the Ousel today, so as not get too behind in School news. I always thank God I was in the Chapel Choir as it makes such a difference; don't you get awfully home and School sick? I do and it's quite natural.

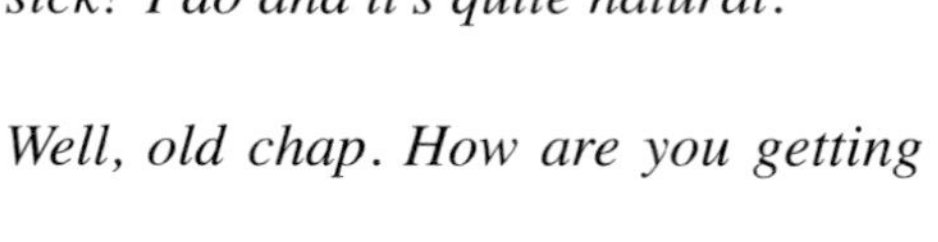

Well, old chap. How are you getting

along? I don't expect you have too much time for letters, but I'm sure you don't forget that I'm thinking of you everyday.

When I get my hols I hope I shall see you, and also when you come back from the Front, if you go; we mustn't lose each other. One never knows whether his pals will come back, isn't this war fearful? But I've given over worrying about friends and relatives, I trust only to God's mercy and prayer.

Good bye and good luck
I remain ever your affectionate friend
Cyril B Cook

Back to Colchester

July 27th 1915
From Colchester to Mum

This is very poor tack indeed. I arrived here last night and no luggage had arrived leaving me without bed, washing or anything whatsoever.

Now for this Battalion.

If I were to enumerate all the events we have to undergo I couldn't. I feel much more like mutiny than anything else at present and can see no hopes of improvement.

Because

There are 130 officers of the 8th Batt. itself and 30 from the 5th, 6th, and 7th. The 8th officers get all the preference that there is which is not much at present, but some of them and all of us are together in misery [and it is misery I can tell you] of being in an officer's class. This means that we act just as if we had never done anything before in the shape of soldiering, and do drill, bayonet fighting and all the squad drill in front of the men of the squad. This by itself is Hell, almost literally, because I can't get used to it, and it seems to me degrading and unnecessary, and I fume like anything all day.

But to make it worse we are taken for it not by a decent instructor but by a young idiot [a 2nd Lt of the 8th!!!] who by virtue of being on a week's bayonet fighting and physical drill course comes on funny or tries to be, and promptly tries to tell you that everything you have been taught at Codford by Captain Campbell and a

Sergeant Major of the School of Musketry is all wrong.

More, by token that old Colonel Ripley has forgotten to write after all this, and this CO, an old ass, practically informs us that we are junior of everyone else because seniority here and also as afar as we can see, from what he said, seniority in going out goes by the date of joining the Battalion! Consequently our likelihood of ever getting out of here seems to be dwindling to vanishing point all together.

That is enough gall and wormwood by itself, but I ain't finished yet.

As I said we are 15 together in a men's hut. Consequently we have the more riotous members of the community coming in at unseasonable hours of the night, making a row and waking us up. Also a good few are very junior. The worse was a Corporal in the Sussex Regiment and for an arrant bounder I couldn't want a worse.

One is reminded of a paragraph in Robert Grave's "Goodbye to All That" when he wrote "What I most disliked in the Army was never being alone, forced to live and sleep with men whose company, in many cases, I would have run miles to avoid!"

The letter continues.

The long hut is lit by 3 electric lights. These have to be shaded with red covers and no more light is allowed even if you have a good oil lamp. Why? Because of aeroplanes. [There were German bombs dropped on the camp in February 1915]. Consequently letter writing and reading is very difficult. You are not allowed to write letters in the mess anteroom, which is seemingly some sort of sacred place. I think I will be driven to the Officer's club to write letters

Next there is no one here I have the slightest liking for. The hours of our doddery work start at 6.45 and go on until 5.30 and with little interval. I have already described the work itself!

In fact the whole thing is one long series of disheartening events, and not even the blessed relief of privacy at any moment of the day.

My word this gentleman's in love with the army!

All this is aggravated by the want of a bed etc. The nuisance was eased today by the arrival of the parcel with my pyjamas, one comfort. Also my portmanteau turned up at the station, but, of course, the valise did not and that contained my bed and washbasin, blankets brushes and everything important. I wired to

Paddington but they can't trace it, nor can the GER, but I have written to the lost luggage office at Paddington and the GER and hope to hear shortly.

August 2nd 1915
From Geoff

The vicarage
Mullion, Cornwall

To Herr Von Hertz Schmidt.
I suppose you are wondering what I have done for my duty, as I am not in uniform. Well, as you know, I have had a year at a Tech College in Manchester, living in rooms there and now I have got a job in an engineering firm turning out war material.

It is extremely agreeable to live on ones own and altogether I have had a fairly good time. In holiday time I have been camping with friends in the Lakes and Shropshire. I enjoyed the former more than anything I have ever known.

I could quite sympathise with you being bored with your surroundings. I know a good many who had nearly a years training whilst others have joined and were sent out in just 2 months.

It certainly doesn't seem right that such should be the case.

Rex came down for a weeks leave about a month ago and I hurried to see him. He thought it would be his final leave but he has not yet left for the front and he expected to go by July 1st.

Tessie is coming down here for some time in order to read for her BA. Just think of that frivolous spark being a bluestocking in disguise. I shall see her for 4 days and I don't think she'll forget as I am going to zag her as much as possible".

August 2nd 1915 to Mum from Colchester
I will not give my opinion about Kessingland. I don't think it's safe after all but I don't know. There have been 2 air raids on Harwich in the last fortnight that didn't appear in the papers.

Launches into a diatribe about America sparked by something his dad wrote.

If someone would only sink a shipload of American dollars they might come in, but they'd rather lose 1,000 American citizens without saying a word, and it's unfortunately true, as a German paper says, that this war will leave us in head over heels in debt to America, who seem to be beneath contempt as a lot of bum bailiffs, useful but contemptible.

This must be about the sinking of the Lusitania.

Back to Colchester
The whole show is horrid but one gets used to it. When I shall kick up a stink is if any 8th men are sent out to the 6th, but till then mum's the word.

I went to All Saints and the Vicar gave out that he wants more in the choir and that anyone who could sing could apply. I met him after the service and he has given me carte blanche to sing in the choir whenever it suits me.

August 3rd
BEF

Dear Heriz-Smith

You might send me on my wristwatch as I have finally busted mine.

We are billeted in a ramshackle old village within sound of the guns and will be moving up to our killing warrens in a few days. We are all keeping very fit and well and are very comfortable under the circumstances. The only fly in the ointment is the variability of the weather. We route march most days and when it is hot it is bloody hot and when it isn't it rains. We were wet once today and twice yesterday and we haven't many drying facilities. We had Hell's own bombing practice yesterday with an almost unlimited supply of real genuine government made mortars – some bang.

Beasley, Burrows and Evans here present join me in sending love to you all.

Yours sincerely

A Loughlin

August 7th 1915 from R Beacham
It was nice to hear any news of you although I wished you had been able to write in a happier vein. I'm afraid you are not too comfortable in your new surroundings. Colonel Ripley has already written to your CO with reference to

you being sent out early and is going to send a reminder. But if things are not going as you would like don't play into their hands by showing resentment and sulkiness, rather show them what you are capable of doing, then you won't give you any reason to keep you back. We move up behind the line tomorrow and shall probably enter the trenches next week. Everyone is well, the Sergeant Major has gone to the Divisional Base as S Major and Sgt Major Fletcher has taken his place. We are within sound of the guns and that is all, but next week will remedy that.

With kind regards to you all and trusting you may soon join our happy band.

You may rest assured that the Colonel will do what he can.
August 9th
Northwich
Cheshire

I heard yesterday from Lambert, from the front, and he says he's writing to you as you hadn't written to him in ages. He seems to be enjoying himself on port wine dinners.

Well, how are you getting along? I expect you will go out in one of the first drafts as you are fully trained.

I heard this morning from Mackenzie and Spencer. Mackenzie is in town at present, he is trying to get in the navy, and if he fails he's going into the Inns of Courts OTC.

Spencer has been staying here for a few days. He came up on his motorbike and returned in safety. It took him only 5 hours to get home. He has got a commission in the East Anglian Engineers. He is in Sauer's Coy; Sauer is practically a captain now.

Last week we had the Cheshire Volunteer Regiment reviewed. It was fine. I'm in the Regiment, and I'm quite efficient now.

We were reviewed by General Creigh VC who said he had studied war all his life, and was certain in his mind that there would be an invasion of England and that we would all be called up. There were 10'000 of us and 400 cavalry who looked fine. We have our own silver bands, signalling corps and ambulance corps etc. One of the features is the motor transport. The whole Regiment can be transported by means of motorcars and wagons, about 800 to 1000 of them. [We are looking out for an aviation corps to be complete].

Colonel Sauer, Sauer's father, is our colonel.

Etc

Ever your affectionate friend
Cyril B Cook.

August 9th 1915
From Colchester to Mum

General chitchat and telling how he found his valise that somehow had got to Purfleet.

We have heard from the 6th. The Colonel is very sorry for us and is going to write, so they, our correspondents, say. I suppose you saw the list of officer's casualties from K1 in the paper yesterday, mostly Rifle Bde. and KRRC. It looks as if the 14th Division has been a bit cut up. The 6th themselves are now occupying trenches that no English troops have yet occupied. [Where can this be?]. Also they can only understand the patois of the country with some difficulty. Also "we should be surprised if we knew where they were". It sounds as if the French have given up some of their line to us, but where? Also their trenches are less than 30 yards from the German front line!

Also the troops opposite them are those devils of Bavarians, so it looks as if there would be some hot times, as if the B's try any of their mutilating tricks on our division our fellows will assuredly give no quarter, I know this for a fact.

All this looks like us getting out fairly early always supposing we go out before these 8th people.

I got a service line from Lambert and a letter from Loughlin.

They don't look tremendously bright in Roossia do they? My Cossack gent said "No ammunition".

We were going to go down to Shoreham this Friday and the advance party actually went down there on Saturday but they are coming back and departure is postponed. I need say no more about my life here. It's boring to a degree and the Colonel is an old beast. Geoffrey Peel is down here.

August 24th 1915
6th Battalion Northamptonshire Regiment
BEF

My dear Lizzie.

I am glad that my letter was "most excellent", but I wish I could say the same about yours. It is neither long enough nor sufficiently chatty.

I had a nice letter from Cyril Cook. He told me he was going to write to you, so I suppose that was your second letter from him. I should like to think it was your first, but I'm afraid I cannot bring myself to do so.

I saw the casualty list with Maurice Simpson's name in it while actually in the trenches. I have heard from Bob and Jack but neither of these knew what had happened to M. However they are going to let me know as soon as they can. I hope it is nothing really serious. I agree with you that it was probably at the new landing.

I suppose your Zep raid enlivened the proceedings much to your satisfaction. I have seen between 150 and 200 shells fired by the Huns at our aeroplanes in the same afternoon, but without bringing one down.

Have you heard from Ian Black at all? I have written to him but have had no reply, so I'm afraid my letter has gone astray. I see that Noz has done very well, 2nd into the Indian Army. Does that mean he is abandoning the JP?

The General commended little Corporal Denton the other day for assisting in the capture of a Hun, and for remorselessly pinking a British soldier who had got in the wrong place. The last was a fine shot.

So George is a consolation to you? I'm glad you hit it off so well. Our "A" Coy is a fine institution. Willows, Grace, Shrine and Pig, and the old man are all splendid fellows to get on with. Stokes, Simpson and Mick are our most frequent visitors, and of them Stokes is more often than not to be found around "A" Coy. I'm afraid that none of us, with the possible exception of Willows, hit it off with Woulfe at all. Grace, the Old Man and I positively hate him. Schreiner, who very rarely passes a judgement on one of us, says that he is the absolute limit. The actual words he used were considerably stronger than that. Tonight we had a row with him, and we were discussing him very freely, when I happened to turn round and saw him at the table just behind us; he heard every word. Poor beggar his ears must have tingled. It will do him some good though.

I personally have been enjoying the life immensely. So far the trenches have been anything but unpleasant. The nearest thing I have had was a bullet fired by one of my own men, who let off his rifle just as he got into his dugout, on coming off sentry. The bullet went between Captain Barford and myself, about 3 feet from each of us. We have had a goodly number of rifle grenades and some trench mortars, also some whiz-bangs, which are the German field guns. They are pretty harmless, except the rifle grenades. These don't often get in a trench, but when they do they are quite useful. At the piece of trench my platoon held, we were at one place only 15 yards from the Huns. Everything, however, was very quiet. We had 2 minnenwerfers over one night. They go whoosh –oh-oh-oh, polop —-bang! They make a hell of a noise but their bark is worse than their bite.

We have now moved, and are settling down opposite one of the hottest parts of the line; very different to where we were I can assure you. Still at the worst we can only be killed and that will suit you people fine —- n'est- ce-pas?

By the way if you have found a solace in George I have certainly found one in Mick. I can assure you he is one of the best, whatever his faults may be. He is usually found around at "A" Coy or else I am to be found at "D" Coy, when we are doing nothing in billets. I like him better than anyone else in the regiment. That is quite a fine panegyric from me, as you know I'm not as fine an enthusiast as you.

By the way I am at present in consultation with the R Pros over a sort of bomb projector which is [I don't think] going to engrave our names on the tabloids of posterity, if they don't use gelatine camels instead of tabloids. Schreiner is planning frightfulness with the largest salmon rod on this earth, and a reel that looks more like a capstan than anything else which I know.

I want you to remember me to everybody, especially bloody old Morton, and Spencer if he has not left you.

If you go on leave at any time, I also want you to remember me to all the old crowd, especially Bob, Ian and Atchy. Also to Batterbury.

Well I have written what, is for me, a long letter. Please do not allow yourself to be out-done.

Yours ever
Pudding

J Lambert.

August 27th 1915
To Dad

My Dear Old Dad

Gotcher letter
My what a waste of ink
Why you can't write a betta
That's more than I can think.
Yet Oim inditing an ansa
By no better light than the moon
Anything I can but you can't sir
While awaiting the Zeppelin's zoom
You may think it's a foolish fad sir
While the sausages cruise in the heaven
To write to one's darling old dad sir
With the world all at sixes and sevens
Yet here goes an answering epistle and quite a challenge to bet
And though my wit makes you all whistle
You ain't seen the end of it yet.

In other words thank you very much for the letter received this morning.

What do I want to say? I don't know! I have no news except that you unscrew the muzzle cap and strip the lock and the fuse spring. Sorry! You can see that my brain never had very highly developed cells for Maths, engineering, mechanics etc and that I am on a machine gun course. I hear it said that they are going to form a machine gun corps now like the German one, and like the artillery.

Also there's a tale from a fellow back from Felixstowe that they have German submarines in Harwich. That one or two have actually come into the harbour —- and haven't got out. Also mines are sown in the North Sea by a special kind of submarine only discovered by the capture of one a little time ago, having an ingenious false bottom whereby they drop mines.

Also there are rumours that they are moving troops for France and the Dardanelles.

Maurice Simpson is back home. He fell in to a Turkish trench and got stunned and came to when all his men were either still someway behind or shot down by the Turks, and he had to defend himself from the Turks with his revolver. He is now at Oxford suffering from slight concussion.

It's a very hard life you know, and I'm living in a perpetual ferment of discontent varied by gusts of fury, and envy of those already out at the front. They are certainly adept at here in finding out fresh ways of annoying one. My hat I'm fed up with the place and the Battalion.

Enclosed please find a letter from Lambert. The 6th have repelled a German attack, and captured 1 Hun. The Companies trenches were also shelled and knocked down in places but quickly repaired with few casualties. My, ain't I longing to be safe there from all these worries.

The Zepps didn't come last night as expected.

I am prepared to bet you that America will not be in the war by the end of October – a good offer in a way, as you haven't a ghost of chance of winning. A sorrier lot of skunks, money grabbers, degenerates than the Yanks I've never seen. She and Bulgaria is a pretty pair. One would sell it's soul for money, the other for power. I almost prefer German bestiality to American grasping and hollow sounding vapours. I've never had much opinion of the Yanks, but by goodness they've descended so low as to allow themselves the insults by Mexico and Haiti. A sort of "This way please, plant down all your dirty baggage here" attitude. I used to be afraid that the USA would conquer Canada, now I shouldn't be surprised if Canada doesn't eventually establish a protectorate over the USA! China has ordered 100 submarines, I see. Why she and Japan would walk over the USA with ease. *One thing is that whatever side wins will eventually reduce the USA to very small beer indeed and a good thing too.* [He was wrong with this prediction!]

One thing looks bright and that's the 6th Bde. are now in the hottest part of the line, so a chance of getting out does seem possible. They were at Ypres were they? I wonder.

September 2nd
To Mum

I hear the 6th have not been in action yet, so going out there seems almost as far off as before.

The 7th battalion has been out 3 weeks and only just marched to the trenches before being flung in after a very long march into the thick of the fighting. Consequently they had some time. The colonel was killed as were the adjutant, and 5 captains killed or wounded, and so we hear, 600 men gone, and the Battalion commanded by the Quartermaster! Consequently our 7th fellows expect to get out at once

Sept 11th 1915
To Mum

We had another Zep raid on Wednesday. The Zeps came over but either can't find us or don't trouble about us. The latter is likely, as they seem to know their route very well. I have heard plenty of details of the last raid. There was a panic at Millwall. The poor people went out in to the street screaming I'm told. There isn't a whole pain of glass left in Broad Street, and they came within 400 feet of Liverpool Street Station and dropped a bomb or two. One missed the station the other fell on the line between Liverpool Street and Moorgate and tore it up a bit. Another fell on a busload of people and killed the lot. They succeeded at last in killing a soldier after one year. One bomb fell on Fenchurch but didn't explode. The damage at Millwall they say was very great. The Zeps seem to be justifying their existence at last, and they weren't far from Woolwich Arsenal.

Something has to be done to relieve the hopeless monotony of this place. A fellow who I rather like here is always asking me to go to the Hippodrome or pictures and really I'm fed up making excuses not going. The former I simply bar as it is vulgar and unrelieved by any wit. The pictures are a delight but I usually only go there to scream with laughter. However one does meet some good things occasionally. However few officers go to the pictures.

Sept 18th 1915
To Mum

Yesterday we vacated the Reed Hall 'utments and came here to Meeanee Barracks. The Colonel was in a frightful temper as usual, so much so that he made us load the lorries with our own bags rather than by a fatigue party. An unheard of thing and one which only intensifies everyone's dislike for what the senior major in the regiment called "An insolent, ignorant, unmannerly cur", or words to that effect.

Granted that among the subalterns there a number who never should have been made officers, and who have no idea how to behave like gentlemen; still for a CO to make officer's do Navvies work, or to allow the Sergeant Major to be rude and insubordinate not only to subalterns but also to Captains, to call two subalterns "the scum of the earth", "lazy loafers" and "idiots" to their face is a bit strong. You can guess what state the Battalion is in when I say that the two Senior Majors are only waiting for a suitable hold to enable them to run the CO before the Divisional General, that the senior Captain is only waiting to get a few more instances of insubordination on the part of the Sgt Major to order him to his quarters and have him up before the CO, that the subalterns, one and all, except for 5 or 6 who toady him, loathe and abhor the CO as a loud, ignorant, vapouring and unmannerly cur, that the men and especially those who have been in the Regular army, or in the 5th, 6th and 7th Battalions, hate the sight of him! Some Battalion to be in! Yet there are decent men and officers if it weren't for the spirit of meanness and unfairness personified in the CO, which permeates everything here.

However we are now in the barracks and what is very much to the point is that I and Fawkes are sharing a nice small room which we have furnished with two carpets, wash stand, chest of drawers, slop pail, easy chair and small chair and all modern conveniences at the price of 12/- per month between the two of us. What ho! We aren't 'arf comfortable, not 'arf. You see we aren't in the barracks but in a large house nearby whereof there are two, which accommodate 20 officers. Of course the regulars had these before the war so they would be luxurious—not 'alf In fact everything apart from the CO and parade are nice.

We are much nearer town and nearly in the grounds of the Officer's Club. In fact quite in clover.

September 24th 1915
From Eric Piercy
B Coy
16th Middx.

I was sorry to hear of your rather unfortunate position but I envy you just the same. I have now been in this battalion 12 months and it is quite doubtful whether we shall go out before the spring. We were inspected by Sir Archibald Murray and he said we were one of the finest battalions he had ever inspected. General Maude, who was for a time our Divisional Commander, was very pleased with us and General Paget said we were in such an advanced state we were to be equipped and sent out a soon as possible. Yet in spite of all this we have only about 100 short rifles, and are not being equipped as far as I can see.

The rumour is that we are being sent to Shoreham for the winter. This camp seems to have a bad reputation so it is unlikely that we shall stop here for the wet season.

My cousin, "lout" Lawless, is a Captain in the 18th Middx [pioneers] who are attached to our division.

I am presently on a Grenadiers course, and we have an excellent trench catapult for bomb throwing; it is almost exactly on the lines of those some naughty boys used to use at school, only, of course, much bigger.

18

"First Friend"

The death of Jim Lambert[22]

The earlier pages in this book provide illustrations of the affectionate relationship Heriz-Smith and James Lambert had. They went through school together and lived very close to one another. Denzil lived in St Georges Road and Jim in the Grove, both in walking distance of School.

Occasionally the relationship was prickly but the sentiments that Jim's mother mentioned in a letter after Jim's death showed the huge bond there was between the two. Denzil went into the Northamptonshire's because Jim was there and both were on the road to Oxbridge and then the Church.

They frequently used nicknames for each other, Denzil being "Lizzie"[23] and James "Pudding". Both of them always wished to keep up to date with school news even when they were in the trenches.

Jim had an outstanding school career being a Monitor and playing for the First teams at both Rugby and Cricket. In his last summer at Bedford Grammar School he scored a century against the Leys and averaged 24 with the bat.

On 14th September 1914, James Lambert was commissioned into the Army as a Temporary Second Lieutenant. On 3rd November 1914, 2/Lt. Lambert was appointed Temporary Lieutenant in the 6th (Service) Battalion Northamptonshire Regiment. Lt. Lambert went to France on 26th July 1915 with the 6th Northamptonshire's.

This caused some envy and frustration in Heriz-Smith as he was left behind as a Subaltern in Colchester, a place he learnt to loathe, and he was desperate to get to the front, be it in France or the Dardanelles. Lambert writes

BEF September 13th

"My Dear Lizzie"

So you have deserted Bedford for the sombre pleasures of Clifton and Ealing. You

seem very down on your luck. As you say, your power of letter writing has deserted you [to some extent], and you no longer reel off page after page of irreproachable literature. All the same it wasn't quite a hopeless letter, for some bright spots were in it. Anyway I will try to cheer you up!

To begin with, we are stuck in a delightful bit of trench that varies from 12 to 50 yards from the Hun. We live in an atmosphere of rifle grenades and trench mortars, and mines. There are mines galore in every sector and there is always something going on. So you see this part is so much more exciting than the part where we went for instruction – there is no comparison between the two. Their snipers are very good indeed. You put up your head for a mere second in daylight and it is "actum est". Sergeant Holley who was in your company did it with fatal results – he was in my platoon. I think they must use a clipped bullet, or else it is at very close range, as they make a horrid mess of anyone they hit.

I have had one or two close shaves, but nothing really bad. I was on the latrine in the sector next to mine [our own was a rotten latrine], when they dropped several trench mortar shells around me and covered me in dirt and pebbles, and again they put up a trench mortar on the parapet the day before yesterday, and I was busily employed with my field dressings, when they put another one over, luckily 5 yards over the trench over the parados! We were covered with parados but nothing worse. Their trench mortars are good but our howitzers are very good. I saw them put three running into their parados, through a periscope, and their trench was well under 50 yards from ours. I think that was pretty good shooting.

I see that the Welsh miners have gone on strike again. They ought to be decimated or bayoneted or have ball bombs dropped among them, or, better still, rifle grenades. The Colonel is very strong on the subject, and thinks they all ought to be shot.

Podmore is a bloody fool. He was told that he had to send in the name of a subaltern for the Cyclist Coy. Pod said he didn't want to lose anyone, but thought the fairest way was to toss up. So he tossed up between Gilbertson and Webb! Fancy putting them in the same footing. Fancy too, leaving out Palmer and Unwin. Of course, Gilbertson lost, and his name was sent in. Fortunately he is second reserve Machine Gun Officer, and also he may not be wanted, so I hope to goodness he won't go. Grace says anybody not wanting to get rid of Webb is incomprehensible to him. I agree with him entirely.

We are in support trenches and have just come out of the fire trenches. We had some rapid fire and some of the men got over the front of the parapet! They were devilish anxious to get after the Germans, but really there was nothing at all doing. So Simpson told me, as C and D went in last night relieving us.

I have had very few letters from Bedford recently but I suppose that is natural during the hols. The mater is in Wales so I get letters from her at odd times – about half the number she gets from me, but she always was the limit as far as that is concerned. I have not heard from Cyril for a long time, but I think he owes me a letter, in fact I'm sure he does. The last letter he wrote was some letter though and I'm not grumbling yet awhile. I got a very nice letter indeed from McFarland and I was glad to get it. Tell me, is Fawkes still with you as I ought to write to him to thank him for taking back my motorbike to Bedford?

Mind you tell me what is going on in Bedford, when you get time, as these people who write never – or very seldom – give the interesting little details that one likes to know. You know what I mean. Remember me to everybody, especially to Bob and Ian.

We still get on rippingly in "A" Coy, as cheery as anyone could be. The Colonel and his Adjutant are also topping, as decent as could be, especially the Colonel. Even old WDW is cheerful. He came into my section the night before last and he went round the whole trenches of the sector with me, and said it was very interesting. Very interesting it was, too, and I have really enjoyed it very much indeed. As long one is not worried by whiz-bangs etc you can enjoy yourself very much. It is, of course, hard work at times, and after these nights I have had a total sleep of four hours for the three, it is tiring however much you sleep in the day. ***But I don't think you could find better sport anywhere****.*

I must really stop now so cheerio and best of luck. I can't bring myself to say I hope you come out soon, but I hope you get out somehow – you know what I mean.

Yours ever
Jim

7-10-15
My Dear Lizzie

Again we are out of the trenches, for seven or eight days. They are working us hard. We have been out for four days now and I have not had time to get a bath. We have to go two or three miles for one, and all the men have had theirs, but none of the "A" Coy officers have. This afternoon we are for a conference. It is enough to make even Neville swear. I hear that Neville has been mentioned in despatches and the Adjutant has got the Military Cross, and our man "C" Coy, the DCM. It was over a German mine. I have only just heard the news and will go and see that it's true before I send this off.

The Germans let off their mines while we were up there, two in a night. I was rather lucky about one, it was nowhere near me, but I was just ready to go out patrolling when the second one went off. If I had been out when it went up last night I might have been badly strafed, as everybody thinks a mine is a good occasion to let off whatever they have got handy from Very pistols to West Guns.

Later.

I believe it is quite true about Neville and Beecham. I had four men from a new depot a short time ago. One of them is just like Ian Black. I knew he reminded me of someone, but for a long time I could not think of whom. Suddenly it dawned on me and whenever I look at him the likeness is clearer. He has got the same rather thin neck, large ears, rather prominent nose, highish cheekbones and wide level eyes, and, most typical of all, the same sudden smile. He has a few teeth missing in the upper jaw that makes a slight difference. Really though it is a most extraordinary resemblance; just Ian Black but a little older. He is a pretty good soldier, a trifle too good tempered.

I hear you have had a whole week in Bedford. Lucky fellow— if it is true. I think that even an Anglo Indian Colonel with a greenish yellow liver would be preferable to sleeping two hours at a time in every four when soaked through, and without anything but a light doze. As a matter of fact I only averaged 1-1/2 hours to 2 hours per night asleep in my dugout, as I was out every night with a patrol. Patrolling is really the only interesting job we get.

Most Bedford people seem to have deserted me —. I mean in the writing line. I have only had one letter for over a week, and that was from the mater as a matter of fact, and I got another one from her today.

Tomorrow we dig, and in the afternoon there is a rugger match, Officers v Men. I think the officers ought to win don't you? Our team may amuse you. Roberts – Grace, Beasley, Shepherd, Palmer—Bennett, Burrows – Schreiner, Gilbertson, Clark, "Old man", Wilcox, Fowler, Evans and Myself. Simpson will take the game. I hope it will come off alright. I am having the backside sewn with a pair of red pyjamas for the occasion, and shall have the legs cut short. Fowler, Wilcox and the "Old Man" have not played before, and Roberts just a few games.

We were inspected yesterday. Everything went very well and we got high praise. That was very satisfactory as Sir Charles Munroe[24] *is not a man who praises things unduly.*

I have finished. It is a goodly letter and I want a good long reply. "Old Man" says "remember me to the old boy and say I hope he is not too mournful at Colchester." I personally am very well and feeling most cheerful.

Yours ever
Jim Lambert

25-10-15
My dear Denzil, alias Lizzie.

For your letter my thanks in proportion to it's length which was great. I did not realise that you people were at Meaane Barracks. I kept thinking for some reason that you were still in the Huts at Reed Hall.

Do you do bombing? If not you should take any possible opportunity of doing so. Bombing is the **most important** *factor in capturing the present complicated system of trenches. Do you know that one battalion used no less that 6,000 of them in one attack.*

We have had a riotous evening, as Simpson and Neville came to dinner; riotous but sober, for there was nothing but whiskey and French beer. We shall go up to the trenches again the day after tomorrow, I think.

I had a letter from Maurice Simpson a few days ago. He must have done splendidly. I also had a ripping letter from Bob yesterday, the first I have had for ages. He told me you had been there. I also heard from Kirky about a week ago – he wrote me a very nice letter indeed.

You seem very anxious indeed to get out, but I am not sure you would like it out here. Stand to in the evening, then alternately two hours on and two hours off during the night, an hours stand to in the morning and then a tour during the day, does not give much time for sleep. I think my chief grumble at this trench warfare is that it is tiring and monotonous. As a matter of fact you are lucky if you get 3 hours sleep a night, as you are probably on patrol every other night, and there are various other things to be seen after in "off duty" time.

28-10-15
In the trenches again and raining like the devil. Simpson transferred to A and Grace to D. Simpson temporarily in charge of A, while Willows and Gigantine Williams are home on leave.

31-10-15

Grace and Burrows got their Mons Stars[25]*. I had a night's patrol work on the 29th. The Brigadier got some word late from a deserter and the Colonel sent me out to see if it's true. I went with Sergeant Bradbury and our company patrol and all we got were a lot of bombs unpleasantly close. The Colonel wanted us to get into the trench, but they unfortunately found us out when we were five to six yards away, and how they managed to miss us beats me, but they did.*

By the way, I don't know how I forgot it; the Old Man – who is in great form—has got his second star. This is excellent, but I'm afraid it might mean some transfers from "A" Coy, as the Colonel told Willows that he had too many loots over a week ago.

I am going to shut up now, as I'm so cold I can't write. Raining like the ——!

Yours ever
Jim Lambert

Jim Lambert was killed the day after this letter

Meeanee Barracks Colchester
November 9th 1915

My darling Tittie

I said I would write to you on Sunday or Monday but as a matter of fact on Monday I heard from the front that Jim Lambert had been killed, and it rather did for me yesterday, because I'd only had a letter from him two days before and it came so suddenly. It is taking all my time even now to visualise it and I confess that it is the first loss that has really hit me hard. I have lost some acquaintances and two friends, Curlett and Roy Cameron, but neither of the latter two were, though much more than just acquaintances, nearly such close friends as Jim, and though I was fed up when the news of their deaths came it was of course quite different from this. To lose ones first friend whom one has played and lived with and gone about with to camps at Aldershot and all over the place, whose people one knows and who was responsible for my joining the Northampton's, is a fact I find most difficult to realise and it hasn't improved my spirits.

A week ago Sergeant Major Wolsey, formerly my Sergeant in "C" Coy, a regular who was wounded at Mons, and who was transferred to "A" Coy [Lambert's] on promotion to Sergt Major, came back on leave, as did several other officers of the 6th. He came up to see me, and told me all the news particularly saying that Jim had told him to give me a message. Further he said that Jim was a very fine officer, who had already been complemented by the General on his courage and coolness. He used to go out the front at night right up to the Hun trenches and bomb them. A short while ago, Nov 1st to be correct, we blew up a mine in front of our lines and then rushed out to fortify the crater at night. Lambert and Wilcox with 3 men went to cover the digging operations by bombing the Huns. In the darkness Jim was separated from the others with one man and a little later this man returned saying that he had been shot dead by the Huns. Dawn was just breaking so they could not get the body in but next night the only officer went out and got him in. he was buried by the Padre that day, the first officer casualty in the 6th. I wrote to Mrs Lambert today. It is rough on her and I don't know how she will take it.

39 The Grove
Bedford
November 12th 1915

My Dear Denzil

Forgive me calling you this, but I look upon you as Jim's very dear friend, and because of this it is very difficult for me to write to you. He was very fond of you, and in a letter left with 6th Northants to be given to me should he not return, he asked me to give his love to you. I know you will be glad to have this last memory. I can hardly realise he is gone, but I have some comfort in knowing that he gave his life nobly for his King and Country. I must try to remember that others have the same sorrow, but in most cases they have someone else left but I am alone.

When you come home I should be grateful if you would come and see me, and if there is anything I can do for you at any time, please tell me.

I shall remember you in my prayers always. Thanking you for your kind sympathy.

Believe me
Yours very sincerely
Lucy Lambert.

Letter from Dad
November 13th 1915

My own dear son,

Mother wrote yesterday giving the sad news of Lambert's death.

I am so sorry, dear. You know how I would love to be able to comfort you – but what are words in the face of such a loss?

It was a glorious death to die, doing great deeds for one's country's sake—a speedy and gallant ending to another good life. We can only take comfort in the thought that all these things are "meant to be", although it is so hard.

You did not answer my last letter – which I wrote ages ago—just after my return to town. Now here's another that simply must be answered, by a card if not by letter. Mother said something about you being able to be home for Xmas – is this right? The point in question is this – could you possibly come home at the New Year instead? I have been offered a fortnight's war work at Guildford and so couldn't possibly be home for the 25th. We break up on the 18th I think, and I should have to go straight to Guildford College and would get back to Bedford on January 1st. It should be too sickening to miss you and yet I feel I should do my little bit when possible.

Letter to Mother November 15th 1915

Enclosed the cutting from the Northants Independent, which may be put away in my cuttings and papers draw. So glad to hear about Mrs L; it has been a terrible shock to her. I hear the old boy left his motorbike to Bob Simpson which a very nice thing to do. I hope you may be able to see Mrs L occasionally, as she must, as you said, be terribly lonely.

By the way Jim promised me his photo about a year or so ago and had been promising it for some time, but he hadn't given one to me because he always forgot when he had one spare, so if you see Mrs L could you might mention the fact, as I forgot to mention it in my letter.

I have applied for a transfer to the Machine Gun Corps, now forming at Grantham, but I am not likely to get it, I believe, as out of the nine who applied, three were first reserves to the 6th, and 3 to the 7th. However we shall see. You see we are trained officers and I consider it unlikely that the W.O will sanction the transfer.

I'm afraid that the Reed Hall touch is now a certainty, and the prospect is horrifying to say the least of it. Goodbye to all the small comforts that made life bearable in the evening. What it will be like in midwinter in one of the men's huts with the class of officer we have here is unthinkably beastly. However there it is and it's just got to be stuck.

In early November 1915, the 6th Battalion Northamptonshire Regiment was in the trenches of Sector D1 near Fricourt. Just after dusk on the night of the 1st-2nd November, the miners of 178th Tunnelling Company Royal Engineers exploded three large mines that formed two large craters about twenty yards in front of the British front line.

Northampton Independent 13-11-1915

LIEUT. J. E. D. Lambert
FIRST OFFICER OF THE 6TH TO FALL

Killed in Action on 1st November 1915 at Fricourt, The Somme

The first officer of the 6th Battalion of the Northants Regiment to give up his life for his country is Lieut. J. E. D. Lambert, whose home is at Bedford. This gallant young officer was killed on the night of the 1st and 2nd November [1915], while in command of a party of bombers, who had been sent out to the right flank to cover the operations of a digging party subsequent to the simultaneous explosion of three mines in the sector held by the regiment. As Lieut. Lambert and his party came under very heavy fire he ordered his party to return to their trenches, but he courageously determined to stay out himself for a little while to locate where the fire was coming from. As he did not come back to the trenches it was feared that he was wounded, and several search parties went out and made most gallant efforts to find him. As no trace of him could be found it was feared that he had been wounded and taken prisoner. When dawn broke, however, his body was seen on the outside of the crater formed by the explosion at a place thoroughly searched by each successive party. He had been shot through the head, and it is conjectured that after he ordered his party to retire he crept into the mouth of the crater either for cover or to make a further reconnaissance and that he was overcome by gasses formed by the explosion and did not recover consciousness until some time after the last party had come in. He then probably crawled out of the crater and was killed by a sniper. As his body lay nearer the enemy's trenches than our own it was impossible to recover it in the daytime, but next night it was brought in by Lieut. Shankster and two men of the deceased officers platoon. By his death the Battalion has lost a most courageous officer. His Commanding Officer (Colonel Ripley) pays the following tribute to his character: "So beloved was Lieut. Lambert by his men, and respected for his absolute fearlessness, that when volunteers were called for from his platoon for this dangerous task every man of them came forward. He was a splendid stamp of fearless young Englishman, and is a great loss to his Regiment."

Lieut. Lambert, who was 20 years of age, was the younger son of the late Rev J H Lambert, rector of All Saint's, Vernon, British Columbia, and Mrs Lambert, Bedford. He was educated at Vernon and at Bedford School (1909-1914). He represented the school with distinction in football, cricket, running and fencing, and was sergeant in the O.T.C. and a leading monitor in house and school. He passed eighth in the Woolwich examination in 1913, but them resolved to take Holy Orders, and would have entered Magdalen College, Oxford in October 1914 had the war not called him to the service of his country. He was gazetted to the 6th Northampton's in September 1914, and promoted Lieutenant the following November. From the first he became popular for his many good qualities.

Extracts from Reply to Mother November 16th 1915
Thanks awfully for the sympathy for me regards Jim's death. It was a bit of a knockout to me at first, but what must it have been for his mater, heaven only knows and she is splendid about it. I got a letter from her today – such a nice one too that shows me that although I have lost my first friend, I have me in her. He died a credit to the school he loved and as I know it is, as he would have wished, had he known he was going to die. I only hope I will be half as brave at the front, when I get there.

Letter from Lambert's mother Nov 19th 1915
I saw your Mother yesterday and she told me you would like a photo of Jim. I am sending you the one I like best. We agreed that it would be better to send you a postcard right now, and I will give you a larger one whenever you want one.

I want you to tell me how many men there are in a platoon, for I want to send Jim's men some plum puddings. Will you let me know how many officers there are in his platoon, please? I hope I'm not giving you too much trouble. Your Mother has been so kind to me. Did Jim ever get any praise for anything he did? He never told me anything about himself, and I should be grateful if you would tell me everything you know about him. I know Jim would want me to bear up bravely, but it is so difficult. He was such a dear boy to me.

Part of her reply to Denzil's letter that gave information.
Jim never told me that the General had congratulated him, or anything about the bomb expedition, so I was glad to hear all about it from you. I believe that had Jim lived, he would have done something great, and been mentioned in despatches, or perhaps something more. His kit came home yesterday and it was a very sad day,

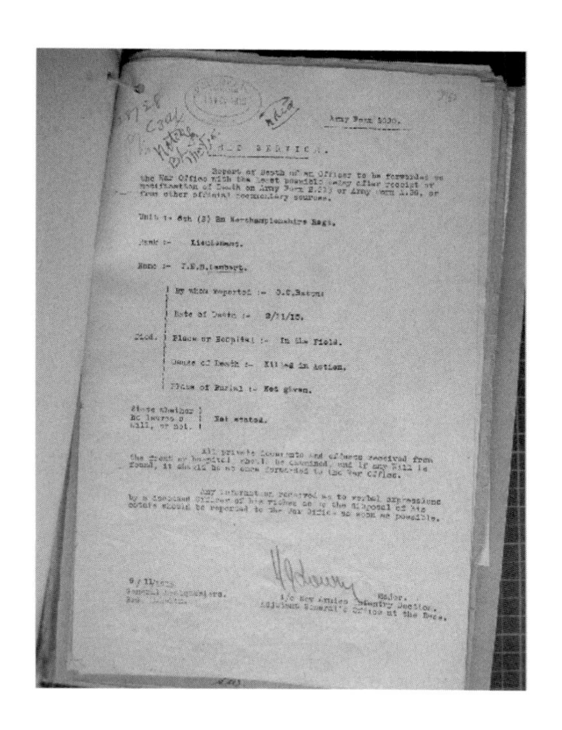

Army Form B.2090.

ON SERVICE.

Report of Death of an Officer to be forwarded to the War Office with the least possible delay after receipt of notification of Death on Army Form B.213 or Army Form A.36, or from other official documentary sources.

Unit :- 6th (S) Bn Northamptonshire Regt.

Rank :- Lieutenant.

Name :- J.E.D.Lambert.

Died. By whom reported :- O.C.Battn.
Date of Death :- 2/11/15.
Place or Hospital :- In the Field.
Cause of Death :- Killed in Action.
Place of Burial :- Not given.

State whether he leaves a Will, or not. Not stated.

All private documents and effects received from the front or hospital should be examined, and if any Will is found, it should be at once forwarded to the War Office.

Any information received as to verbal expressions by a deceased Officer of his wishes as to the disposal of his estate should be reported to the War Office as soon as possible.

9/11/15
General Headquarters.

Major.
i/c New Armies Infantry Section.
Adjutant General's Office at the Base.

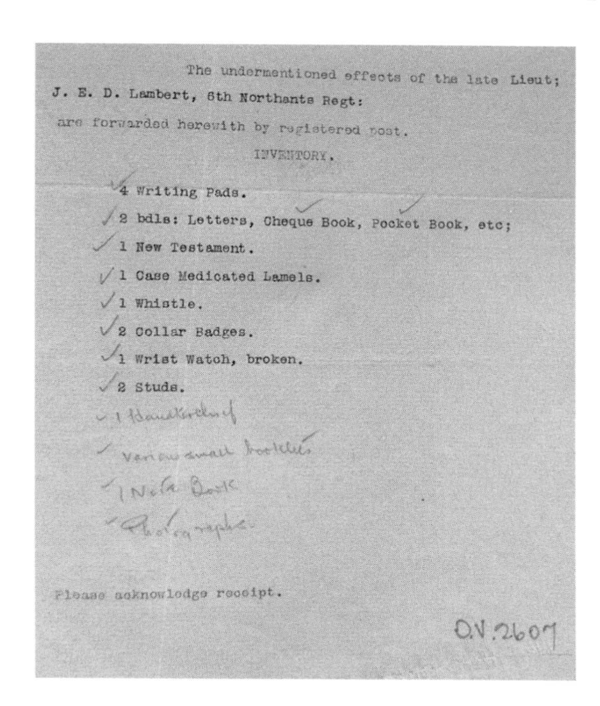

The undermentioned effects of the late Lieut; J. E. D. Lambert, 6th Northants Regt: are forwarded herewith by registered post.

INVENTORY.

4 Writing Pads.
2 bdls: Letters, Cheque Book, Pocket Book, etc;
1 New Testament.
1 Case Medicated Lamels.
1 Whistle.
2 Collar Badges.
1 Wrist Watch, broken.
2 Studs.
1 Handkerchief
Various small booklets
1 Note Book
Photographs

Please acknowledge receipt.

O.V.2607

for it made me realise more than anything that I shall not see his dear face again.

I shall be very pleased if you will give me one of the pictures you had taken the same time as Jim. I know they are good, as I have seen one.

Do you think if I send 25 packets of cigarettes and 25 packets of chocolate the amount will be enough? As you know, I am not very well off otherwise I would send more.

The reality for Mrs Lambert

The Times 10-11-1915

LIEUTENANT JAMES EDWARD DOWNES LAMBERT, 6th Northamptonshire Regiment, whose death is officially announced today, was killed in France on November 1, aged 20. The youngest son of the late Rev J H Lambert, rector of All Saint's, Vernon, British Columbia, and Mrs Lambert, Bedford. He was educated at Vernon and at Bedford School (1909-1914). He represented the school with distinction in football, cricket, running and fencing, and was sergeant in the O.T.C. and a leading monitor in house and school. He passed eighth in the Woolwich examination in 1913, but them resolved to take Holy Orders, and would have entered Magdalen College, Oxford in October 1914 had the war not called him to the service of his country. Thorough, cheerful and fearless he became an excellent officer. He was sent forward on the night of the 1st November with a party of bombers to cover an extension of our trenches. "It was a position of danger," his Colonel wrote, "but he was always first to volunteer for anything of the sort – the bravest of the brave." They came under heavy rifle fire and he ordered his men to go back under his sergeant, and stayed out himself to cover their retreat, when he was shot through the head.

Colchester routine

The following letter is the only correspondence in the archive between the death of Lambert and the beginning of active service in December 1915. It illustrates the despair of Denzil still "trapped" in Colchester with a unit he does not like or respect, and how important to his frame of mind the beginning of active service was, despite the obvious dangers.

8th Battalion
Colchester
November 27 1915

Letter to Mum. Parts of.
I had a little tiff with Herr Colonel Superman half way through last week as to whether I was or was not late for parade, which results in me having leave stopped for a fortnight, so my next leave will be Saturday to Monday December 5th which I hope to spend at KG. Inference obvious.

We were to have played a rugger match at Richmond against the South Africans, which they have just scratched because they are off to the front. It wouldn't have been of great interest to me I confess as I have ***no pride*** *in this Battalion and I refused to play as I wasn't going to risk grogging my knee, which may easily go out again under very little provocation. I think that might stop my chance of going to the front. But it was rather annoying to stave off the rugger enthusiasts who said that various parts of their anatomy were bad but that they were going to play so why wouldn't I?*

The early darkening of the weather has had the effect of cutting off half an hour from parade which is a blessing, but we still parade half an hour longer than any other Battalion, for some reason best known to the CO, who is just as obstreperous as ever. I am getting rather tired of this life. No one but a pack of young men of various stages of gentlemanliness and beastliness.

19

On active service December 1915

Heriz-Smith went to France to join the battalion on December 17th and joined the 6th battalion at rest billets at Buire on 22nd December 1915.

Robert Graves said that after five months in the trenches an officer had passed his prime. For the first three weeks, an officer was of little use in the front line; he did not know his way about, had not learnt the rules of health and safety, or had not grown accustomed to recognising degrees of danger. Between three weeks and four weeks he was at his best, unless he happened to have any particular shock or sequence of shocks.

Denzil's accounts certainly showed that he was feeling his way in the first few weeks but there was nothing to show a decline after five months.

The first letter on active service

Well, here we are with the battalion at last and we go in the trenches for eight days or so on Christmas Eve. Some way of spending Christmas day and rather different to what I had hoped, my own little darling, but still it is so ordained. The trenches are feet deep they say in mud and water, and men have to be dug out because they are stuck fast. No dugouts either I believe. Still, we shall see.

The officers all pity us coming out now, so I suppose it must be thoroughly bad. I am posted at "A" Coy, Lambert's old Coy, and my servant will be Jim's old one, but I shall not have his platoon. We are worked very hard indeed, and it's probably as well as it is werry wet and muddy, socks Reed Hall into mere damp ground! Altogether very discomfortable but one knows one is doing or trying to do one's bit, and in good time, with God's mercy, I shall see my old dad and my darling sisters and my wee Tit again. Meanwhile darling you are not to fret about me more than you can possibly help, as I shall be all right. My Coy Com and second in command with the other two subalterns were all with me at Camberley, and in fact four of the five who were there are in the Coy. Neither Lys nor Batty are with me. By the way my Tit, whether one does or can do letters actually in the trenches actually I don't know. I should doubt it very much, and you must not be anxious if you don't hear from me after tomorrow for eight or nine days, but of course if there is any possibility of writing I shall do so. We started from the base in the small hours of the morning and had a very tedious journey lugging our valises about, but that is over now thank goodness. We are having our Xmas dinner tonight instead of after Christmas, and then I shall to bed, as three hours sleep was our total last night or more like two. The Hun is uncommonly pleasant to us at the moment but won't be shortly I expect!

You can send parcels to the address I mentioned in my last letter; simply name, battalion, BEF. No cigarettes please, a refill of paper this size would be acceptable for my case, yours and dad's photos, and small ones of the kids if poss.; socks as thick as poss. and a hankie or two. They say waders are issued, as the water is too high even to make my trench boots in the least degree useful, so that will be all right. The adjutant at the base [of the 25th Division to which I was attached] asked me directly he heard my name whether I had any relations in Devon. He knew Geoffrey Heriz-Smith well. There were several subalterns at the base, awfully decent fellows and wittier and more completely gentlemen than the adjutant himself, I don't think I ever met. We were only there two nights but we were a very jovial and merry family party even so. I was quite sorry to leave them.

We were at once detailed to censor letters by the dozen and also detailed to look after drafts coming in. I had one of the Cheshire's, quite a nice fellow too. I don't quite know if I ought to tell you more, so I won't about our movements up to this day. Actually our nights were spent in the train and very cold, until we reached the Base, and the days were rather pleasant otherwise. Two of them I enjoyed no end. It was the nights at the base that were nice after work, but it wasn't bad there at all times. My French is strong enough to carry me through nicely in most cases, shops etc though lots of people know some English where we have been. Still I have used French quite a lot and get on quite well. I must go and shave and look for my soft cap, which I suddenly couldn't find when leaving the base camp at 2am. It may just have been packed away, but I doubt it. Well I must go and get my boots off and will finish off after mess. By the way just find enclosed which I might as well just send on as I have it [presumably letter to dad]. It is of a day or so ago as you will see. The mail Captain Willow says is utterly unreliable. You may not get letters for a week after the date sometimes, he says. By the way I found my trench cap. My servant at the base had packed it away like a fool in my valise. Incidentally please send a small flask here. The base does not supply as many things as one was led to expect.

Thursday.
Yes it is trenches for eight days tomorrow. The mud up to our knees they say. We are just within sound of the guns now, but the front trenches are several miles

away. What it will be like in the trenches, of course, I don't know yet, but we are at present, I believe, in a fairly quiet position, which is nice to start with. We had a first rate Xmas dinner in the schoolroom of the village here. Crackers, plum pudding, champagne etc, so biscuits will be some change tomorrow. We are billeted in farms here. All have the same characteristics, a large yard enclosed by buildings, stables etc, vast heaps of manure in the middle and pigeons, rabbits, poultry etc running about in confusion. Well, my little Tittie, I can't think of anything more to say at present. Please write soon, my own, as letters from the family were as valuable as anything could be at Colchester, but here, well, they're the things one hopes for everyday.

Good-bye from your ever-loving son, Denzil.

Continues in letter to father

Thought I'd better just add a line today if I don't decide to write again tonight because for the next three days or so I won't be able to get in any letters at all bar the occasional lines at odd moments. Fear no news today yet. The Hun put over two futile shells yesterday night but they didn't do any damage. I am not going on the ration party tonight as we go up into the frontline tomorrow, so I hope for a quiet evening. Our own strafe yesterday was very effective and our big guns did a lot of damage and blew the German village to blazes. Fritz hardly appreciated such a do.

I should think that one does get bored with trenches around here. I must say to set eyes on London again will be a great joy. Please don't send any more papers as we can get the dailies out here a day or so late, or a picture one sometimes.

I got a large box of Russian cigarettes this morning from Van Raalti's, but have no indication who sent it! Please don't send over fags more than once a month as we can get them easily behind the lines when we are not in trenches.

Ha! There goes Fritz again. Just put 2 four inchers into the village, the old brute.

I want to send my wristwatch home soon to have the strap repaired. Please get me a 5/- Ingersoll and send as quick as poss. Have just discovered that the Town Mayor is the officer i/c this village, a Capt of the Northumberland Fusiliers with whom we mess, and he is a very good fellow too, and an Old Bedfordian; a small world n'est ce pas. Also he met Ronald Maclean out here a day or two ago. The latter is a major and had not seen an Ousel for eleven years, so we've arrived just nicely in time.

6th Northants. Regt
BEF
Christmas Day

My little mother

Christmas this year I will spend and am spending in a ruined French village, deserted by all inhabitants and well within range of the Hun guns. Poor tuck weren't it. We came in early yesterday being the supporting and ration carrying Coy for the others in the trenches. These are our billets and yesterday the Hun sent five or six HE shells slick into our village just in front of our quarters. One was so close that it shattered the window of the room I and another officer were sitting in, with mud and stones. I don't like it one little bit I confess. Worst our artillery has been very busy this morning especially the bigger guns, strafing a village behind the German lines, which will lead to reprisals on us here, which is annoying. Still nous verrons. We marched in here yesterday and I got my baptism of fire on the road, when the Huns were trying to pick out our guns. Yesterday evening I went up in charge of a ration party to the front trenches. The trenches are simply undesirable and they beggar description, up to your knees and often more in a quaggy clayey mud. We had an hour and a half of that awful mud, but got there safely eventually and delivered our rations. I got a drink at the Coy HQ of the front line, and then we got out of the trench and returned along open. Once a machine gun opened up and we flopped down like goodness only knows what flat on our faces, but it wasn't for us luckily and we proceeded untouched. On the way back to our billet we found the officers of another battalion quartered here and their sergeants having a Christmas Eve dinner and singsong. They sang in parts beautifully. It was lovely. They had songs of all kinds, part songs, comic glees, snatches, and finished up with carols and Auld Lang Syne, and then God Save The King. They then dispersed and we thanked them for their entertainment very heartily. It was very nice as it reminded us of home and peace, although the guns were making the windows rattle at intervals. It was also nice for me coming off that other journey to find this going on. Tonight I have to go up again worse luck and then every night till Tuesday when we go up ourselves to the front line for four days before going out again behind the lines for a week or so's rest. I got back last night about 10pm and after the finish of the concert and really had a splendid night's sleep although we may not take our boots off here. I hope to get back earlier tonight as I am not going to waddle along the trenches for miles. No, I don't like war at all not a little bit and everyone is the same, but we shall go on until Fritz can't go on, that's all, and as far as one can make out from the papers etc he is pretty well fed up now. My darling little mother I can imagine and picture myself the fambly sitting round the fire having a pleasant gathering as we have always had, happy and contented, and I figure myself next year with the family. Just two things my darling, I want. Please send me out a pair of new socks each fortnight, also a hankie or two. Then a small lot of Dubbin would be useful once in a way. We get great gumboots served out reaching up to the thighs and we jolly well want them.

On active service. Boxing Day 1915

My own old dad

Just a line to say that I am all right. We had some exciting doings this morning. We all had to clear out of this ruined village we are in this morning as the heavy guns were going to strafe the Germans. We departed to outside the village to a deep road where we waited. The bombardment was pretty severe and made the devil of a noise absolutely. The Germans began also and unfortunately for us in their search for our batteries began dropping heavy shells exactly where we were. We had a very bad sans cous time indeed. Once the Captain and I made sure we were for it, the shells came through with a tremendous noise and rush where we were lying in the bottom of this place, hurtled over our heads and burst with a terrific explosion, some twenty, some forty yards off. Five or six though came within five yards of the Coy and one, as I said, frit me and the Capt to blazes, we made sure it was for us, luckily it just went over us and burst with a boom about five yards away, shattering us with mud but luckily no splinters. I hated it I tell you. However the beggars didn't shell this place and we went on to our dugouts after lunch for the next strafe, which finished except for a desultory shell fairly early. This is a frightfully dangerous place though, I think, liable to be strafed at any minute. Luckily so far the Huns don't appear to have such numbers or such heavy metal as we have. We messed them up proper this morning I can tell you. Bro' Fritz must have got some fright but he'll probably do his best to get even tomorrow, though it will be very dangerous for him too.

Just come back from conducting the rations party to the front trenches. It was rather more "touchy" even than before tonight, as both Fritz's machine guns were going like the blazes in all directions, with Very lights in abundance; these latter do give you the jumps and occasionally you think they can't possible help seeing you. While I was there the Huns shelled our front trenches for a short time but I got back safe and at some pace, but I don't love these expeditions. Just got the post after a good dinner, with it especially your splendid letter. I was awfully bucked with it, it gave me one of the few moments of pleasure, real heartfelt pleasure, that I have felt since I came here. My Christening, you see, has been acknowledged as "un peu fort", anyway it was "fort" enough for me, and must come when I go in front of our first line to the wires. Over! Poor tack! Anyhow I had a very narrow escape this morning and feel sure God will spare me to come back and see my Dad and Mother, who I'm perfectly certain are the best Mum and Dad anyone could possibly hope or wish for, however much they expected.

I got the Christmas Ousel and a card from Mr Carter. I shall try to write, but I shall not send it back as I want you to get me another for my volumes. Just Christmas number and supplement put away for me. I also got an Xmas card from Leyton Halliday, ditto from Fitzpatrick and a card from Forge, and it was a very nice post for me I can tell you. As to matters generally I think Fritz is very sick of this, so of course are all of us, but he must be quite bad. It was good to get back from Suvla, but we never seem to do much more than conduct successful retreats. Still, I believe, we have only to go on like this to win sometime, in the next year.

Well I'm going to shut up tonight. So goodnight my dear old dad and tons of love to you mother and the kids

December Raid
29th December 1915

Heriz-Smith was fortunate not to be involved in this famous raid

The War Diary for the 6th Northants is as follows

4th to 11th December 1915
The battalion occupied D2 Sector for the first time relieving 11th Royal Fusiliers. Weather wet throughout. The trenches were in a very muddy state. Casualties:- 2/Lt. Gilbertson and two men wounded.

24th to 31st December 1915
The battalion relieved the 11th Royal Fusiliers. On the 27th our artillery fired about 800 shells into the trenches in and close to FRICOURT. On the 29th the enemy retaliated with about 2,000 shells from guns and trench mortars on D2 Sector from 3.30pm to 5.30pm and among them were a number of gas shells. Towards the end of the bombardment a party of the enemy entered our trenches west of the Cemetery and captured twenty of our men who had taken cover in a dugout. These men were made prisoners and taken away to the German lines before the posts on their right and left were aware of the occurrence. The point selected for the attack was right by the enemy's gunfire during the

operation and the parapet had been partly blown in. Our men shot a German soldier who had strayed from the party.

Total casualties during this tour of duty in the trenches were four killed, 17 wounded, 20 missing. The weather was continuously wet but mild and the trenches were in a very bad state.

From the Brigade History

The Germans retaliated the next evening hammering trenches 86 and 89 in D2 sector (held by Nos. 4 and 5 platoons of Northamptonshire Regiment) until they were almost flattened and also sending over a lot of tear-gas shells. After a while the fire was lifted from these trenches and put down on the support trenches in rear, and also on trenches on either side. This "box barrage" isolated a part of the Northamptonshire Regiment's front in the region of the sunken road running from the station, which we held, into Fricourt itself. A party of about 20 Germans then came over, bombed out some cellars, and marched about 16 of our men back. Three of our men, including one wounded by a bomb, did not leave the cellars, and, escaping attention, managed to reach the rest of their battalion. The whole affair was a chapter of accidents. The officer commanding the platoon which suffered, was absent, bad weather in the Channel having delayed his return from leave. The platoon sergeant had gone on leave that day, and a lance-sergeant left in charge had gone to see his company commander and had been gassed on the way back. The day sentry had been knocked out, and in the absence of a responsible leader all the nineteen men took refuge in a cellar without leaving a sentry at the spot the Germans entered. The platoons on the right and left stood to when the bombardment opened, and as soon as it was known that Germans had come over bombing parties were sent out. One German who had apparently lost his way was found in our trenches and dealt with. This was the Brigade's first experience of a trench raid; indeed, it was the first on the Divisional front and the use of tear-gas shells was also a novelty to us, accounting for a good deal of confusion. It was noted that the Germans wore gas-helmets of the "snout" pattern.

German Trench Mortar commonly known as a sausage

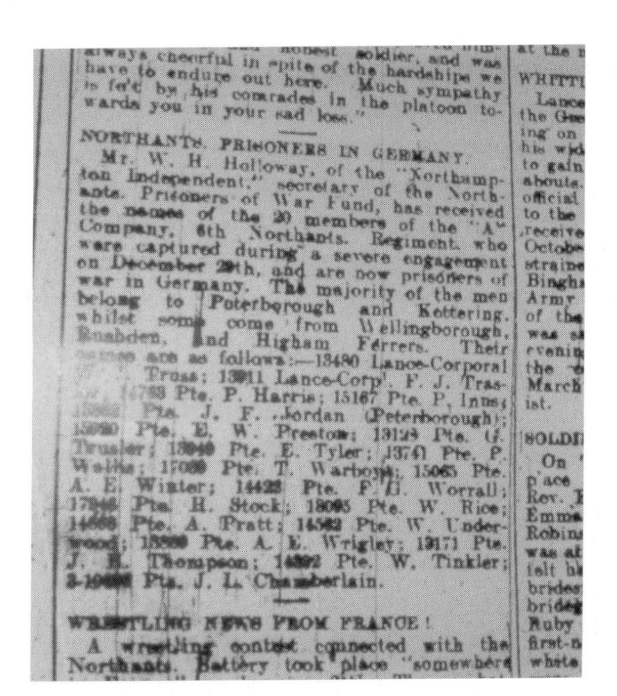

always cheerful in spite of the hardships we have to endure out here. Much sympathy is felt by his comrades in the platoon towards you in your sad loss."

NORTHANTS. PRISONERS IN GERMANY.

Mr. W. H. Holloway, of the "Northampton Independent," secretary of the Northants. Prisoners of War Fund, has received the names of the 20 members of the "A" Company, 6th Northants. Regiment, who were captured during a severe engagement on December [illegible]th, and are now prisoners of war in Germany. The majority of the men belong to Peterborough and Kettering, whilst some come from Wellingborough, Rushden, and Higham Ferrers. Their names are as follows:—13480 Lance-Corporal [illegible] Truss; 13[illegible]11 Lance-Corp'l. F. J. Tras[illegible]; [illegible] Pte. P. Harris; 15167 Pte. P. Inns; [illegible] Pte. J. F. Jordan (Peterborough); [illegible] Pte. E. W. Preston; 1312[illegible] Pte. G. Trusler; [illegible] Pte. E. Tyler; 137[illegible] Pte. P. Wallis; 170[illegible] Pte. T. Warboys; 150[illegible] Pte. A. E. Winter; 1442[illegible] Pte. F. G. Worrall; [illegible] Pte. H. Stock; 180[illegible] Pte. W. Rice; [illegible] Pte. A. Pratt; [illegible] Pte. W. Underwood; [illegible] Pte. A. E. Wrigley; 13171 Pte. J. H. Thompson; [illegible] Pte. W. Tinkler; [illegible] Pte. J. L. Chamberlain.

WRESTLING NEWS FROM FRANCE!

A wrestling contest connected with the Northants. Battery took place "somewhere

Heriz-Smith makes references to this German raid in the letters that follow.

New Year 1916

1st and 2nd January

On the 2nd the Battalion was relieved by the 11th Fusiliers and marched to rest billets at Morlancourt.

Casualties during 1st and 2nd were nil.

Remain at Morlancourt till the 10th Jan.

Part of letter to father New Year 1916

I hope to write more in a day or two but we don't get the time for writing as we did in England by a long way. We have not time at all except for duty and sleep. Well I guess I wasn't listening for bells on New Years Eve. Contrariwise I was waiting for an attack with rapid fire going on all around, machine guns beating away like nothing on earth, and an occasional whizz-bang to increase the "liveliness". Indeed I narrowly missed not seeing the New Year by half an hour. The excitement had died down by 12 and a quiet prevailed except for the growl of our guns in the rear. But, as I said, I thought it was really "joy" to be in a scrap and was too much excited to care much about whiz-bangs. So I thought of you, my dear old dad, and of darling mother in the first few minutes of the New Year, as I tried to get a little sleep if possible.

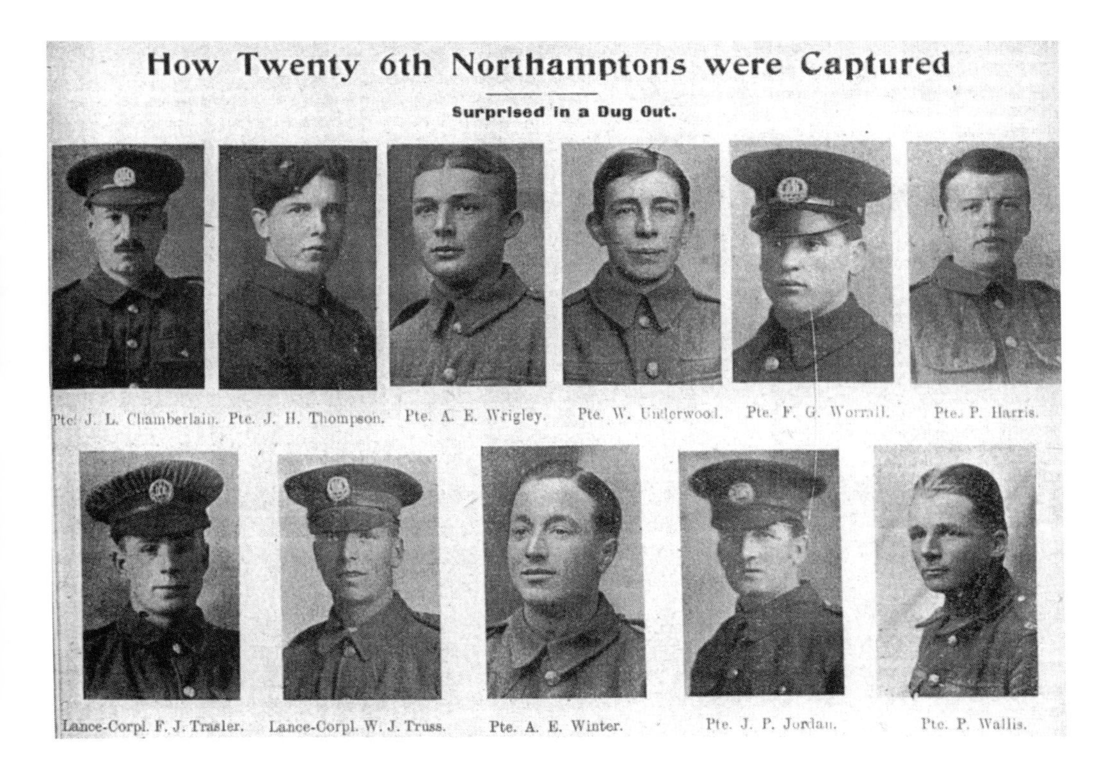

How Twenty 6th Northamptons were Captured

Surprised in a Dug Out.

Pte. J. L. Chamberlain. Pte. J. H. Thompson. Pte. A. E. Wrigley. Pte. W. Underwood. Pte. F. G. Worrall. Pte. P. Harris.

Lance-Corpl. F. J. Trasler. Lance-Corpl. W. J. Truss. Pte. A. E. Winter. Pte. J. P. Jordan. Pte. P. Wallis.

Jan 4th 1916

Extracts from letter to mother

I don't remember if I told you about the bombardment we had. It was a very nasty affair. The Hun strafes us properly I can tell you for two hours, but you will have seen about it in the papers. It was poor tack indeed, but is quite a dim recollection already though only six days old. There is no doubt that he did very well, but the claim in the papers was exaggerated.

[Reference to Fricourt raid at end of 1915]

We had a fairly quiet time of it for the next two days except that the Hun got "funky" one night and delivered rapid fire all along the line, but nothing came of it, except that I again dodged a whiz-bang, or rather ducked towards one which exploded in the parapet above my head.

They say we had the Bavarians opposite us last time and that it is easy to know whether Saxons, Prussians or Bavarians are opposite as the latter are far more active and hate us much more than the other two. Looking over my initiation in to trench life I can only say that in eight days I had three, possibly four, narrow squeaks, especially the one when the 6 inch shell nearly got me and Captain Willow, making a hole eight feet across. Ooer! It makes me homesick to think of it. However these will become commonplace in time, at present they are particularly unpleasant experiences. By the way due to the bombardment we spent an extra day in the trenches, which was very annoying.

The communication trenches are still up to your thighs in thick mud and one always run the risk of being sniped at when struggling for hours in mud and water up to your knees. I never knew what mud was before coming here, yet in the papers a month or so ago it said " There is now scarcely a wet trench left in France owing to measures taken after last years experience!!!" ***Lies****, that's all!*

I had a letter and a copy of the Ousel and the Christmas supplement from Mr Carter.

I really miss my Colchester little church, but Sundays are like any other days out here.

I was glad to hear of your Christmas celebrations and I was there in spirit, but it doesn't seem in place here amidst the guns and horrible sights, yet one is profoundly thankful that England has been spared sufficiently to celebrate Christmas in the old way.

Letter to mother Jan 9th

How do I write in the trenches? Why, in the dugout by the light of a candle, sitting on a bench.

Yes it was curious that one of the whiz-bangs should have killed that sergeant and eight other men and that about 2,000 other shells, many of a far larger size, did no harm to anyone. This is the kind of accident that happens out here. This man had just had an extraordinary escape. He was dishing out food to his platoon and walking around in front carrying a Dixie, when a dud whiz-bang came over and fell right amongst them but didn't explode. He observed that it was a lucky escape. Three minute after, another shell came over and hit the parapet, carried away half the Sergeants head and killed the other men. He was a tall, fine man and a really good sergeant, and unlucky, as not one whiz-bang in a hundred would have done that.

H-S refers once again to the German Trench raid in late December.

The Huns came over during the bombardment as you will have seen in the papers, but although it was poor tack, the papers exaggerated. Still I don't think there should be any doubt that though the Hun will have some local successes and scupper everyone in the front line in some district somewhere, we have them cold on this front and we will win sooner or later. That's certain.

10th to 18th January

The Battalion relieved the Fusiliers. This period of eight days was a quiet one. On the 17th our artillery fired about 800 shells into and around Fricourt.

Weather fine and mild. Casualties were 1 killed and five wounded.

Letter to Mother Jan 13th 1916

Well, here we are again after our four days in the front lines, in the second line where we have been for two days. The first four days were comparatively quiet. No particular excitements, no narrow shaves.

But it has been far more beastly in terms of cold. For the first two nights in spite of all I could do, I could not get warm as I have no decent dugout and I have to lie on the floor. Consequently I got little or no sleep whatsoever. I used to consider myself an A1 at sleeping, but I found I couldn't now, which is awfully disappointing. The third night I got about four hours sleep, good sleep, but I woke up, or rather was woken up at 1am for my second two hours spell of trench patrol, feeling as sick and horrible as a cat. I confess I had a dreadful two hours, cold, almost dead with sleep and afraid I was going to be sick any minute. I felt very hopeless all the next day. However, by dint of eating nothing all next day and sleeping in the Captains dugout all the afternoon, I was much better than before and have recovered almost.

The trench patrols twice a night are the lid, absolutely right down lid. You go up and down seeing what you can of the Hun trenches over the parapet at intervals. Worst of all is the waking up every two hours to a weary boredom. It is only a relief when one is cold, miserable and been trying to sleep for hours without success. Then one welcomes getting up, lighting the candle and putting on a cup of cocoa to boil, and after 20 minutes or so on gulps it down and feels refreshed.

Incidentally please send the following things

Bivouac cocoa in squares. Two boxes

Refill of brandy for the flask [I can't stand the rum ration]

Jan 18th–25th
Morlancourt. The Battalion were relieved by the 11th Fusiliers, and returned to rest billets

Jan 22nd
Rest billets
We are now at the rest billets in a village about three miles behind the front lines. Rest billets does not mean rest, it only really means relief from nerve strain, cleaning and smartening up equipment, clothing and the men themselves. I have taken the men down to some baths about one and a half miles from the village. I gave them some bayonet fighting instruction and then more drill etc. Still we gave the men as easy a time as Brigade and Division will allow, and also the limited facilities for amusement in the village. This has a fair amount of inhabitants and is rarely touched by shellfire, as it is beyond the reach of everything except really heavy howitzers.

We got two or three shells from Fritz as we came out of the trenches and down the road as we marched back, but no damage. The trenches now are very different from what they were three weeks back. The pioneers have taken them in hand and one can walk along dry foot and clean on the boards all the way back to the front line.

Glad when the Welsh come out but pity them for shouting with joy on hearing the news. Reminds me of a story of a veteran of the Retreat from Mons standing in a French station watching some new troops going to the front in the early stages of the war. They were cheering and roaring and singing like blazes. He watched them with interest and when the train moved out they yelled to one another down the train, "Are we downhearted?" The others shouted back "No." Said the veteran as he turned away "You bloody well soon will be."

26th to 31st January

In the 26th the Battalion returned relieving the Fusiliers. Weather fine and mild. Casualties, three killed and one wounded. There was little activity on the part of the enemy during the period in the matter of machine guns, which were very busy. The majority of casualties were caused by two shells, which burst inside the men's billets at Becourdel

Letter to Mother at end of Jan 1916

My own darling little Mother
Well it's some time since I last wrote a real letter, isn't it, and I'm afraid you may be

getting a little anxious. Still, one thing and another have combined to put it off and I hope you get this before you begin to worry whether I am journeying in a different way from what I always said, towards Munich [You see I don't by any means give up the idea of that Bier Halle and the best umpah German band procurable, in spite of my experiences here].

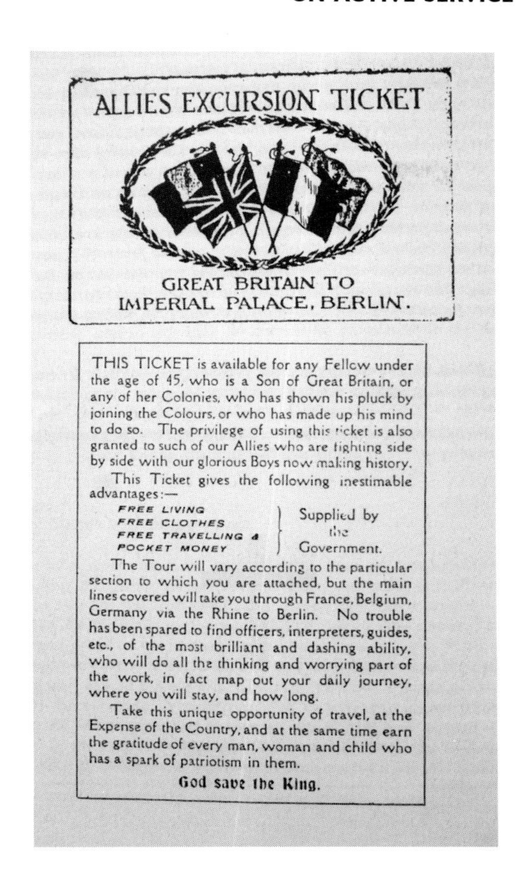

ALLIES EXCURSION TICKET

GREAT BRITAIN TO IMPERIAL PALACE, BERLIN.

THIS TICKET is available for any Fellow under the age of 45, who is a Son of Great Britain, or any of her Colonies, who has shown his pluck by joining the Colours, or who has made up his mind to do so. The privilege of using this ticket is also granted to such of our Allies who are fighting side by side with our glorious Boys now making history.

This Ticket gives the following inestimable advantages:—

FREE LIVING
FREE CLOTHES
FREE TRAVELLING &
POCKET MONEY
} Supplied by the Government.

The Tour will vary according to the particular section to which you are attached, but the main lines covered will take you through France, Belgium, Germany via the Rhine to Berlin. No trouble has been spared to find officers, interpreters, guides, etc., of the most brilliant and dashing ability, who will do all the thinking and worrying part of the work, in fact map out your daily journey, where you will stay, and how long.

Take this unique opportunity of travel, at the Expense of the Country, and at the same time earn the gratitude of every man, woman and child who has a spark of patriotism in them.

God save the King.

Perhaps Denzil was becoming a victim of British propaganda!

Well, as for news, I shall have to begin from the last day of our last stay behind the lines about a fortnight ago. Also I imagine I shall have to do it as a serial for the next seven nights, for this reason, always by and with the leave of the gentle Hun, i.e. always supposing he remains normally quiet during the next few weeks or so and does not try any attacks as I see the papers have it he is going to try. We shall be in billets several miles behind our front line for a rest from the trenches for three weeks or possibly even 6 but that is unlikely. We are a good ten miles behind now in a village distinguished only by the fact that it is too small for the number of troops who have to be put up in spite of the Mayor's frantic attempts and also by the fact that until we get going on it, it is not over clean. This is due to the fact that after about seven months out here the brigade is now in reserve. Of course, if the Huns open a general attack on our divisional line we may be rushed up there at a minutes or so notice, but that's part of normal contingencies out here. So if we stop here over the three weeks I might find myself in the same predicament as one gets complaints of from home i.e. "No news". Still if it comes to that I'll go on with dissertations about French "mores". And even, if necessary, the colour of a German Land-Sturmer's trousers, so I have you "cold" in that direction too in any case! Suffice it for the present that we're here out of range of anything except naval guns, which means as safe as you are from Zeps until we get suddenly called up. I will therefore venture no more upon descriptions of this place until I get there in the due course of the narrative because much water has run along the Somme since then and much has happened also which I shall do my best to describe without giving away secrets.

I told you last how on the last day in the village three miles behind the line we went for a battalion route march, and had just gallantly marched out of one side of a small village when a Hun aeroplane dropped a bomb from out of the blue [literally] on to the other side. It made an extraordinary sound coming down and, like I said, but Archie prevented his having any further truck with us, not a good deal to our dissatisfaction.

The next day we were off to the trenches again and this time I definitely took over command of a platoon, No. 1 or Lambert's old one, so I'm no longer in instruction but have my own 50 men or so. We went straight up to the front line and got there without the Hun spotting us or shelling us at all, which is always a bit of relief, as it is displeasant to be shelled when reliefs are taking place because there are an extra numbers of men overcrowding the communication trenches. That being done satisfactorily we settled down to the ordinary trench life, but it wasn't ordinary. There was some very heavy firing going on to the north all one day and the thunder and growl of the guns was absolutely incessant. We surmised an attack, but nothing that happens perturbs anyone out here, so long it isn't in or near one's own lines. We take as great interest of course and are agog for news of it but it hasn't the same personal meaning for one. It came in due course that evening on my first tour as officer on night duty in the trenches, and I was standing on the fire step near a sentry post of ours trying to locate a machine gun of the enemy which was sweeping our parapet and making life very uncomfortable for our sentries, when in a silent interval I suddenly heard the far away sound of a bugle behind me. I said "well that is a ripping sound to hear out here and very surprising to hear it out here." Then two or three peals of a church bell at the back and it came to me suddenly that things weren't quite as pleasant as they seemed and in a minute everyone was getting gas helmets ready. I suddenly remembered that this was a signal for a gas attack. However it turned out to be a gas attack on a division of ours several miles to the north and so that excitement died down. At least it wasn't any excitement but it was new to me. Gas was reported to have cleared in a little time and it never reached us.

Next morning we heard the furore of guns going full lick down south. This was the Fritz attack on the French, practically next door to where our division was when it first came out. This went on for the whole day and a lot more. Just as I came on duty in the early hours of the morning and had just finished one tour of the trenches I suddenly sniffed the desert air and smelt a strange smell very faintly. I sniffed my observer sniffed and we both sniffed and sniffed. I said, "oho, what about very strong water cress or dead geranium stalks", and went off full lick as all my sentries had by this time sniffed it and reported it as gas. Sure enough thicker and thicker it came and my eyes began to water and it hurt like blazes. A sort of mist it was [not the chlorine stuff], but lachrymatory gas and the smell got worse. One began to cry like anything, at least some did. My eyes were sore and watered but I didn't cry with it. Well it passed off in about half an hour and we found it had come straight down from the Fritz attack a few miles away.

Another day we had during which the Huns knocked nine of ones company's men in the ruined village I have told you of. We also had a day of extraordinarily thick fog during which I came out from brekkers and got on the fire-step. I observed to my astonishment shadowy figures about 100 yards out wandering about. I found it was half of my company crawling about, some next to the Hun lines, looking for souvenirs! There was only the occasional shot going about at the time, but it did give me a fit to see them all coolly wandering around, and such a collection of German bombs, grenades, shell nose caps, bells from the Hun, French rifles and bayonets etc and they brought back stuff I had never seen, also German Gas helmets etc etc. Well we recalled them all except a strong party who were out not for souvenirs but for the wily Hun! I had to go out nearly 200 yards to get some of my platoon in. What would have happened had the Hun opened up with his machine guns, sakes only knows. The business party had poor tack luck. They were waiting in a shell hole having taken two Hun alive when another party from the next Coy spoilt the game. The Huns tumbled to it and opened rapid fire, our fellows at once dropped one of them and the other went down and they think they got him too, which was good but we would have preferred them as prisoners. We had no casualties. The Hun's stretcher bearers whistles went several times to our joy, that morning, but in spite of not being able to see more than 50 yards we let no-one go out and sure enough the Hun thought we were at it again and he had his machine gun knocking bits of our parapet for one and a half hours, almost incessantly. We were pleased!

Next day we went out of the front line, of which more hereafter.

Things I want

50 Gold Flake and 50 De Reza[26].

Nail scissors wanted urgently and applied for three weeks ago!

A cake; this is a great luxury out here. Get Aunt Flossie to send one as well.

No more Socks, Hankies, collars, vests. I am already over regulation weight for these, and if we had to move at short notice they would be thrown away.

February 1st to 4th

The Battalion completed it's tour in the trenches on the 4th when it was relieved by the 8th Battalion Devonshire Regiment, and was marched to Mealte. Weather was fine except the last day when it rained heavily. Casualties—2nd Lt Wilcox and one man wounded.

5th to 10th February 1916

The Battalion marched eight miles to billets at La Houssoye, the 54th Brigade now being in Divisional reserve

Feb 10th 1916 BEF
6th Northants

To Dad

I'll think I'll take up the story from where I left off a day or two back to Mother.

I left off I believe where we were just going back into the 2nd line for our last four and as it turned out, five days.

Well I went straight back to the redoubt about 800 yards from the front Hun line on a hill, and became OC this redoubt. It had a name but I can't give it to you, of course. It was rather amusing having an independent command and I didn't mind it a bit. Besides the first thing that met my gaze as one went in the communications trench was a board to OC.Coy's Dug out and over the door of the said dug out was also a board "OC. Coy". "Some" nut wasn't I? Of course if the Huns had broken our front line I should have been reinforced by three more platoons for the defence of the redoubt [a redoubt as you know a separate system of trenches, having all round defence, stores for a siege and a main eminence], but it was I who was OC of the redoubt with my platoon, six dugouts, communication trenches, stores, a water tank, two or three artillery observation posts etc. What's more I was Infantry Observing Officer of the 54th Brigade. I had my observatory and had to watch all enemy movements on the horizon and in the village below me, all single Huns, what they were dressed in, what they were up to. And also report all activity of any sort with a powerful telescope and with a splendid view of miles of the country in enemy hands, added to the comfortable knowledge that my observatory was not even proof against a pop gun and that I had to be there all day almost with the artillery spotting officer and my observers, and that the Hun probably knew about the existence of the observatory if not the exact location, as they put 20 heavy shells between it and the wire in front one day.

All these things I had to send in a report every day to Brigade HQ, and I saw a good lot of exciting things including two mines go up, three heavy bombardments and about 100 Huns fooling about at odd spots. Still let that rest for a bit.

I got my men settled down and then after a thorough look round I returned to my new dugout in the evening. There were two beds rigged up one above the other in which my servant and me slept. I dined at Batt HQ every night, luxuriously. Port wine etc, but brekker, lunch and tea I had cooked on my primus that arrived opportunely with the other good things that Mother sent in her parcel, on the very day I went to the redoubt, and as I had a bed, table and a comfortable, if not shell proof, dugout, I sent for my servant to get hot water for my shaving etc. I was as snug as a bug in a rug and the men had a good easy time as well.

Well, there wasn't a lot of interest first day except watching our artillery shell various places, and seeing my first Hun on the horizon with my telescope in their blue, grey uniform. Next day nothing much again except the usual shelling and a very narrow squeak when a rifle bullet actually shaved my sleeve when I was superintending a working party on top near our wire.

A very good dinner followed at 13HQ where I described my Colchester experiences to the Colonel to his huge amusement. By the way, did I say that I had now got poor old Jim's platoon? Also a methylated stove of his as well as my primus.

Next day was a series of exciting experiences. In the early morning I saw several Huns at quite close telescope range. Late on the Hun began pounding the portion of our front line exactly opposite my observatory, up and down with heavy shells and continued for two or three hours. It was a fine site viewed from comparatively safe quarters, of course, or rather, not safe but out of the way. The odd thing was to watch their big shells. You'd hear the distant muffled report of them a few miles away then you'd hear the crescendo of the shell shrieking through the air nearer and nearer, then you'd see the shell hit on the trench, sending up a great column of earth, then smoke and debris, twenty foot or so into the air, then you'd hear the screech and the roar of the shell a it got to close quarters, after [several seconds after] you'd see it explode, then finally you got an enormous crash! The sound of the shell bursting. An extraordinary thing, but of course, the reason is obvious, but it seemed wrong to my senses somehow. Well our guns didn't do much more than send over a few heavies in ditto fashion on the Hun trenches immediately opposite those they were shelling.

However, late in the afternoon they suddenly began, and my Christopher, it was a sight, putting down a long succession of shells going overhead hard on the heels of each other and sometimes four at a time. The Hun trenches looked one mass of columns of dust, earth, debris, and terrific explosions, crashing, roaring and shrieking of big and small shells, here several white puffs of smoke, here enormous pillars of coal black smoke, here a great deal of tawny yellow smoke, and an inferno of crashes and roars. The artillery officer with me in the observatory was frightfully bucked, as was I, and my observers were very excited. It must have been a bit of a bad time for the wretched Huns, but I didn't feel a bit sorry for them, only intensely bucked and excited. Well old Fritz got wild about it all and got it so badly in the neck that he proceeded to do a real bit of heavy hate against the Brigade on the extreme left, and sent over a colossal number of shells on to our lines there.

It was now dusk and as we at once answered with a terrible counter hate which lasted longer than theirs, there was a perfect hell going on, and on the left of from where I watched the sky was rent by great bright stabs of light, the roars and crashes were incessant and the shells were going whistling overhead for ours, even after the Hun got tired. Whew-w-w-wed ad infinitum. Besides this there was a perfect firework show on the horizon over the big lines of trenches, huge flashes and stabs of light, like a grand firework display. It was a grand sight.

Incidentally I suddenly got the message about halfway through the bombardment, by telephone orderly from my telephone office [Yes I had one!], that the Huns were using gas shells on our left and sho'nuff in a few minutes the gas mist came rolling up. I went to my men and warned them and told them that we were on high ground and would not get a great deal of it. However we got a fairish amount of it as it happened. It was beastly tasting and had a nasty effect on one's eyes, but it was not the Chlorine stuff and we didn't make a great deal of it. Some men put on goggles but it wasn't really worth it. It was, however, much worse on the low ground and when I went down to Batt. HQ for dinner everything tasted of it, including the port! The Hun was very active that night with machine guns four or five at a time going full blast all out. When I got back at about 10pm I visited my posts and found one of them very much tormented by this MG fire which was putting bullets into the parapet too near to be nice, they said. As it was too far back, 800 yards, and our lines were in front it was not essential that we were in the same place, so as a preliminary to our move a bit further on, I got out on the fire-step to see if I could locate the mg that was paying such particular attention to my parapet. All was quiet for a minute or two, and then crack, crack, crack, 20 times repeated like a typewriter at full speed, and I jolly soon ducked I can tell you. The blighted bullets were very uncomfortably close under three or four feet or less from my face, so as we were not the front line I thought I wouldn't go on taking unnecessary risks and I moved my group down a bit, and then went to bed.

One feature of this of the dugout was the good nights I used to have. The excitement next day was a spy hunt. One was reported near my dugout in one evening, so I sallied forth with my servant and explored the whole redoubt and without success. However I took means to ensure his being "chopped" if he got into my little command at whatever hour, and then I went to bed.

Next day we were relieved by a new division, a regular one, and we marched back to the village with the Church intact, that I have told you about, a mile or so back, where we slept the night. The Huns put 30 or so shells 200 yards away from our billet during the day, but they all went all in a field and no damage was done. By the way I forgot to tell you about the mine that went up one evening. A fine sight! Suddenly the earth rocked and swayed and one saw about 1000 yards off a huge umbrella shaped tree of fire and smoke that spread aloft, flaming, and then subsided. It was a great sight

After this night we were marched back about 12 miles and we are now that distance from the line in a small French village in Divisional reserve for a month, so I will stop my story for the present.

Please tell Mother the parcel she sent arrived safely two or three days ago and was splendid indeed. Three of us had parcels at the same time so there was a regular "beano" in the mess. Also please tell Mother that I cannot do with any more clothes, towels etc now, nor socks, nor nothink, save only one thing if sent at once, a pair of footer boots. I have an old pair haven't I? But it must be absolutely at once. Also I want a pair of puttees, smooth ones, not rough outside, and smooth to feel. Please write down £2 for these in my book [Denzil meticulously noted down the cost of things his mother bought for him and paid her back on visits home]. *Thanks very much for the novel, the Ousel and for the tins of biscuits, sweets and dates. I was properly tucked! Novels are enormous boons out here as are such things as cakes, biscuits, chocs and such. The periscope is fine but I haven't used it yet.*

Well now, my old dad, accept tons of love for you, my little Tittie and the kids. Shall get abreast of the times in my next.

Your loving son

Pops

Letter to Dad
Feb 15th 1916

I saw about dear old Mr Nixon's death in the Times a few days ago. I should awfully have liked to see him once more, but he was getting very old, and some how these times one feels that the England he knew would not be the same for him after the war by any means.

So many of one's young friends are falling nowadays that when an old friend dies one wonders what will be the end of it all.

On 16th February the Battalion marched two miles to Pont exchanging billets with the 7th Royal West Kent Regiment. The weather was wet with light winds, during the last week.

Letter to Dad Feb 16th 1916

Yesterday's letter was poortaag wasn't it, but I thought you better hear of me so I wrote in great haste before the letters went. Well, I have arrears to make up. In my last I got as far as our removal back from the line. We arrived at a certain village down a long, straight main road, situated quite high and in a very bracing and healthy atmosphere. The billets were very portaag indeed but better couldn't be got as we are pretty full up round about here. We were with the Bedford's, which was nice for a Bedford man. They are the nicest battalion in the rest of the Brigade.

We at once started settling down, overcame with our wiles the objections of villagers about various things, such as football grounds and parade grounds. I organised a platoon soccer league, battalion soccer and rugby matches, Brigade boxing contests and a rugger match between our village and another one, and whist drives, revolver and shooting matches. Then the order came that we were to move out today to a village further back but still only two miles away, but this has absolutely done in our arrangements of course. Such is life. We are now in the new billets that are worse than the others, the village is low down instead of highish and it looks as if we will find difficulties to get any ground to play on. You have no idea how difficult it is to get grass ground. Nearly every inch is cultivated out here. I was elected chairman of the Coy Athletics Committee, and played soccer for the Coy against a pioneer battalion. My first game of soccer was therefore a match, and it is more curious still that in spite of me playing we won 4-0. Also I have got to play for my platoon in the soccer league. Then we got a rugger match, Northants v Bedford, and for once I played against Bedfordshire. We lost by a goal and a drop to nil. The drop was splendid in a strong wind although it was uncertain if it was a goal. I think it was but even if it wasn't it deserved to be. On the other hand the try was certainly not one, as the fellow was tackled twn yards from the line and instead of putting the ball down and playing it with his feet, he scrambled along on hands and knees and scored. However they kicked a beautiful goal for it and altogether, though beaten, we had a ripping open game with no feeling except that of sportsmanship and we all enjoyed it immensely.

Rugger always seems so different from soccer. In spite of the officers efforts a soccer league always seems to have bad feeling about it. All the players question the Referee's decisions repeatedly, and the onlookers also do [Does this sound familiar?] I told my platoon that if I played for them it was on the understanding that if players or onlookers questioned decisions wrong or right, or did any barracking, I would not consent to play again. What affect that has remains to be seen.

We are to smarten up all round; there are battalion competitions on smartness of turnout, drill, rifle firing and bayonet fighting. I am at present the Coy expert on bomb and bayonet fighting and give lectures in them. My platoon is smartening some as you have no idea how dull, slovenly and listless trench life makes everyone. The result is that the authorities have gone back to close order drill.

Also we are smartening up like mad and here my Colchester course of bayonet fighting and my liking for it, and my course on physical training at the same place, also my course on bombing out here, are very useful. I have always been good at drilling men even though I do say so myself. Incidentally, while I remember it, the Captain told me the Bde Major was very complimentary about my observation reports.

Well in the village, which we have now evacuated, we had trouble at first with the villagers about certain things but when we left they seemed sorry to see us go, and told us we were trés gentile. The Battalion in before us was not considerate of the inhabitants but we have got on well with them. Von Kluck was in the village we are leaving today, at the beginning of the war and the Huns murdered an old man there. The old girl we stayed with has had English, French and Germans at her house at odd times. She is 93 and you see more old people, hale and hearty, in this village than you would in 20 English ones. I have got on well with them because I try to converse in French with them

School House
Bedford

February 20th 1916

"My dear Heriz-Smith

I was very glad to have your letter, and I'm ashamed to have let so much time go before answering it. It was good of you to give me so full account of your experiences—everything and anything from the front is interesting to us and helps us understand in some degree, at any rate, what you have to face. It seems absurd to be sitting quietly at home among these peaceful surroundings when our friends are going through what you describe.

The more I read and hear about modern warfare the more surprising it is that we were able to hold on as we did a year ago when our artillery was so weak. It's some consolation to think we have plenty of guns now, and, I hope, munitions are being piled up, for the expenditure in the summer will be enormous. Here we are doing our little share. We have about 400 or more 13lb shells at various stages in the workshop, and the first batch has passed the test. Squads of all ages are at work, men, women and boys, and I hope we shall turn out our 40 a week. It will give particular satisfaction to any OB gunners who came across our shells to see "BGS" stamped on them.[27]

I am glad you got the Ousel in due course. Things are going along quite well at the School. I dare say you knew that we took the first two places in the Woolwich exam – Yates and Williams—a fine performance especially on the part of Williams who was in the Classical VI, that magnus parens of so many eminent men, last March. King has taken a temporary commission, or is about to, in the Artillery [at present I think he is bombardier], and Hill is in Sandhurst this week, and has been undergoing a hasty preparation in the ICIV; so now Malcolm is now left top of the 6th. It seems a very juvenile front bench compared to the grave and reverend seniors of 1914. The Monitors are dong well and keeping things going capitally, and our first XV this term is really quite good – when it is at it's best. We beat Merchant Taylor's comfortably despite one or two naps indulged in by the forwards in the course of the game.

Woolwich beat us on their ground; we had to play uphill in the 2nd half against a heavy and aggressive pack, but we gave them a hard game. Next Saturday we play Eton on their ground and next year they come to us.

Chapel, OTC, Choir and the other societies are going on as usual, except that Colon has joined the army and gone into training at Romford. Mr Batterbury plays the organ and is doing very well. In the Choir we are doing Stanford's Battle of the Baltic, a fine work but distinctly hard. What to do for a dramatic performance I cannot think at present for practically all the leading actors are in for exams in the summer.

We have had very cheerful letters from Dick, who is somewhere up north—his movements are shrouded in mystery and his letters are chiefly filled with descriptions of a pantomime which is to be performed soon.

Dear Mr Lambert—he was one of the best and I can understand how his men loved him. I hope you will get his platoon. I'm glad to say we have a memorial of him in Chapel – two fine candlesticks above the altar, which Mrs Lambert presented to us on the same morning that he left. We shall never forget him.

Write again when you have time.

Our best wishes
Take care of yourself
Yours ever
Reginald Carter

Head Master
Bedford School

Letter to Mother Feb 22nd 1916

I was suddenly off to the Army sniping school. I rushed off at very short notice with my servant and got settled there. It was a six day course, and by virtue of reporting to the Commandant first I got the best billet, and the old girl was "trés gentile" and did all she could to make me comfortable.

We have in number six officers or so from different battalions, and a pretty silly lot too. We had the first day's course lecturer and a lot of shooting with all sorts of telescopic, optical and aperture sights, and a hugely interesting syllabus in an 8-hour day. I was terrifically interested in the work. My particular instructor was Sergeant Fulton, a famous shot and Old King's Prizeman at dear old Bisley

Letter to Dad. Feb 27th 1916

He describes how he has become the Sniping Officer as the holder of this post is on leave; previously H-S was the Assistant Sniping Officer [sinecure]. Has the reputation of being the best shot in the Battalion. He says he's good with a rifle but less so with a revolver. Tells that his old Platoon Commander, Wilcox, has been severely wounded by a rifle grenade.

Mentions the belief that they will push soon to help the French at Verdun.

Describes a dinner he attended

1 Delicious curry soup
2 Chicken with potatoes and beans, bread sauce and Escoffier sauce
3 Mutton roast hot
4 Jam puddings
5 Cocoa wafers
6 Hors d'oeuvres of sardines with tomato sauce on toast; I forgot this should be on top!

Washed down by copious amounts of Champagne

Compares this with trench food which is Maconochies Bully Beef,[28] tinned fruit and cocoa

Feb 28th 2nd Lt Shankster slightly wounded

March 1st 1916 Pont Noyelles

Battalion in Corps reserve with the remainder of the 54th Brigade

Corbie 2nd to 7th March

The Battalion marched to Corbie, three miles and went in to the town. Weather wet with some snow.

Letter to Father March 8th 1916

Well here we are again within sound of the guns and going up nearer still before the day is out into the reserve trenches. We marched to this place late last night and rolled at once into bed, as we were very fatigued after the long march. It was a very curious march, pitch dark and lights and flashes all round going up descending and floating. You could see flashes but not hear the guns owing to the distance. On the right, lights and the occasional growls of guns straight ahead, and again on the left more lights going up and occasional flashes. Only behind was there unmitigated blackness. It seemed like marching into a salient.

He speaks of going to the dentist to complete what was started in Bedford, and to save a tooth. He also says the French are doing well at Verdun and that the Hun in general is "getting to the end of his resources".

Also that we are great pals with the French.

11th to 15th March 1916 Bray

The Battalion marched to Bray, 11 miles, remained there that night and the following afternoon marched to Bronfay Farm and Billon wood, two miles. One Coy and HQ's being at the former, and three Coy's at the latter. Colonel Ripley and Adjutant R Beecham wounded.

11th to 15th March

The Battalion went in to a new sector of front line trenches just north of Carnoy village replacing the Bedfordshire Regiment. The trenches were in a very bad state of repair. The enemy fired a mine on the 13th. Weather fine. Captain Burrows killed and two men wounded.[29]

Letter to Mother March 12th 1916

Since I last wrote we have had some adventures again. We were in a big wood in huts and tents and in reserve for four days, latterly, yesterday, coming up into the front line in a new sector. The said wood has been heavily shelled for some time and at odd intervals by the Hun so it is not over safe. Also it snowed and we had a moderate time, not by any means frightfully uncomfortable, but not comfortable. We slept eight officers in a wooden hut but on the floor.

The Colonel and adjutant came up on the first day and unfortunately were shelled by Fritz. A big shell dropped about on top of them, with the result that the Adjutant was found lying in the shell hole with a compound fracture of the leg above the knee and an arm wound, while the dear old Colonel got off with a chunk of flesh out of his arm. They were both very cheerful about it all. The Colonel will be out for a few days, but the Adjutant we will lose for good, as he will get a better job if the war is still on when he recovers.

We are now under command of our Major.

The day after we moved into the woods and not a single wink of sleep could I get as our guns are in the neighbourhood and the noise they made all night was simply terrific.

It was horrid but we are getting accustomed to all that. Yesterday it happened that Fritz did not disturb us with his shelling very heavily. We passed by guns of ours on the way in, and two were fired when my platoon was just passing. It was horrid. The shock, roar and flash were so great that we had no time to be anything but dazed and the flash left me blind for about three seconds. I would not like to be an artillery man for some things.

Well, we came up into the line last night and I was on duty in the trench visiting sentries, patrolling the trench etc which one officer at a time does during the night, when suddenly I stopped to get on a fire step between the two sentry posts each of which was a little distance away, and lo and behold, three figures in the blackness were walking along our wire not 20 yards away, not yet seen by the sentries. My observer got up with me, trained his rifle and my revolver on the others. I challenged, and they didn't hear, but suddenly stopped and I heard "Och wasser — —" or something like that clearly and distinctly!! Well, my revolver went like lightening at once and my observers also. The sentries joined in and later a machine gun. There were loud groans and all three of them dropped to the ground. Two were hit and the other one got up after a time and ran away so we had to fire again. It was the most unpleasant and morally repugnant to me than anything I have ever experienced. Well, to cut a long story short, at dawn we heard groans outside, and as we couldn't stand the idea of that fellow being out there all day, we got out and I and another officer went to search. It was rather risky as we got badly fired on by our own people and got hit by a little bit of bullet which didn't cut me or hurt me at all, only stung a little. I found that Hun and got to him, but the poor fellow was past any help. I called him Kamerad and he put out his hand towards me. Well, I got his rifle and bombs and went back to the trench doing a tremendous speed over our wire through everything and hurtling myself literally into the trench. Our people further down to the right were sending bullets all around and my escape was narrow. The other officer stayed lying with Fritz lying in the ground that was a wiser course than mine. In a minute or two we stopped the people firing on our right, and I went out again with a Sergeant and a man, and between us we lifted Fritz and carried him to the trench, but it was a horrid job getting over our wire especially as the Huns saw us in the quite good light and opened rapid fire on us. Never did four people, I warrant, get over the wire with a 13 stone man so quickly, though we had to drag him through the wire without regard for his groans, and we simply went into the trench head first, pulling Fritz in after us. He was mortally wounded we found out and died in a few minutes. I was glad as the sight nearly made me sick. I saw the other one dead a few yards off. The other got away. They were bursting with bombs, but what they intended to do I shall never know. We got his rifles and bombs and sent them to Brigade, who were pleased with our work, I think. We have been forbidden from going out to the dead man, that is, no officer is to go. His rifle is my property, having gone out to fetch it off him, but I didn't take it, as I didn't want to be reminded of that scene and it would only be a nuisance to me. You see, darling, I have a good lot to be thankful for in my escapes; we have probably thwarted the intentions of the enemy on us, but Oh, I felt very sorry for the wounded man and very queer too. ***War is so beastly my little Tit, there's no doubt about that, and I haven't got the required coolness and deliberate recklessness for it yet, and I doubt I ever will.*** *Schreiner was splendid as usual. I was in doubt as to whether I should go out or not as it was absolutely light and the Huns were only 2-300 yards away, but together we decided to risk it for the fellow, and the Sergeant came too.*

By the way, thanks for the last parcel and for the Ousel that I received with great joy. The School seems to be getting on quite splendidly by all accounts. Have they played Eton yet or has it been impossible this year?

I have heard from Batterbury and Atchie and news about Cyril Cook and Maurice. Geoff has been transferred to Ipswich, lucky beggar!

It's a bit steep being asked to give up tea! What's next! I could not exist without my tea.

15th to 19th March 1916

The Battalion returned to rest billets at Bray.

Letter to Mother March 16th 1916

Bedford is to be "strafed" is it? My word, I do hope not. If Zepps come over Bedford and do anything of that sort I shall kill Huns with much greater pleasure, nay with zest. You seem to be using the Chaplain to your advantage.

19th to 23rd March 1916

During this period the weather was variable. The enemy snipers who were very active at first were much quieter. Casualties—two killed and one wounded

March 22nd

I had a shave from a sniper first night. I popped my head up near one of our sentries and hadn't been there a second before a really good shot hit the sand bag about 3 inches from my right eye and filled the same eye full of earth and stinging it no end. Lucky it wasn't worse; it was a really near thing.

You told me you were going to the intercession service. I love the school chapel as you know and will be able to picture you there and at St Andrews. I can see you tramping up the Kimbolton Road.

23rd to 27th March. Bronfay

The Battalion returned to the intermediate line.

27th to 30th March

A quiet period but for artillery fire which was chiefly done against work in constructing dugouts and shelters. Casualties – two killed and four wounded

RAID BY BEDFORDSHIRES.

Last night the Bedfordshire Regiment carried out a very successful raid near Carnoy.

The raiding party rushed trenches, and, after fierce hand-to-hand fighting, drove the remaining Germans into their dug-outs and bombed them there.

Our casualties, eight wounded—all brought in. German loss considerable.

To-day hostile artillery has been active about La Boisselle and Hébuterne. Last night enemy exploded a mine south-east of Neuville St. Vaast. To-day hostile artillery has been active about Monchy au Bois and Neuville St. Vaast.

Yesterday evening the enemy carried out heavy bombardment on our trenches east of Armentières and about Frelinghien. South of Frelinghien enemy entered our trenches at about 8 p.m. under cover of the bombardment, but was immediately driven out by a counter-attack.

Last night, after heavy bombardment, followed b. the explosion of a mine, the enemy attacked our trenches on Hill 60, but was repulsed. At the same time the enemy gained a footing in one of our sapheads north of Hill 60, but was driven out by our bombers. Our trenches west of Zillebeke and north-east of Hill 60 and battery positions in rear were heavily shelled from 6 p.m. to midnight.

An attack at St. Eloi was repulsed. To-day hostile artillery has been active against our trenches south-west of St. Eloi.

Last night enemy gained footing in one of our craters in the Hohenzollern section, but was driven out at once.

During the night enemy sprang mines south-east of Souchez, north-east of Double Crassier, north-east of Vermelles, and west of Hulluch. We sprang a mine in Hulluch sector.

Beds Raid April 1916

The famous "Raid on Carnoy" of the 7th Battalion Bedfordshire's.

26th April 1916.

Letter from H-S to his father April 1916

"The old Boche is very much cut up in his feelings opposite my battalion section, as not only did he lose the patrol that I scuppered early on, and all the men we killed with bayonet and rifle during the strafe, to say nothing of the artillery, but, as you will have seen in the papers, the Bedford's, our "Chummy" battalion which relieves us in the trenches, cut out the Germans the other night, three or four days since. They strafed them first with artillery then rushed them with a raiding party. All the men were out for blood not prisoners. The Hun was thoroughly demoralised, and they killed about a dozen by bayonet alone, besides bombing two dugouts filled with Boche. They reckon our old Hun opposition trenches lost about 60 killed in the raid. "Some business". The old fellow must be scarified some by now I should say. All the raiders got back

safe though some were wounded. That following the thrash we gave them in the loss of a patrol or two, all the same lot of Huns, can't have improved their morale much. What ho for the red Beds!"

It was in the Times & all sorts.

The War Diary of the Bedfordshire's says:
"A2 26-4-16 Relieved 6th Northants in A2 Sector early morning. Relief complete 12.40pm. Hostile aeroplane dropped bombs just by Bray Church. A Hole in road and windows etc. broken was the only damage. No casualties. ***We raided German trenches night of 26/27th****. No killed but 2/Lieut. H. Driver wounded & 13 others."*

General Officer Commanding 54th Brigade requested the C.O. to publish in Battn. Orders the communiqué appearing in the Times of 29th April respecting the raid carried out on night of 26/27th April by D Company.

It was decided that such was the success of this raid that all ranks in the Bedfordshire's should be told about it for purposes of the morale of the Regiment

"BATTALION AFTER ORDERS
By Lieut.Colonel G.D.Price Commanding 7th (S) Battalion Bedfordshire Regiment

30th April 1916 COMPLIMENTARY ORDER.
At the request of the General Officer Commanding 54th Infantry Brigade, the Commanding Officer has great pleasure in notifying to all ranks the Communiqué published in the "Times" of April 29th 1916, which referred to the recent raid. "Last night the Bedfordshire Regiment carried out a very successful raid near CARNOY. The raiding party rushed the trenches and after fierce hand-to-hand fighting drove the remaining Germans into their dugouts and bombed them there. Our casualties – eight wounded, all brought in. German loss considerable." The General officer Commanding 54th Infantry Brigade is of opinion that in publishing the name of the Regiment in the newspaper, which up to now has scarcely ever been done, a high honour has been conferred on the Battalion. The British Communiqué has also been published in all French papers.

(signed) J. H. Bridcutt, Captain Adjutant 7th (S) Battalion Bedfordshire Regiment"

This is a good example of the use of propaganda and the use of National and Local papers. It brought kudos to a Regiment that was not well known up to this point.

20
April to June 1916

OAS Thursday night 12.30-ish 1916 April?

Darling own Tittie

Just back in my little dugout [comfy but not safe] after a stroll in no mans land with my servant Chantrell. We went out at 11.15 having muddied our steel helmets because with a bright moonlit night and about an hour and a half examining our wire in front, Brer Boche was obliging enough to put up few lights and still fewer shots, and also kindly refrained from using either his searchlights or machine guns anywhere near us. So we had a moderately easy journey apart from the soaking wet long grass, and the conglomeration of loose trip wire and rattling tins strewn all over the place to make a noise, the mud and the scrambling over wet dykes. I shall have to prepare my report on the wire now so I shall shut up my wee Tit until tomorrow. My dugout is quite nice and cosy with a candle near the bed, and for a change there is plenty of water to be had. So it looks quite the little dressing room with my shaving kit and washing kit scattered about amidst Very pistols, nose caps, trench daggers etc. I'm not going to bed tonight as I am going out for a walk round my platoon soon, so nightie, nightie, my own darling sweetest of little "Titties", with pounds and pounds and tons and tons of love. I carry yours and Pa's faces in my mind and I feel quite happy!

April 6th 1916

Just another short letter to acknowledge, as I forgot to do last time, the parcel and cake, which arrived safely in the trenches. Misfortunately however a cake from Aunt Flossie arrived same day, and not only that but three other members of the mess had cakes on the same day. Also, taking all this in conjunction with the fact that I could only carry one cake back to Bray with me, and you'll see how unfortunate it was. Never mind. The platoon enjoyed the cake immensely. The sections cut a pack of cards to see which one was going to have it for tea and they liked it no end, and as privates out here get none to good food by a long way you won't grudge it falling into other hands — or mouths — from that which it was intended for. Better luck next time.

April 8th

Here's just a note before we go into the trenches again tonight. We've had some bad news today and that is that we have got to give up our ripping mill to another company. It's considered the best and we are not to have it always. It's a beastly nuisance, unmitigated beastly in fact, and feds me up to the teeth. There are also wild rumours of all sorts about going shortly for a rest, another about moving to a completely different part of the line. To vacate the mill means that instead of being in the midst of the river we shall now be in town itself.

Did you see in the paper that poor old Griffiths has been killed? Another of my pals! He was only recently slightly wounded I believe. He was a ripping fellow, one of the best.

April 9th

Here we are again in a front line trench and in the same old game. Trench life is a good deal better than it was, but that is not saying a great deal, now that the sun makes things look a bit more cheerful.

One of our officers in the Coy had a bad accident this morning, playing about with the detonator of a "dud" German rifle grenade – a very foolish thing to do at the best of times. The poor fellow has paid for it with the loss of sight of one eye and a mauled hand, but I can't think what made him do it. The Boche is fairly quiet though he treats us to rifle grenades and trench mortars every now and then, and quite a few times he catches a good deal more that he bargained for.

I need hardly say that the idea of catching a glimpse of you and dear old dad, and the kids after a whole five months is wonderful but I can't build on such hopes as so much can happen in a month.

April 13th

Well, well, what a life it is to be sure. Please excuse a very hasty scrawl with a blunt pencil, and a scarcity of ideas.

You wouldn't believe it but we've just, in the grey of the morning or somewhat earlier had a repetition of December 29th. I have to thank God for a much more extraordinary preservation than the December 29th one even. There you see I was not in the vortex of the whirlpool at the time. We had a very thin time of it for 80 or 90 minutes starting at 2am. There were heavy shells of all sorts crashing and bursting about the trenches, and much worse than that the sausages. Sausages are 100lb mines. You see them coming with a gentle trail of sparks ever so high and then descending steeply, and when they burst they are much worse than a shell, an awful blast and the pieces! If one gets into your trench, well, your body may be found up to 200 yards away, and they did test us. One fell, smack, onto our platoon latrine and the results were not salubrious over in the front trenches! That was almost worse than anything.

A perfect inferno it was. Luckily to put it down to luck, ***which it wasn't of course****, the shells all went a little over and the wind was against the sausages causing them to burst short and some over, and only one or two in the trench while others nearly drove you out of your senses by bursting two or three yards from the parapet. The local papers will certainly make a fuss of it.*

NOTHING is to be written on this side except the date and signature of the sender. Sentences not required may be erased. If anything else is added the post card will be destroyed.

I am quite well.

I have received your letter dated April 2 / parcel " April 3

Letter follows at first opportunity.

Signature only. Dm Henry Smell 2/Lt

Date April 9. 1916

[Postage must be prepaid on any letter or post card addressed to the sender of this card.]

FPC

Our casualties were much heavier, and there were some awful sights, but my platoon, which caught it almost worst, certainly worst of any Coy, only had one casualty, when a sausage fell on the parapet and flattened the trench out. He was buried and hit in the head; I dashed down with my platoon sergeant and pulled him out with difficulty amidst the crash of the shells, and started to bind him up. He is, I believe, doing fairly well now thank goodness, but looking back at it I can only call it another extraordinary escape for all of us, and with a little difference in the wind we might of lost nearly the whole platoon. Of course we weren't idle all the time. I simply cannot describe my men. I bolted out of my dugout when the whole thing started and dashed into the fire trench with two sandbags. One puts one's feet into sandbags when going to bed to keep the mud of the bed. Well I forgot them and dashed out with the men, nearly falling on my face several times, but I got to the trench first almost of everyone except the sentries who are always there, and presently the fun began! Fun!!! Rather I should say Hell!!! Yet my men came tearing up to the fire step amidst tons of shells and began as rapid a fire as they could, yelling "Come out you blighters", "Show your bloody faces, yer (excuse the language)." I dashed up and down looking for bombs and ammunition supply with my sergeant. I was bucked by my men. They fought like blazes, doing it with a grin and a smile. They are fine I must say. By the way the Huns came over in some numbers and there were several deeds of bravery. The affair ended to our advantage. The Huns were pushed out where they had got in with greater losses than ours and we have got several Hun bodies in front of our wire now. We captured one alive but he was wounded and frit to death, evidently thinking we were going to murder him. One of our men did an extraordinary brave thing. He was badly hit in the legs and the Huns got him and took him across. When they got to the wire one guard was left with him to bring him there as he could hardly walk at all [all in the dark of course], when he suddenly pushed the Hun headlong into their wire and then turned and heavily fired on the Hun trench. He lay out in shell holes gradually getting closer to our lines, and suddenly when it was light made a bold dash with a last effort and flopped over the parapet into the arms of the officer on duty. He will be on his way to England and home. A plucky lad! The General was very pleased with our efforts and when he came round this morning to hear of our success, complemented the Company Battalion highly. Three men's names are in for mention and one was this fellow who escaped, and well he deserved it. Well darling we have had a rough time and lost some good men, besides seeing some revolting sights but my Coy and platoon particularly were very fortunate and ***I think I can say that God comes with us.***

We got our own back for December 29th.
All leave is stopped again!
More!
Rumour has it that I am going to Divisional School for 3 weeks.
I got the Ousel yesterday and enjoyed it as usual.

HCP is getting married and is enormously happy. I'm selfish enough to feel sorry he's getting married. I'm truly afraid that marriage does ruin a friendship, a bachelor one I mean. Still I'm awfully bucked for his sake.

School of Instruction

Headquarters 18th Division
BEF

April 17th 1916

This is my new address but only for a fortnight and a little over to be precise 18 days. I got here yesterday and we now have started work. It looks like being an interesting course and a pleasant change from the trenches, numbering amongst other benefits a good bed, no night duty, a hut to myself, stove etc. Further more curiously enough, the Commandant was in command of my Coy at the Staff College last March; very nice to it is, and I know that I can look forward to his lectures with real interest. It was he, you will remember, who took me in his car when I dislocated my knee playing RMC Sandhurst.

Curiously I have met an OB here who was goodish but junior to me and we were not very well acquainted. He was the fellow whom Mr Sanderson offered me the tutorship for in Ireland at the commencement de la guerre. Now the lucky blighter is in the Machine Gun corps, has only just come out here and has two stars up. Such is life!

Robert Graves continued with his view that after the first few weeks an officer went into decline, and that though at six months he was more or less alright, by nine or ten months, unless he had been given a few weeks rest on a technical course, or in hospital, he usually became a drag on other company officers.

May 1916 was six months after the beginning of active service, but Denzil was showing no signs of decline, partly because of the distraction of a course he had been on but also because he was very optimistic about the outcome of the war. The next few demanding and exciting months were to see Denzil at his exceptional best.

The background to the Battle of the Somme July-November 1916

1915 was to prove the most costly year of the war and major offensives such as at Champagne, Loos or the Dardanelles achieved no breakthrough at a terrifying expense in lives. For the most part the Somme had been a "quiet" sector with some trench raids and mining but little else.

An allied conference in December 1915 at Chantilly discussed the possibilities for offensives in 1916, in Russia, in Italy and on the Somme, but the charnel house of Verdun changed the Somme initiative to essentially a British affair over a shorter front. The Somme became essential to take the heat off the French at Verdun, despite the misgivings of some soldiers and politicians.

The path to the Somme offensive in July can be traced using regimental and brigade diaries, and Heriz-Smith's notes and letters back home. This two-month period starting in May is the background to what turned out to be the biggest single loss of life in one day in all British military history. The Somme remains a topic of great controversy with some referring to it as "Lions led by donkeys", and others saying that the cost to the Germans was so high that they could never win the war from this point. Certainly the combined impact of Verdun and the Somme on the

German Army was a very serious one, but it was the impact of the entry of the USA into the War in 1917 that led to the German gamble of the Spring Offensive in March 1918, a gamble that came close to victory, especially as Russia had increasingly dropped out of the War in late 1917 after the Bolshevik revolution.

Planning

If you were on a fatigue or a working party, it was easy to believe that yours was the only platoon or company doing any real hard work in the whole of France, and, further, that the job had been organised merely to annoy you. So it was that few people, even among those on the spot, realised how great were the preparations necessary for such an undertaking as the Somme offensive of July 1916.

In his despatch on these operations Sir Douglas Haig gave a vivid picture of the tasks involved.

"Vast stocks of ammunition and stores of all kinds had to be accumulated beforehand within a convenient distance to the front. To deal with these many miles of new railways – both standard and narrow gauge – and trench tramways were laid. All available roads were improved, many others were made, and long causeways were built over marshy valleys."

"Many additional dug-outs had to be provided as shelter for the troops, for use as dressing-stations for the wounded, and as magazines for storing ammunition, food, water and engineering material. Scores of miles deep communication trenches had to be dug, as well as trenches for telephone wires, assembly and assault trenches, and numerous gun emplacements and observation posts.

"Important mining operations were undertaken, and charges laid at various points behind the enemy lines."

"Except in the river valleys, existing supplies of water were hopelessly insufficient to meet the requirements of the number of men and horses to be concentrated in this area. To meet this difficulty many wells and borings were sunk, and over 100 pumping plants were installed. More than 120 miles of water mains were laid."

"Much of the preparatory work had to be done under very trying conditions, and was liable to constant interruption from the enemy's fire. The weather on the whole was bad, and local accommodation totally insufficient for housing the troops employed, who consequently had to content themselves with such rough shelter as could be provided in the circumstances. All this labour, too, had to be carried out

in addition to fighting and to the everyday work of maintaining existing defences. It threw a very heavy strain on the troops, which was borne by them with a cheerfulness beyond praise."

As far as the Brigade was concerned, preparations began as far back as May 4th when the battalions were relieved in the line by the 21st Brigade (30th Division) and were engaged for nearly two months on work in connection with the long-anticipated offensive.

The Fusiliers were in camp at Bois Celestine employed chiefly on road mending; the Bedfordshire Regiment in billets at Bray, working under the 30th Division; the **Northamptonshire Regiment** in billets at Frechencourt and Querrieux, building railways between Carnoy and Daours; and the Middlesex Regiment at Grovetown Bay, also on railway work.

The following will give a general idea of how the next few weeks were spent by the battalions:

"Huts had to be erected by the score, roads to be made and other repaired, barges unloaded, ballast procured from quarries, and many other arduous tasks carried out. The parties on hut building soon began to see some result of their labours, and before many days a snug little town had sprung up under the shadow of the budding trees."

"The valley of the Somme was indeed superb. In the early morning you would awaken to the song of birds in the trees above you; dragon-flies, at least six different colours, which drift noiselessly through the air, and beautiful butterflies, made every moment of the day really enjoyable." You are recommended to read "Birdsong", if you have not done so already.

"In Chipilly village there were some baths alongside the canal, and our men had a hot bath and a change of under-clothing, and a hundred yards away was an open-air swimming bath where our men splashed about."

"There were magnificent views of the Somme and the lagoons from the woods, and some of the officers got a boat and rowed from one lagoon to another to Sailly Lorette. On the way some indulged in a swim, while the others prepared tea in picnic style. For the men, we arranged cinema shows, concerts and football matches."

Among the work to be done on the front from which the great offensive was to be made was the preparation of Russian saps. These were tunnels under No-Man's

Land, leading to within about six yards of the German lines. They were to be filled with stores of all kinds and when the attack had been launches, all that was necessary was to blow out the end, and a way was made for carrying parties to get rations, water, ammunition, etc., to the advanced troops.

There were two of these saps on the front on which the Brigade attacked, and the digging of them led to an exciting moment. Work was going ahead in good style, when, to the general consternation, they broke through into a German dugout. Luckily, it was unoccupied at the time; the hole was carefully patched, and apparently the Germans never knew of our visit."

During this period 54th Brigade headquarters were at Oissy, where Brigade Machine Gun, Trench Mortar, Bombing and Signal schools were instituted. Sir Douglas Haig and Staff visited these schools on May 12th.

June came, and with it more active preparations. On the 9th the Fusiliers and Northamptonshire Regiment began digging near Picquigny trenches which were an exact facsimile from the aeroplane photos of the enemy system opposite Carnoy, which they were to attack three weeks later. By the 11th, Brigade headquarters and all battalions had arrived at Picquigny, and practice attacks over the facsimile trenches were actively carried out.

On May 16th 1916 Denzil wrote to his mother

I went into ———, the big town I told you about last Sunday, waylaying one of the ASC lorries and demanding a lift, thus getting into A——, with the minimum of trouble and the maximum of comfort. It was a real treat to see a big town humming with life, tram cars, a big Cathedral, very nice too, long green shady boulevards, well dressed ladies, crowds of French officers, and soldiers and English ditto.

Next day was interesting in that we visited a British Aerodrome and later had a lecture from a RFC officer at school. I cannot of course give more details.

In the course of work here we had two contests between officers and NCOs in wiring by night and bombing and won narrow victories.

An order has come out here that officers are to reduce their kit to the absolute minimum, so you may expect a consignment of woollen things to come to you soon.

I have had letters recently from Cyril Cook, Cyril Mudford, Percy, Rix, Auntie Flossie, and Geoff Bull etc so you see I'm not forgotten.

I see Maurice Simpson is gazetted for a MC. Good! Some Stunt!"

There are no prizes for recognising the visit to Amiens, and, by the way, the Cathedral today has many plaques and areas that show huge gratitude to the British as well as Commonwealth countries, particularly Australia. It was the defence of Amiens in March and April 1918 that prevented a catastrophic German breakthrough to the Channel coast. Haig's instructions to troops to fight with their backs to the wall and to the last bullet show how desperate the situation was then.

"A" Company marched to Corbie to be attached for demonstration purposes to the 18th Divisional School at LA HOUSSOYE. Lieut. Schreiner the OC [of] the Coy being appointed Adjutant of the School.

May 21st 1916 *I left Waterloo at 4pm and Dad and Auntie were at the station. I had had lunch and a walk with Dad before starting. I left Southampton about 8pm without destroyer escort. The sea calm but it was foggy.*

May 22nd *I arrived at Le Havre at about 4am and trained at once to Montrodier, and had an omelette. I arrived at Amiens at about 5pm, detrained and got to Corbie by 6pm. I left Podmore [Captain Hubert Podmore] to go on. I found the Company acting as Demonstration Coy at a Divisional school. I took over command of Coy*. [The short tenure as Company OC, 22-5-16 to 3-6-16, was too short to trigger a promotion to temporary or acting captain]

May 23rd *There was an attack demonstration before the School. A game of cricket followed, and on May 24th I started the platoon cricket league.*

May 24th. **Colonel G E Ripley** returned from England on recovering from his wounds and he took over command [Both Ripley and Schreiner were hugely charismatic soldiers].

25th May 1916. SAISSEVAL was the Brigade HQ's

A draft of 38 NCOs & men joined from an entrenching battalion, and these would be involved in the highly dangerous mining activities that some say were counter productive on the first day of the Somme, July 1st 1916

26th May 1916, SAISSEVAL

Two drafts of 50 & 56 men joined from Base.

May 28th 1916 Letter to Mother

"I've had as nice a week as any since I have been in France. Nice weather, a camp in a clearing in a wood near the School, light work, much cricket on a very bumpy and dangerous pitch, and the duties and privileges of being OC Coy, have combined to give me a very pleasant time. You see I've not really had very much to do; yet one gets so much to do as OC Coy. ***I found my experience as Head of School rather useful during the week. I have had some difficult cases to deal with and I find the same principles apply to men as to boys.***

We are quite a happy family in Coy "A". There are a number of really good NCOs, very decent fellows. I'm alone with only one other officer to run the Coy, and Woulfe who is slightly senior to me and whom I can never really get along with, is away, though he is very pleasant. Schreiner, the OC Coy is a very good fellow as I told you, and is Adj. of the School now and so not actually in command of the Coy, but he is quite close at hand and we are, of course, under his orders as regards demonstration attacks and such like wanted by the School.

My word, did I have a nice time at Bedford and everybody was so decent to me, but above all it was so nice to see my own wee Tit, dad and the kids.

It was simply lovely seeing you and father again after the longest interval I have stayed away from you all my life, n'est ce pas?

Yeh! It was nice and one felt very poortaag on getting back at first".

30th May 1916, SAISSEVAL

Major S H Charrington from the 15th Hussars, joined the Regiment and was appointed 2nd-in-Command.

May 25-31. *There was work as usual, and physical drill. The cricket league is in full swing – I took a good few wickets and scored some runs. No 4 platoon won with four out of five wins.*

June 3rd 1916

Some time after he had left the School of Instruction, Denzil replied to his father's question of what did they do all day!

"We do demonstration attacks from the trenches and in the open in front of the

School and such like, and for our own edification do arms drill, company and platoon drill, bayonet fighting and bombing, besides my parade at 7am when I superintended the Coy at Physical training. Bayonet practice and bombing are my specialities. Besides that we have various working parties mending roads, digging trenches, putting up specimen revetments, putting up and staking barbed wire entanglements and wiring by night and occasional patrol practices; added to this, a Barr and Stroud rangefinder has just turned up and I find myself doing range finding instruction by virtue of having done a course when with the machine guns. There are occasional lectures and clerical work of sorts fill in the work time.

The Western Front June 1916

To occupy spare time I got up an inter platoon league at cricket and we play this valiantly and with enthusiasm on a bumpy pitch which is quite dangerous, with a compo ball and home made bails that blow off in every gust of wind, and home made wickets. You can't tell for toffee what the ball is going to do. Sometimes a good length ball will hit you on the hand, sometime it will shoot along the ground and we bat like demented lunatics. Aye you dance out to hit the ball and it suddenly develops great speed and spin and breaks 6 ft or so. Other balls come as you would expect. Altogether we get great fun out of it and the league has gone with a swing. My platoon had won one out of five matches till this afternoon, owing to a curious habit of collapsing utterly at batting, getting the others out for very little and fielding like lunatics. However roused by the absence of the really good bat of the side, they proceeded, I having been bowled off my feet after one natty boundary shot, to put in an amazing total of 124 and we got the others out for 64. The other side was the one that had won by virtue of having up to this afternoon five matches out of the total six to be played. It was extraordinary as we had several of our second team playing due to absences, and I, who have taken about 30 wickets in the other games as the chief bomber, failed utterly with bat and ball. I rather fancy myself at cricket for style of batting!"

On June 3rd Heriz-Smith handed over to 2/Lt. Gerald Woulfe on his return from

Divisional School, as the latter's commission was about 2 months earlier in 1914 than that of Heriz-Smith.

June 10th

To Dad

"The paper I got a week or two back was interesting only as a slight surprise. You see we were never transferred to the 8th at all, only attached – the four of us, I mean, who went there last, so why they should they transfer us back, goodness knows! Still, there it is!

Rumour has it that going around to the effect that no more letter writing and sending is going to be allowed shortly, for a period of some weeks. Whether, if this happens, we will get posts from home, I don't know, and also whether we are to be allowed to send FPC's or not, I don't know. The only reason I mention this is that in case it does happen, don't get alarmed and worried if you get no letter for about a month or more. It is poortaag, but one of the blessings of trench warfare is regular posts, which have been a bit of a marvel compared to other wars, so one must not grumble if one doesn't get much communication for a while."

June 10th to Corbie for bath. This was always a high point if possible!

June 10th to Mother

"Talking of relations, I hope Rex is pleased with life. I expect he is. A nice "blighty" is a thing not to be despised, sometimes by a long way. I wish him the best wish I can that he has a long stay in England. Any news of Eddie? I want to hear some so if you have got some, don't forget. I want to know "'twonce". I suppose he was in the naval battle the other day? I see the Warrior is down at last, poortag. Still he wasn't on it. How did his ship fare? [Obviously a reference to the Battle of Jutland].

The Italians and French seem to be holding out well, and the Russians doing well. As for us, Kitchener has got to be revenged!" [Kitchener had earlier drowned at sea]

June 4th-11th.There was cricket as usual.

11th June 1916, SAISSEVAL

"A" Company arrived at PICQUIGNY by train from CORBIE.

June 12th. *Schreiner takes over command. Train to Amiens and then on to Picquigny. I settled in a billet near canal with Capt Golding.*

12th to 15th June 1916, PICQUIGNY

The battalion trained in assault on trenches.

June 13th. *This was an off day, and a day to clean up. There was a Conference for all officers led by the Brigadier General*

16th to 18th June 1916, PICQUIGNY

The Brigade trained in assault on trenches; and was inspected by the Corps and Divisional Commanders.

June 14–18th. *These were battalion and brigade days. The weather was hot and muggy.*

Letter to Mother

June 18th

"Just when I might need it I have lost my trench dagger. It's a beastly nuisance. Please do not send me clothes or things to carry, as we can't carry more than our little 35lbs, and are going now to be rigidly kept to it. Only eatables are any good.

We have nearly finished in this place and I don't know where we going after it exactly, though we know the whereabouts all right.

We now have daylight saving in place and we curse it heartedly as we get up early enough as it is, and it took an hours sleep away from us."

June 19th. *This was a rest day. We heard of Russian successes* [This must refer to the Brusilov offensive that was a severe defeat of the Austrian army by Russia, a victory they failed to reinforce, almost as much for political and military intrigue than for any other reason. Brusilov was not of sufficient birth and was conspired against by noble commanders for reasons of jealousy! The Russians did well against Austria in the War but found the German Army a different nut to crack]

I practiced revolver shooting against bottles on wall with GLW [Gerald Lascelles Woulfe, "A" Company, KIA 14-7-16], CGK [almost certainly Clement Geoffrey

Keys, also "A" Company], Percy Harrowell Higham, and Capt G. [presumably Captain Golding]

June 19th to Dad

"There is not much news. We are still comfortable, but not much doing and not much time to be comfortable left. We feed well, sleep well and have got over the bulk of the work we are doing.

We have been doing an average of 12 to 14 miles per day or so, for the last week and we are now resting for a day or two, but expect to be dans les tranchés before very long.

I had some pistol shooting practice this afternoon down by the river, and great fun it was strafing a small tin from some distance and see who could make the tin sink first. I see in this weeks Shooting and Dramatic several photos of the School Cricket XI and St Paul's together.

All things bright and beautiful! We have 4,000 odd bombs, live ones too, underneath my bedroom."

20th June 1916, PICQUIGNY

The battalion went on a short route march.

June 20th. *We marched out to the army ground for an address by Colonel Ripley. It rained on the way back. We went through a gas chamber in smoke helmets.*

21st June 1916, PICQUIGNY

The battalion performed a final assault practice over trenches.

June 21st. *This was a battalion day. We marched out to the training ground*

22nd June 1916, PICQUIGNY. Battalion transport left for HEILLY.

June 22nd.*This was spent packing kit. I had a nice bathe with the MO, Captain Golding.*

Battalion orders were issued by Colonel Ripley the CO of the Northants 6th, and these orders were for the decisive battle which the 18th Division will soon be in.

The attacks were to be proceeded by a five days bombardment of all calibre of guns and mortars.

There will be 12 Stokes guns [trench mortars] and 4 Vickers machine guns for the front.

The days were to be designated by letters of the alphabet and the assault will be carried out on "Z" day.

It was imperative that the land taken should be held at all costs for a prolonged period against enemy counter attack.

During the waiting period the Battalion will be at Bronfay Farm, and prior to the attack the Battalion will occupy the trench in Carnoy. Battalion Headquarters will be at Piccadilly.

23rd and 24th June 1916, PICQUIGNY

The Battalion marched from PICQUIGNY at 10.30am and arrived at AILLY at 11.45am. *The weather very hot. Our train, due to leave at 12.18pm, did not leave till 4.45pm. We arrived at HEILLY by train at 6.30pm. We marched through MERICOURT, "A" and "B" Companies went to BRAY, "C" and "D" Companies and Headquarters to BRONFAY FARM into dug outs which were not reached till 2.30am. Rain fell throughout most of afternoon and evening.*

An artillery bombardment of the German trenches commenced at about 2.00am.

June 23rd. *There was a long and tiresome train journey, in full kit. Then we marched from Picquigny to Heilly- Sur- Somme and then on to Bray. We had heavy packs, full equipment and it was done in pouring rain. It was a very wearying march and we arrived at 3am. I dossed down in a house by the river and slept on the floor.*

June 24th

Letter to Mother

"My own little Tittie

Quelle existence to be sure. Yesterday we moved from where we were and are now in the midst of things. We didn't enjoy the march one little bit. It was one of the most tiresome I have ever been on. I had a colossal pack and haversack and all my equipment, and carried a rifle, and other people's bombs as well, for a good distance. It was terrifically hot and oppressive when we started and the first part was too perspiringly hot for words. The whole of the last part was in pouring rain and owing to the trains we got nothing to eat for nearly 24 hours also except Oxo, which we made at one of the halts. We arrived at 3am, and as it was entirely unforeseen that we should pitch up just when we did, had no billets. So in the pitch darkness we got billets for the men. In looking for our own we couldn't get any success, so as this town is deserted of all save troops, we were at liberty to put ourselves a place anywhere we could, so four of us crawled into a open window to find unfurnished rooms and proceeded to explore with the aid of numerous matches. We soon found it belonged to someone as we heard snores upstairs and I personally lumbered into a room full of sleeping servants. We then discovered that it was a mess. However, being wet through with rain and perspiration, and being dog tired and fatigued, we weren't over-particular as to who it belonged to or what we did, drew our wet raincoats over us and soon were snoring on the floor in a minute.

Six surprised officers came down to mess the next day and found our recumbent forms on the floor. One of the nice things about the Army is that you can do all these sorts of things and only meet with civilities in exchange instead of a having a terrific rumpus. I broke off curiously enough at tea-time owing to one of these same civilities. We appropriated a room from the mess of the billets, and at another mess we walked into the next morning sat a man called Carrington who was at school with me and who I hadn't set eyes on for about six years! We had a long chat and I found out how many OB's are knocking around in this direction, and, curiously enough, saw one of them after tea in the square of the town! However, to return to the civilities question we were all leaning out of the mess window watching aeroplanes flying about when an officer came up to us and asked if there was a café anywhere he could go to. He turned out to be a new arrival from Blighty belonging to the RFC, and had had nothing to eat for a long time. So, of course, as there was no café available we gave him a huge tea and sent him off to the destination he was going to. That's the beauty of the Army. In many cases, if not all, you are free to drop into someone else's mess if hungry and have a meal with them.

When he had departed we all went out to the little square where a very interesting sight was to be seen. The band of a French regiment was "discoursing sweet music" in the square, which was literally packed with French and British troops like sardines. There must have been two or three thousand there. Little groups of English, Scottish, French and Algerians talking together and fraternising. The band played very well, and there was a ripping blend of Horizon Blue, Khaki, Kilts and Red Fezzes. It was an inspiring sight.

Went up to the trenches again this morning for a fatigue [and other jobs also], and the Huns were nasty enough to put some big shells quite close to us, but they were at the time distinctly piano, or if I may say, pianissimo, and for very good reasons too—but I shan't go on though I should love to do it, to tell you what was up, and what I saw. Had a good mornings work and got back at lunchtime to find that our billet had been appropriated by the authorities for some battalion, and as we were, so as to speak, chance comers, we had to get out. So we walked across the road and installed ourselves in another house, originally a shop; I am writing now on the counter, and, of course, we slept on the floor as before.

Oh! I forgot. Before we left this place in which we were in station, and we had a last night of it. We went to a café and ordered a big dinner and had two guests, consisting of the Town Mayor and the OC Sanitary section. We had a fine time, Champagne and about four courses. We were asked to dine with another Coy so broke off our celebrations and went there at about 10pm, only to find they had forgotten all about it, were playing cards, were not in the best of tempers, and could only offer us whiskey which I hate. I didn't care much as the tone would not have attracted one much. I'd had two glasses of Champagne and an aperitif before dinner, a vermouth and Curacao liqueur afterwards, and that was just enough for me at that moment. Still we had expected to find merry makers there and to enjoy ourselves for an hour, so we were pretty sick to find all there with "stink faces", and nothing doing, so we returned to bed and just in time to stop the men who were also kicking up the Dickens of a row, long after lights out. Still, this was last night and we didn't say anything except "Shut up now". We had a very good time, if rather long hours and hard work, at that place.

This morning I came under shell- fire for the first time for two months! It was an extraordinary morning for many reasons but I can't tell what and why."

By the 23rd preliminary training had been finished, the whole Brigade was moved to the Bray area, and on the following day it took over on the front that was to be attacked.

"On the way up from Bray we were delighted to see guns of every calibre dug in – it seemed everywhere. In fact, the whole ground seemed alive with them, and in every valley behind the line was a very hot-bed of destruction to spit at the enemy."

"A good deal of our time was now occupied in cutting steps in and erecting bridges

across the assembly trenches. The steps were to be used for quickness when we left the trenches to attack, and the wooden bridges by reinforcements who would come up across the open."

In the week or so before the big offensive, the Brigade carried out two or three successful raids for the purpose of information.

June 24th. *The house we bagged this morning turned out to be the mess of a Wiltshire Regiment. There was nothing much doing today as far as we are concerned. The Bedfordshire's go up into the front line. Our artillery was firing all day and night, to cut wire and shell trenches. The Hun reply was feeble so far. There was heavy firing from the French all along their line, and French 75's and heavies all up road to Bronfay; the whole valley was stinking with guns. It was some noise.*

The battle really began on the 24th June when an artillery barrage began that was to continue down to the early morning of July 1st. Unfortunately bad weather and poor predictions meant that not all surface installations were destroyed by this barrage despite it being heard as far away as London.

25th June 1916, BRONFAY FARM

There was reconnaissance by officers of the "forming up" trenches of the Battalion for the coming attack.

June 25th. V Day.

I took my platoon to Carnoy to dig out assembly trenches at 7.30am and the guns were going full swing as usual. I went with the NCOs up to the 2nd line, and came in for a few 5.9 shells from Huns. There were no casualties. A French band was playing in the square after tea to audience of Scots, English, French and Algerians. It was a picturesque sight. I saw PG Humfrey [an OB who survived the war], in the distance. There was heavy damage to trenches by our artillery and the firing was much heavier on our front. The Hun's reply was feeble. He is puzzled by extent of front probably, but anyway there were only a few shells from him today.

A Hun sausage balloon was brought down in flames by one of our planes. Another was hit by Archies and brought down.

26th June 1916, BRONFAY FARM

We worked on the forming up trenches.

June 26th. W day.

There was increased firing by our guns, and bursts of concentrated bombardment, giving smoke clouds at intervals. Gas was sent over by the division on our right. The Hun was more active today, putting some stuff back but nothing like ours. There were extraordinary sights to be seen in the shape of vast columns of green, yellow and pink smoke besides white shrapnel bursts. Big heavy stuff was firing onto the Pommiers Redoubt, with enormous explosions and clouds. Also Contalmaison was in flames for some time in the Hun lines. Bricqueterie was getting what Albert got from the Huns.

I took a party of NCOs to see Schreiner in Ops in the Durham trench, to observe our line of advance of the big guns. As we got there the Huns shelled it and as the smoke was too thick at the time I took the party in the direction of Peronne to have a look see there, and then came back to Bronfay Farm. I then went to the OP to see Schreiner and was back by 2pm and there was nothing much doing after lunch either. It was a very cold night lying on stone floor with only a blanket as a bed. I made a fire half way through the night out of a cupboard and slept in front of it in the next room.

The German reply to our preliminary bombardment caused a certain amount of trouble.

It was near the same spot that the Bedfordshire Regiment had a very bad bit of luck, having all the officers of one company killed or wounded only a few days before they were due to go over in the big show.

A great deal of rain fell during these days and nights of waiting for the big event, and trenches got muddier and muddier. In spite of hard work and discomfort, the men were amazingly cheerful and full of heart. The worse the conditions, the better their spirits seemed to become.

27th June 1916, BRONFAY FARM

All officers' valises and heavy kit were sent back to 1st Line Transport.

28th June 1916, BRONFAY FARM

It rained hard all day and the condition of the trenches became very bad. The Forming up trenches were completed, the wire on our line of advance removed and all preparations for attack completed. It was thought that the attack would start tomorrow but probably owing to the weather, instructions were received that zero hour would be postponed for 48 hours.

June 28th. Y day.

There was a heavy bombardment as before with smoke clouds. We did not go in the trenches today and it was a slack day till lunch. After lunch we were getting ready to move up to the forming up trenches.

June 30th *The Adjutant informs us that the Push has been postponed for two days!!! Another cold night was in view. A parcel arrived from home in a nick of time. We broke up another bit of shelves to make a store of firewood. The sergeant major kindly brought us a sack each as a sleeping bag. We secured a good night's sleep in front of a good fire.*

29th June 1916, BRONFAY FARM

The weather cleared and the ground began to dry up. This should have been <u>*the*</u> *day, but there was nothing until midday again so I used the time to write letters and got things ready to move. The guns were still active but hardly as before I think. There was a shell or two at night*

The postponement for 48 hours probably was as frustrating for the waiting troops as it was in June 1944 when D Day was postponed due to poor weather. Perhaps the difference is that most soldiers in June 1916 thought that it would be comparatively easy on their D Day as they had been told that German resistance would be weak due to the incessant bombardment that had fallen on them for a week. What they didn't know, though some officers did, was that about one-third of the shells would fail to explode and that the wire had not been cut in most locations, and that the shelling had tossed the wire around making it even more tangled and difficult.

Denzil wrote to his Mother on the eve of battle.

June 30th 1916

"My little mother.

Just a line now to say that I love you and that I will not be able write for a little while, as in an hour from now we move into the front trenches to assemble for the assault. Some time tomorrow we go over the top to strafe the Hun. At that time, my little darling, I shall certainly give just one thought to you and the dear family at breakfast, and then, my dear old dad, to business.

This time we are all out to give the Hun a real bad knock, and with God's help, still do that and move on nearer to the end of the war. I hope with God's grace to get through it safely and to see you all again.

Anyway the Hun is in no enviable position I think. He can hardly be as we have given him a horrid time for the last seven days now with all kinds of guns, so that prisoners say they have been without food for three days. The guns have been tremendously busy and have levelled villages to the ground behind the Hun lines. It has done great damage to their trenches. All hope for good luck and much success.

Well, that's all I need say as time is getting on, except to give you and Dad and the dear kids, all my bestest love and kisses. I hope to write after the strafe on at least a FP.

Well nightie, nightie and tons of love
Your loving son

Pops"

30th June 1916, BRONFAY FARM

We got everything ready and had a parade of the platoon in the morning. The Coy paraded to go up to Bronfay farm at 6.30 and we marched up to go in the trenches, by platoon. We stayed at Bronfay till 12.45 and I spent a little time with D Coy in their dug out, and then waited till darkness amidst the scream of our shells going overhead and the Boche sending a few back.

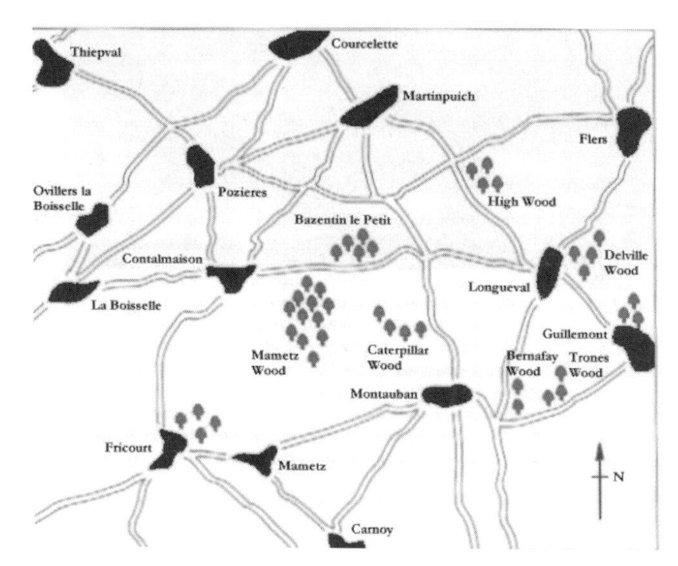

Area of the Somme in which the Northamptonshire 6ths were fighting

By 2am on July 1st all units were in battle positions, as follows:

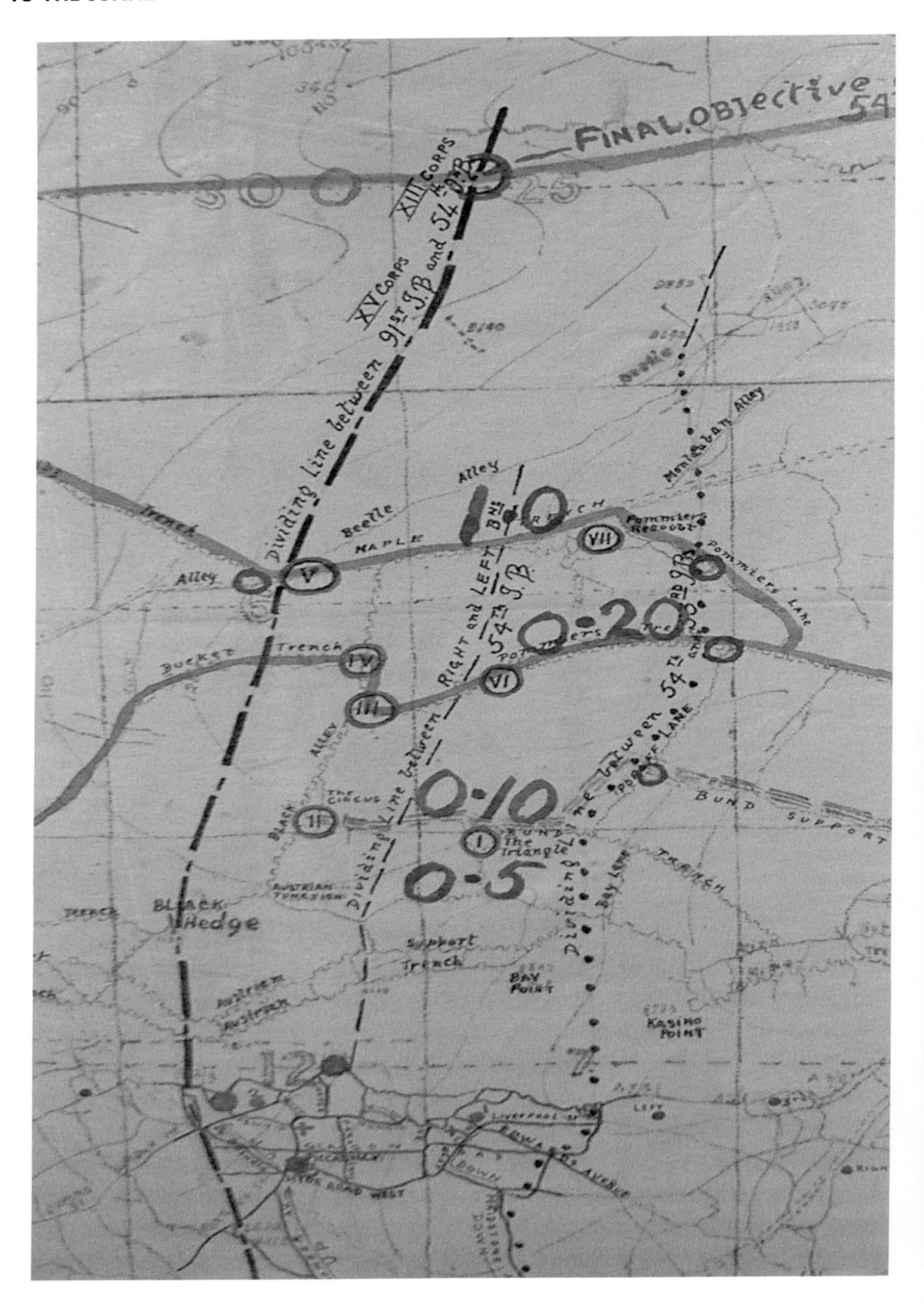
FINAL OBJECTIVE
XIII CORPS
XV CORPS
Dividing Line between 91st I.B and 54th I.B
Beetle Alley
Maple Trench
Montauban Alley
Pommiers Redoubt
Pommiers Lane
Alley
Bucket Trench
Pommiers Trench
RIGHT and LEFT Bns 54th I.B
Dividing Line between 54th and 53rd I.B
0.20
0.10
0.5
The Circus
Black Alley
Bund Support Trench
The Triangle
Austrian Junction
Black Hedge
Support Trench
Bay Point
Kasino Point
Bay Lane
Liverpool St
Edwards Avenue
Dividing Line

Places to note on the map opposite are Kasino Point, the Austrian Support trench, the Bund trench, Pommiers Redoubt, Montauban Alley and the final objective. As it turned out this was one area of the British line on July 1st where reasonable objectives were made for relatively small cost, not the case at Trones Wood two weeks later.

The Northants 6th were part of the 54th Brigade whose first objective was to capture Pommiers Redoubt to the right of the junction of Beetle Alley and Maple Trench. These can be seen clearly on the map above.

The final objective was a ridge overlooking Caterpillar Wood and Willow Brook demarcated by a line on the attached map.

The 11th Royal Fusiliers on the left and the 7th Bedfordshire Regiment. on the right formed the front line of the 54th Brigade. The 6th Battalion Northamptonshire Regiment (less six platoons) were the 3rd or supporting battalion and also formed one company as dug out clearing parties, which were attached to the Royal Fusiliers and Bedford's. The three remaining platoons acted as carrying parties to the brigade.

The 12th Middlesex were in Brigade Reserve.

The brigade had undergone a week's previous training over ground laid out on the plan of the German trenches to be attacked, and were in fine fettle when the day arrived.

The German trenches and wire entanglements had been battered for seven days by our intense artillery bombardment.

On the night proceeding the launching of the attack (30th June – 1st July) the two battalions in the front line were accommodated in our four front line trenches. The 6th Northamptonshire Regiment (less six platoons) moved from BRONFAY FARM at 11.30pm on 30th June and occupied their forming up trenches as follows:

- "A" Company right company supporting the Bedfordshire Regiment in trenches N & NW of Carnoy.
- "B" Company left company supporting the Royal Fusiliers in trenches in Caftet Wood.
- "D" Company (less two platoons) with a portion of the Battalion HQ were in

Reserve and were concealed in trenches in the same wood.

It was no easy matter for these companies in such a restricted area for these companies to debouch from the wood and get into position for the advance, as there were many trenches to be negotiated. Officers and section commanders however had carefully reconnoitred the terrain in previous nights and trenches had been bridged and wire cut.

The 7th Beds and 11th Royal Fusiliers in front and behind our front line will clear all our wire.

Germans on the Somme

The Germans had anticipated a large-scale attack in this area and their defences on the Somme were very strong. They took advantage of the local topography, constructing concrete fortifications, and the defences consisted of no less than three separate positions, consisting of approximately three lines of trenches each.

These ran along the top of the ridges overlooking the British lines and giving the Germans good observation and early warning of attack. They joined up a series of fortified villages and locations, which had been turned into strong points. They contained very deep dugouts, sometimes up to 12 metres deep in which large numbers of soldiers could shelter from the barrage. The German machine guns were carefully sited so that they could fire in enfilade across the lines of attackers. The German defences were much stronger north of the Albert-Bapaume Road, particularly the Schwaben Redoubt at Thiepval and the fortified village at Serre. The positions south of the road to the Somme River were much weaker. In front of the trenches were deep belts of barbed wire. In 1916 the British found these very difficult to cut. In many

Germans dug in on the reverse side of a ravine at the Somme

sectors on the first day of the battle they had not been cut and as a result the attacks 'hung up' leaving the troops in the killing zones of the machine guns. Over the course of the war as whole artillery was a greater killer than machine guns. At the Somme however, particularly on the first day, the machine guns caused massive casualties, because the British artillery barrage was not coordinated properly with the infantry's movement. The German third position was largely situated on the rear of the ridgeline and was thus very difficult to see and therefore to attack for the British Army despite the use of air reconnaissance. The overall depth of the three positions was such that given the range of the majority of British artillery the artillery would have to be moved up a number of times during the battle in order to have sufficient range to attack each position in turn. This militated against a quick breakthrough. At this time the German High Command had ordered the troops to hold ground at all costs. If the British forced their way in to the fortifications the German troops were expected to counterattack immediately and drive them out. This meant that the Germans stationed large numbers of troops in the front line itself. This had the disadvantage of causing very heavy casualties amongst the German troops from the British artillery and the policy was later changed to one of elastic defence.

The Boche delivered small counter attacks with platoons or companies immediately hostile troops gain their objectives. These small counter attacks have had far reaching results and have to be specially guarded against. To meet these small counter-attacks the reserves in the hands of the platoon and company commanders were of the greatest value.

The three sides had upward of 1 million men collectively and 200,000 horses, and both had built "temporary" cities, building roads, bridges, stations and railway lines to bring up food, munitions, fodder and equipment. Also built were hospitals, first aid posts, battery positions. airfields, assembly points, observation posts and communication trenches.

21

July 1st 1916

On July 1st 1916 at 7.30am a series of mines, were exploded such as at Hawthorn Ridge and Lochnagar, and the infantry followed on behind what should have been a moving barrage by the Allied artillery. The British advanced from the north and the French from the southern sector, but at the end of the day it was only the French who had reached most of her targets.

In the British sector the results were appalling and the New Armies of Allenby and Rawlinson were shattered on the slopes leading up to Thiepval and Beaumont-Hamel. The German lines were only breached in part elsewhere.

The casualties were horrific. Of 58,000 men 20,000 were killed on July 1st. 32 Battalions of 800 had more than 500 lost. This was the most costly day in British military history.

July 1st. Z Day.
We moved off at 12.45am by platoons down to Carnoy. One or two were wounded by shells on the way down but not in my platoon. It was a frightfully tiresome journey in which we were continually stopping because of the crowd in front. We got to our forming up trenches after a long halt in Caftet Wood owing to a block in the bottom at about 1.30am.

"Ghastly by day, ghostly by night, the rottenest place on The Somme," Richard Holmes later described this part of the Somme front.

The trench was just outside Carnoy and situated opposite Caftet Wood.

The Huns put no single shell there all the time we were there. We lay at the bottom of the trench to sleep as well as we could, as the noise was "un peu fort", but still many of us slept all right to the accompaniment of the screams of our shells going overhead. The rum ration was served round and we put on our kits ready for action, as the fog lifted and the accompaniment wound down.

6.30am There was an intense hurricane fire from all our guns, and a tremendous unheard of bombardment began. Shells went overhead in their thousands going over to the Hun guns.

7.00 French mortars open up as well. The din was terrific and one could hardly hear oneself speak. The light became much clearer and the fog was rapidly clearing.

7.15 There was fire from the guns, trench mortars, howitzers and Stokes guns making one huge crash and shattering the air.

7.22 It must be concentrated hell for the Boche I would think.

7.27 A big mine goes up under Kasino Point, a prominent projection in the Hun lines which could enfilade an attack. The whole Point was blown up and there was a colossal crater. A number of our men got too close, and many casualties result.

7.30 The 1st wave of the 54th Brigade Beds and Fusiliers got into the German 1st trench and support lines. There was very heavy fire and then the barrage lifted onto Emden Trench.

7.35 The1st wave went into Emden Trench and the barrage lifts to Bund Trench.

7.40 The1st wave rushes Bund. There was some hand-to-hand fighting and men of the 109th Regiment [Prussian] were killed, showing a relief to have taken place in the last day or two.

7.50 The barrage lifts onto Pommier Redoubt and the 1st waves rush Pommier Trench. More hand to hand fighting. Pommier Redoubt was catching it hot.

"All our men in "A" Coy waited in the trenches wild with excitement, yelling and shouting. Masses of assaults were clearly visible moving over the shell torn hill, steadily, the sun playing on bayonets. The Hun barrage was feeble."

At half an hour after zero hour (8am) the Regiment in line of half platoons at about 60 paces intervals and 150 paces distance found themselves launched into the attack. They had to change direction slightly to the right and open out, soon after moving off, but this was successfully accomplished. The battalion advanced as steadily as if they were on the parade ground, their instructions being that it was not to halt until the enemy second trench Austrian Support was reached.

All companies came under heavy artillery barrage before our rear trench Hyde

Road West was reached, but they continued to move forward with admirable coolness, "A" Company even checking in "No Man's Land" to correct their direction. The two leading companies arrived simultaneously at the Emden and Austrian support trenches.

8am I am getting the Platoon together in trench ready to go over the top.

8.05 Over! We went out into the open over the trenches by a bridge laid down previously. We got into small columns and moved steadily up to our front lines.

8.15 We arrived at our front line and went straight across out towards Hun line. A few were hit by shells now bursting just ahead [Friendly fire].

8.25 We arrived at Austria trench with no casualties and then stopped a minute to reorganise. We went on again and the Hun barrage was getting thicker. We arrived at Emden and went straight up to Bund and we lost touch with rest of the Company who stopped in Emden. The Hun was sending large numbers of shells across now, but there were no casualties up to here. We got reorganised and got in touch with rest of the Company. Some Bedford's on the left reported that 53rd Brigade might be held up.

A halt of about 40 minutes here took place, during which the left company ["B" Coy] and bombing parties were detailed and sent up Black Alley. At the same time (8.20am) the right platoon of "A" Company reached Bund Trench and were followed 20 minutes later by the 2nd Platoon, who moved to avoid artillery fire.

From Bund Trench to Pommier Trench both companies came under a heavy artillery fire and suffered considerably, and here Captain Neville, commanding "B" Company was wounded. "A" Coy on reaching Pommier Trench immediately began making strongpoint VI, the three remaining platoons proceeding to Pommiers Redoubt and consolidated that on evacuation by the Bedfords. "B" Coy moved up at the same time and started to consolidate their allotted strongpoints. These strong points were to be prepared for all round defence and strengthened with wire. They were to be held at any cost. Companies were to send officers or NCOs to take over their strong points before the assaulting battalions vacated them.

All troops clearly understood that no reliefs could be expected until their final objectives had been efficiently consolidated.

The men were carrying about 60lb of equipment!

9.25 We came out of Bund in the same formation as before. The Hun barrage was now heavy with shells bursting and crashing all round and worse, there were machine guns to the right of the hill enfilading us.

9.35 We were in Pommiers trench having lost five men including one killed. We could see them lying in the rear, two of them quite close. There were shells bursting everywhere with things becoming unpleasant in Pommiers, and we could get no connection with rest of the Coy. We decided to move on at the double to the next objective.

9.45 So we went out again at the double and through the barrage as fast as possible. There were machine gun bullets flying all round and another 4 men hit were including Lt Boon just at my side. I was hit on the hat with splinters but there was no damage. We all dashed onto the Redoubt. We got men down into the trench, and went round to find our position, which we were due to consolidate. We found a large mass of all sorts of Battalions in the Redoubt and without officers.

I found Schreiner and told him the situation as I did to Colonel Price of the Bedfords when I met him

I got back to my platoon and instructed Sgt Martin to try to go on ahead with Corporals' Tite and Clapham. We heard a bell ringing in the dugout so we cut two wires. We summoned the two dugouts but got no answer, so we carefully went down into one, which had a signalling receiver. We put all wires out of action and went into the other one In this one we heard someone say "Pardon Kamarad, mercy." We couldn't see anyone but we told them to come out. One appeared with his hands up and at the bottom of the stairs he hesitated. We beckoned him to come up and he came up in a terrible fright, saying, "Pardon Kamarad." Others followed and we, carried out a thorough search of each, and then sent all 5 scuttling back to Carnoy. We went down into the dugout looking for letters etc, and then I started consolidating my piece of the redoubt, digging fire steps etc.

The Huns tried to bomb from the right, but we stopped the Hun attack and established bombing parties to counter. I consulted Schreiner and got the men to work quickly. The Huns were putting over a lot of stuff onto these redoubts and were holding two lines in front of the slope above Caterpillar wood

On ascertaining that the 91st Brigade had been held up on our left, which was thus exposed, the officer commanding "B" Company asked for further help and two platoons of "C" Coy who had been bombing dugouts but had rejoined HQ's were sent forward and eventually occupied Maple Trench. "D" Coy in reserve had followed "C" Coy and detached one platoon to garrison strongpoint II placing the remaining platoon in Pommier Trench. This company and part of HQ's. came in for heavy shellfire and suffered severely. By about 10.15am all strong points in the first objective had been occupied and were being placed in a state of defence, and the task allotted to the battalion had been accomplished.

The two platoons of "C" Coy and the two of "D" Coy who went over with the Royal Fusiliers and Bedford's worked through the three front lines of the enemy trenches to a set plan and carried out their work thoroughly and well. Three sections of "D" Coy however suffered very heavily from machine gun fire and were practically wiped out.

Liaison was well maintained between the battalion and the companies on its right and left.

All company commanders carried out their orders correctly and handled their companies with gallantry and skill. Platoons were well led by officers and NCOs.

Signalling was perhaps the weakest point even though runners and bearers worked splendidly.

Battalion HQ's was first established at Piccadilly and afterwards moved to a point in Bund Trench about 100 yards west of the Triangle.

ABOUT half a mile Northwest of the village of Montauban, in the Department of the Somme, is a long, narrow wood, twisting like a caterpillar.

3pm.The Huns could be seen getting guns away from Caterpillar wood. It was frightfully hot and I was terribly thirsty. We advanced and took the whole trench. I found a glass of Perrier water, and a slab of chocolate from the officer's dugout. There were many dead Huns and some of our dead lay all about the redoubt. There was a constant stream of prisoners and wounded coming through. Parties were sent to Caterpillar Wood but they found no Huns.

Fricourt on left was partly surrounded, Montauban fell to the 30th Division, and Mametz to the 7th Beds. Rumours of the capture of Contalmaison were incorrect but we were near it. The French were quite successful on the right. I got a little sleep towards midnight but then there was an hour in purgatory with a 5.9 Hun Gun just failing to drop into our trench or bury one with showers of hot lumps of stones and dirt. A horrid time.

Casualties amongst the Northants 6th were surprisingly light for this day, with three officers wounded, other ranks killed 29, wounded 123, missing four and one case of shell shock

There were orders concerning prisoners who had to be marched back across the open and not down communication trenches, and the Battalion who took the prisoners had to supply escorts. The prisoners were to be taken in batches of 100 with a 10% escort.

Slightly wounded men can be used for escort. Prisoners were to be disarmed and searched for concealed weapons and documents immediately after capture before being marched off and officers were to be separated from the rank and file immediately.

2nd July 1916

July 2nd
Shelling started again next morning and gave us a bad time. I got my platoon out of the Redoubt, but Keys got a shell in his trench that killed eight men, a horrid mess We spent the day consolidating the front and were pretty much constantly shelled. The 12th Middlesex Regiment came up to relieve the Bedfordshire's in the front line. It was a bit like a ship life with everyone doing a turn of duty and then trying to get some sleep in the dugout

Fricourt was taken.

German Bunker at Beaumont-Hamel

Bau des „Leiling-Stollens" in der Spitze der Leiling-Schlucht (südl. Beaumont)

3rd July 1916

"A" Company relieved 7th Bedfordshire Regiment in Emden Trench.

"B" Company relieved 7th Bedfordshire Regiment. in Bund Trench and No. II Strongpoint.

"C" and "D" companies remained in their old positions.

July 3rd
I saw the Colonel in the morning. We did some digging and wiring and further improvements to the men's shelter. The Huns put over a few shells. In afternoon an order came to move down to Emden trench and give our redoubt to the Middlesex. Coy. We got down to Emden at about 7pm and found everyone moaning about the bivouac in the broken down trench all night. Bronfay wood was captured by 31st Dvn with 3 mg's and three guns. Middx found three guns in Caterpillar woods and took them. Yesterday the7th captured Shelter Woods and four guns.

The French had taken whole German front line before them.

4th July 1916

The work of consolidation was continued.

Denzil wrote the following remarkable letter to his parents

July 4th 1916

From a German dug out

In other words we have "pushed" once, have captured seven rows of the Hun's first system of trenches, a big redoubt on a hill and — "ce n'est pas fin". This child came through without a scratch, only a slight hit in the tin helmet and any numbers of squeaks and shaves. I lost only two or three killed in my platoon and a few men wounded.

*There were, of course, many nasty sights to be seen, but the excitement at the time was so intense that, asked at that time, **I wouldn't have been elsewhere for a fortune.** But it wasn't quite as nice by any means when after storming the redoubt we had to dig, turn to, and look around[30]. I myself with one of my corporals captured the German's CO's HQ dug out with all it's telephone instruments, and* *cut the wires. In the next dugout we had the luck to come across 6 unwounded Huns, one officer included, who under the impulse of my section at the top, came out trembling, hands up, exclaiming "Pardon Kamerad, Pardon Kamerad." Well, I looked as fierce as I could [You know how terrible I look when roused!] and accepted their surrender, after giving them a moment of suspense. Then up they all came, and I made each one "Hände Hoch" as he came up, and having searched their pockets and papers etc drove them down over the open big trench towards our lines.*

They were in a funk — great big Bavarians too!

There was plenty of loot in the dugout, but I was foolish enough to forget about it and missed a number of topping souvenirs – helmets, photos, cameras, watches etc. In fact all I got was a bottle of Perrier water than which I never tasted anything so good, after three hours fighting in the boiling sun.

By evening we had reached our objective, captured numbers of prisoners and made some slaughter of the Huns who were truly routed. Consequently we are now somewhat jubilant over the first stage. But holding on and consolidating the line gained was not so pleasant under the Hun's guns but we did it and were secure by morning, except, of course, for casualties by shellfire. I shall not, of course, give casualty figures, but the Hun's were about twice as many as ours, not counting, I should think, a thousand or more prisoners to the Division.

Next day we spent getting shipshape and making our line safer, burying the dead and so on. I sent a Hun field postcard I found and I hope it got through [It did]. The corps, Division and Army commanders have congratulated our division on it's performance in our portion of the job, and our General was very pleased indeed when he was in our dugout yesterday.

I haven't seen any papers and I don't know what is going except for the Division next to us, but you can take it from me that the — 18th Division has done well."

We are at present bivouacking in a ruined Hun trench, and today I got off a four day's beard, cleaned my teeth and washed for the first time for four days, and am consequently feeing bucked with life. Lost my Burberry in the Redoubt, but revovered it two days later reposing in the hands of a private from another battalion as loot! Gave him five francs for finding it and all were satisfied.

The sentence I have highlighted on page 227 really took me by surprise when I first read it. How could anyone really want to be there on the first day of the

Somme? We do have the advantage of hindsight and know that the successes of this action was not often replicated elsewhere, but this is to deny other factors such as esprit de corps in the platoon, getting a job done, an adrenalin rush, a belief that the cause was right and a sense of leadership that Denzil obviously had in his too short life. It was his platoon, he was going to share the dangers with them. He also had strong religious beliefs and this probably tempered his fear of death.

The other sentence that surprised me was the one concerning the slaughter of Huns. Denzil was a very well read and cultured young man of fairly liberal beliefs, but, as with many in the war, he found that the slaughter of the enemy was necessary to end the war soonest, and this would not have precluded him from having German friends after the war was over. He may also have absorbed the frequently produced Government reports in the media concerning German barbarism. Certainly orders about taking prisoners in certain circumstances were left suitably vague by the General Staff.

July 4th

We were in Carnoy early to fetch packs of groundsheets. I got a splendid shower and wash after 4 days. In the afternoon there was a catastrophic thunderstorm and rain that washed out the bivouacs and everything was miserable. We were just getting shelters of wood cut for the first time when orders came through to get back to Pommiers with packs!!! We drizzled back again to the trenches to find them awful, under mud and water. We relieved the Middlesex and settled down again. It was my night on and I did not like the mud and watch, but it was compensated by a good sleep later.

July 5th.

It was a decent day. The Hun was putting over shells two at a time all day on the OP's of 7th Division front line.

I did my rounds at 11.30pm. A direct hit on their shelter buried two of my platoon. but help arrived just in time and they were unhurt except for shock and suffocation.

July 6th.

Nothing much was doing till late afternoon apart from making improvements in the trench. In the late afternoon orders came to move, and we moved away from Bronfay Farm at about 7pm. We occupied shelters for night and were quite comfortable.

These are the results so far. The English have captured Montauban, Mametz, Fricourt and La Boiselle, and. also part of Thiepval and Contalmaison, plus 6,000 prisoners and 12 guns. The French have captured many villages and made a break in the Hun second line of six miles, capturing 9,000 prisoners and 60 guns.

Letter to Mother July 11th

Just a wee line today, as I haven't written for two days. Life goes on as usual at present but we move up again quite shortly, perhaps tomorrow to have another slap at the Boche. Yesterday I went into a small town a few miles from here by lorry, and had a good bath which was a great comfort, brought a few necessary things, getting back to our camp in time for late dinner and then bed, which is, of course, a positive luxury out here. Today we had a ripping and very amusing concert from men of another brigade out here. A hollow of a fair size slipping down to the stage was packed absolutely full like an amphitheatre. It was a topping show and very refreshing

Continued on 12th

I believe we move up again to the front line, perhaps tonight, so I'll just add a line to yesterday's screed.

Saw a further batch of Boche prisoners brought by from where I was exercising my men. 16 in all marched along by two cavalrymen, and I've never seen such a miserable, unkempt, dirty, ragged, small and frightened crowd in my life. I could have smiled but it was such a sordid sight after all. We are hammering the Boche rather hard out here and by all accounts he is not liking it at all, and is in a poor way. Never mind, we will go on hammering him until he breaks and this might be sooner than a great number of people expect. Anyhow, I've never been so confident that the Hun is a complete back number, as I am now.

He is reported as being seen killing our wounded over on our left a day or so ago, after a counter attack. Well, it is a dangerous as well as dirty game that two can play at, and the strongest side—us—can take it out of the other at the end.

Denzil seems, as with most people to have underestimated the ability of the "Hun" to fight on and the end of the war would still be in another bloody two years and four months. Germany was still capable of giving the Allies more than just a bloody nose. The war was to continue for another two years and more, and the Germans came close to breaking the Allies in March and April 1918.

22

Trones Wood

The region of the Somme is not unlike Salisbury Plain, with much gently undulating countryside, but it is punctuated by woods, some of which became notorious in the fighting that took place in the summer of 1916. Names such as Delville Wood and High Wood became synonymous with savage slaughter and huge acts of bravery. Trones Wood is not as well known but it sat like a big teardrop threatening the British lines and it needed to be cleared. Denzil's troops were fortunate to have relatively few casualties on July 1st but they did not escape so easily this time, particularly the officers.

July 13th

Letter to Mother

Here we are once more under shell fire [with a vengeance too], having come up here this morning to a certain village a little way back and in the midst of our guns, and consequently of Hun shells.

I am now looking forward to a good rest, which would be nice. The extraordinary thing is that we get valises and post even up here with lorries and traffic like nothing on earth. Yet the Hun puts over tons of shells and heavy ones too.

Could you please send me some brandy for my flask in the next parcel?

I long to see you and it is two months since I last did

The guns have ceased and the attack has finished. As we've not been called up I hope we have taken the wood all right [Trones]. If so we will not be needed unless the Huns counter attack.

I hear we make another big push tomorrow for the second Hun system of trenches and villages. What part we, the reserve, play, I know not. Although the guns out there are creating a terrible shindig, we are warned to be ready to move in to support an attack on the woods about a mile away.

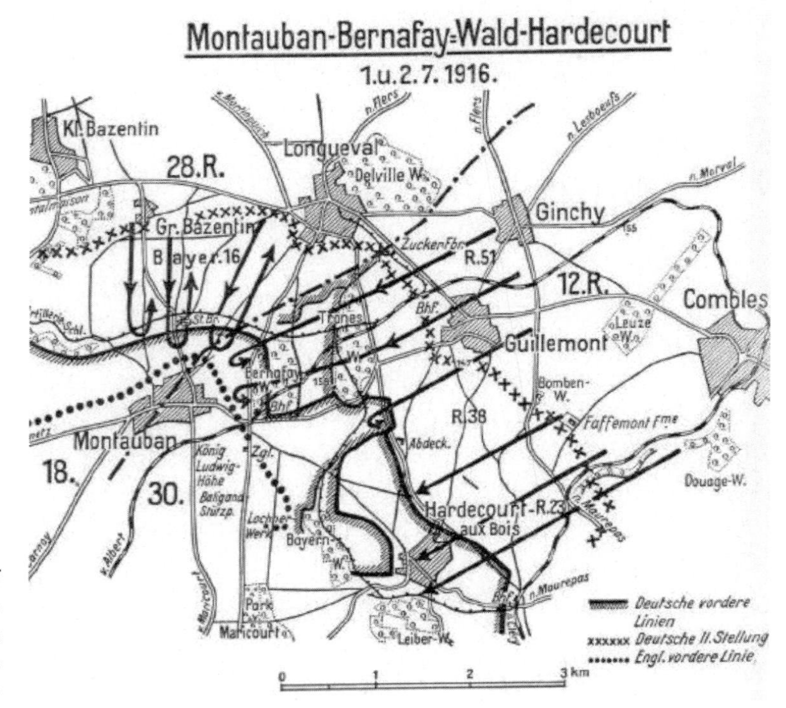

A German map of the area the 6th Northants fought in during the middle of July 1916

Edited entry of the 6th Northants war diary for the action at Trones Wood

Reference to this will greatly aid the reader in following the shifting course of events that day.

14th July 1916

At 2.45am the remaining two companies (A & B) and HQ's were ordered to march to the Sunken Road east of Briqueterie, where they would form up with C & D companies who had been moved forward from Dublin Trench. At the same time, Major Charrington received orders to report himself to 54th Brigade HQs where he received the following verbal instructions from G.O.C. Viz That he was placed in command of the battalion for an attack on Trones Wood – Lt. Col. Maxwell V.C. D.S.O. C.S.I.[31] being in command of the whole operation. Our artillery barrage would lift from the wood at 4.30am. The 7th R. W. Kent were holding a line from East to West across the southern portion of the wood.

The role of the 6th Northants would be that of supporting battalion to the 12th Middlesex, who would be in the front line. The duties of the battalion were to clear up behind the front line and form a defensive flank on the eastern edge of the wood. Major Charrington was himself to report to Lt. Col. Maxwell who would

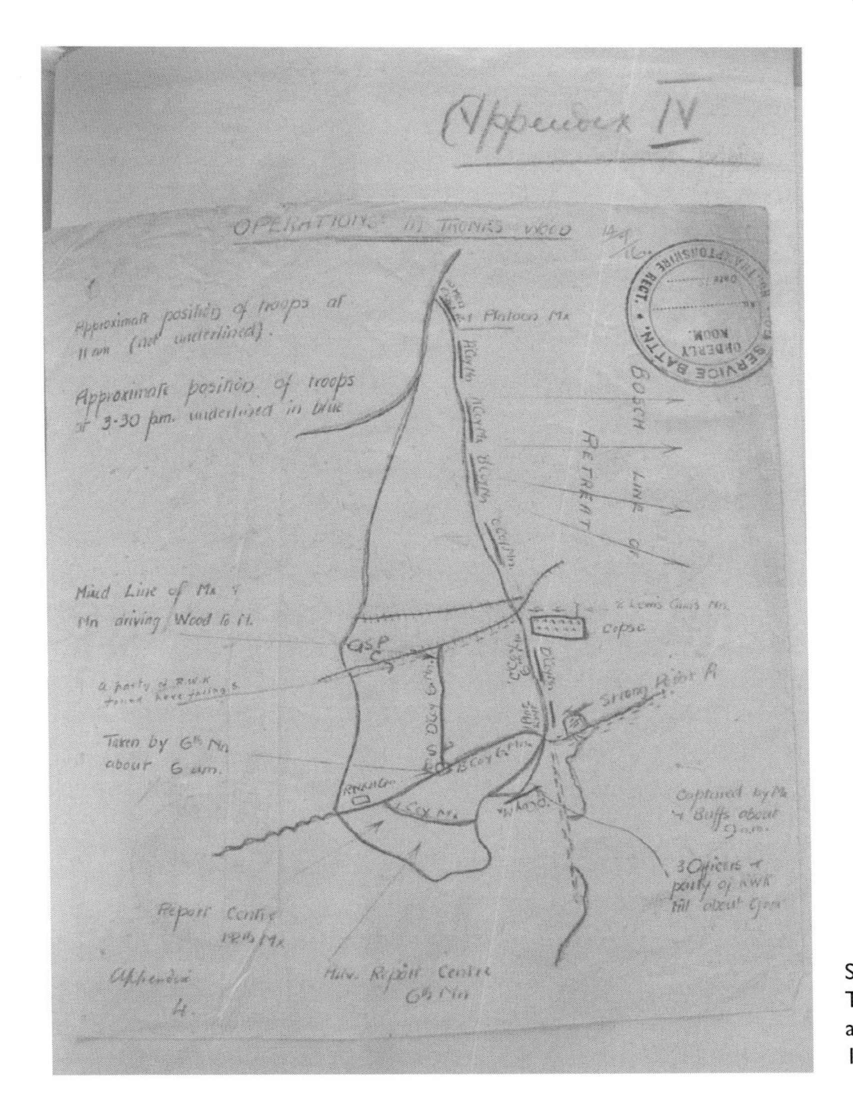

Sketch map of the Trones Wood action July 14th 1916

be found somewhere in the southern edge of the wood. Col. Ripley was retained at 54th Brigade HQ's as liaison officer.

Denzil's letter to his mother intimated that the 6th Northants would be used in a secondary role sweeping up after the Middlesex, but circumstances changed and at about 4.10am Lt-Colonel Maxwell informed Charrington that he was unable to get all his battalion together and that he decided to detail the **6th Northants as the attacking line**. Orders had been given to Major Clark and the battalion were then moving eastwards along the Sunken Road to get into position for the advance on the southern edge of Trones Wood. It was 4.25am and there was no time to obtain any more detailed information as the two leading companies were already advancing across the open towards the southern edge of the wood.

Casualty clearing station near Trones Wood under fire

The advance took place over 1,000 yards of open ground, which was smothered by an intense barrage of large calibre H.E. shells from the hostile artillery. The companies advanced through this barrage with the greatest coolness & steadiness and suffered a good many casualties before reaching the wood. Major Charrington accompanied Lt. Col. Maxwell and Major Clark into the wood to get in touch with O.C. 7th R W Kent Regiment and ascertain the situation. The HQ's of the 7th R. W. K. was found in a shallow trench in the South West corner of the wood. It turned out later that no men of the R W K were found anywhere north of the light railway line that runs E & W through the centre of the wood. The CO of the RWK reported three officers with this party, who said they were short of ammunition and requested reinforcements to be left with them. 2nd Lt. Price reported that this party at first mistook us his men for the enemy and opened fire on them. It was with the greatest difficulty and not until a compass had been produced that they could be persuaded that they were not facing northwards. Many others on other occasions said how disorientating it was trying to fight a battle in woods.

4.45am

In addition to the enemy's artillery barrage, which was kept on the southern portion of the wood, there were sounds of heavy rifle and machine gun fire from a point a little further in the interior. In the meantime, Lt. Col. Maxwell went back to the southern edge of the wood to collect the 12th Middlesex, who had not yet arrived.

5.10am

Captain Podmore reported that his company ["D" Coy] were advancing North East and bombing up a trench running from the South West corner of the wood, and that he was in touch with portions of B and C Coys on his right but not with A Coy. He also reported that he was held up by Strong Point B and that he urgently required more bombs and that Major Clark had been killed, Captain Shepherd wounded, and only about 100 of his company left.

Major Charrington only had one runner with him at the time, so collecting as many bombs as they could carry, he went forward to ascertain the situation. Instructions were left for more bombs to be sent as soon as possible and the men of the Middlesex Regiment soon afterwards brought these up.

Men of B and D Coys were found creeping up to the Strong Point through the undergrowth, whilst those attempting to get round by the trench were held up owing to lack of bombs. Heavy rifle and machine gun fire was coming from the strong point. Captain Shepherd although wounded in the shoulder, was standing in the open cheering on his men in the most gallant manner. On a fresh supply of bombs arriving, the attack was pushed home, and the Strong Point captured about 6am. Many dead Germans were found at this spot.

6.00am
From this time forward, owing to the impenetrable nature of the wood and heavy losses amongst the officers and leaders, units became mixed up and it was difficult to obtain a coherent idea of the situation.

9.15am
Following message was received from Capt. Podmore (timed 9.00am) "Have secured all Trones Wood, except small T head containing about six men by Strong Point on Guillemont Road. Also about 40 Germans in trench outside wood just south of same Strong Point – Buffs are attacking with a Stokes gun. We must have a Stokes gun if we are to take these two places. Am consolidating Eastern edge of Trones Wood."

The above has since been confirmed in a letter from Capt. Podmore (wounded) in which he says: – "I sent Lt. Redhead to work North through the wood. He did so with great success, clearing the wood up the West side up to the north point and then moving down again the East side till he joined us by the strong point on the Guillemont Road."

9.02am
2nd Lt. Price reported that D Coy was now occupying main trench running North to South through middle of wood. The enemy were clear of the wood on East and

South but snipers still in evidence to the North.

9.25am
2nd Lt. Redhead reported that his company were holding a position on E. edge of wood North of Strong Point A. Enemy running away to the East being fired on by 12th Middlesex with machine guns.

This was presumably from Strong Point A, which had been captured by 12th Middlesex and 7th Buffs about 9.00am. From this time until about 11.30am practically no information was received from the front, but Lt. Col. Maxwell was on the spot reorganising units.

11.30am
Message received from 2nd Lt. Price, "Have taken over command of B Coy. Strength at present appears to be about 50. Am hanging onto out position lining the East side of the wood. Line very thin please try and get reinforcements up. Am unfortunately hit in the leg and cannot get along very fast."

About the same time 2nd Lt. Walker arrived and asked for reinforcements for C Company, which had suffered many casualties and was also on the eastern edge of the wood. An officer of the 11th Royal Fusiliers, who were in support, had just reported to Major Charrington with one company, so he was requested to send one platoon to reinforce our eastern flank, which was done. This platoon was later established in Strong Point A. The other three platoons RF were being heavily shelled in the wood & were ordered to fall back to a trench about 400 yards in the rear. The only shelter in the southern part of the wood, which was under a continuous artillery barrage, being a shallow trench already choked with wounded.

11.30am (dittoed)
Approximate position of the troops, as far as can be ascertained at this time is shown in sketch map. The trench shown running parallel to South East edge of wood was found by 2nd Lt. Walker to be occupied by three officers and a party of 7th R W Kent Regiment about 6.00am. They were in a somewhat exhausted condition and were relieved about 9am.

Before this time the backbone of the enemy's resistance had been broken by the capture of Strong Points A and B. **The brunt of the fighting had been borne by the 6th Northants, who had suffered severe casualties both in officers and men.** The wood was now clear of the enemy, at any rate, except for snipers. Lt. Col. Maxwell then organised a drive to clear the northern half of snipers and break up any resistance still left.

2.30pm
Lt. Col. Maxwell returned and gave Major Charrington orders to collect & reorganise the scattered units of the 6th Northants, and as they should be relieved by the 12th Middlesex on the Eastern edge of the wood, to take over Maltz Horn trench from the 7th Buffs, keeping one company in support in the South of Trones Wood.

3.30pm
Unit were discovered, distributed approximately as shown in sketch. 12th Middlesex commenced relieving 6th Northants from the north.

5.30pm
6th Northants were formed up in wood to the West of the COPSE. **After stragglers had been collected, the battalion only mustered as follows:**

Officers
A Coy 2nd Lt. Heriz-Smith
B Coy 2nd Lt Price (wounded in leg slightly)
C Coy 2nd Lt Walker
D Coy Capt. Podmore (slightly wounded, shrapnel in back)
Other ranks
A Coy 57
B Coy 69
C Coy 76
D Coy 45
Total 247

A total of three unwounded officers, including Major Charrington and 247 Other Ranks. This was all that remained out of 17 Regimental officers and 550 Other Ranks that had left the Sunken Road and entered Trones Wood a few hours previously – Lt. Newbery, the Medical Officer, had also been killed whilst performing his duties in the most gallant manner.

6pm
The battalion were then moved into Maltz horn trench, except "B" Company under 2/Lt. Price who were left in support in the trench previously occupied by the 7th R W Kents.

Five Officers were killed during the day including 2nd Lt Lys [OB] and one was missing, 2nd Lt Woulfe, who was later reported dead. Lt Wilcox was later reported killed and Captain Schreiner was severely wounded, though, happily he was to recover and did not die until 1969. Of the other ranks 30 were killed, 198 wounded, 35 were missing and six suffered from shell shock. During the night that followed there were more casualties, two more killed, nine wounded, two missing and five suffering from shell shock.

"A" Company suffered the sort of casualties that they avoided on July 1st, although there was a high proportion of wounded, not killed. We do not know how many of those subsequently died.

2nd Lt Heriz-Smith was one of only three officers to come out of that wood unscathed! Considering the disadvantageous circumstances under which the attack was carried out the operation resulting in the complete capture and occupation of Trones Wood, the capture of which had been attempted and at any rate partially failed on at least three previous occasions, reflects the greatest credit on all concerned. The battalion was thrown into the wood in so much haste, that it was impossible to explain any detail of the attack.[32]

After passing through an extremely severe artillery barrage across 1,000 yards of open country, the battalion was met, before it had proceeded more than about 150 yards into the wood by heavy machine gun and rifle fire.

Without the slightest hesitation the attack was immediately launched and pushed home with the greatest vigour. It was inevitable that in the ensuing fighting units should become mixed up and to a certain extent lose direction, especially in an attack, which had been launched, as this one had, without the opportunity for the least preparation.

There is no doubt that the resistance in the centre of the wood was broken entirely by the initiative taken by the company commanders and other subordinate leaders. It was during the early stages that most of the casualties occurred amongst the officers of the battalion.

Under the circumstances, it can scarcely be wondered at, that after the fight had been proceeding for about three hours, a considerable degree of disorganisation had resulted. A contributory cause was the impenetrableness of the wood, which had been rendered much worse by the heavy artillery bombardment to which it had been subjected from our own and enemy guns, which had laid trees flat in every direction, causing an impassable network of trunks and branches.

Denzil Heriz-Smith wrote to his mother about the engagement. This letter is one of very few primary sources about the action in Trones Wood and it's opening line from a music hall song of the day was a mixture of relief and an attempt to keep up his mother's spirits.

Letter re: Trones Wood

6th Northampton's
BEF

July 17th 1916

"My darling Mother

Herwear, here we are, here we are again! *And this time I write after* ***our second tiddly push****, out of which I arrive safe once more, by God's mercy. This time the luck changed, and instead of two officer casualties we had seventeen casualties out of the twenty who went in! I had simply extraordinary escapes in the woods and I am the only officer in the battalion who has been in both pushes and come out of both unscathed. We took Trones Wood, that wood you will have read about, in the papers. It has been taken or retaken several times but we were ordered up one night to take the whole of it after the assault by someone else failed. We went over the top within ten minutes of arriving, went through a tremendous Hun barrage of shells, gone into the wood, reformed and proceeded to push through. We soon met the Boche in strength. A Hun Machine gun up a tree killed poor old Woulfe and four others. Two seconds after, so I'm told, I strolled with my men onto the piece of ground and stood up in full view of the machine gun, which I didn't know was there. The place was full of bullets, clouds of smoke came from bombs the Hun was throwing and a bullet hit a twig about five yards in front of my eye, drove the twig straight into my eye, but didn't itself hit me. My life was saved by a man who saw the mg and brought the Hun with a crash to the floor from the branch. We pushed but the Hun kept counter-attacking, and one was never certain when one was supported or alone. We drove them back in furious close fighting for five hours until reinforcements came. We finally killed nearly all of them, capturing a few, drove them helter-skelter with serious losses across country. It was an extraordinary fight. Men would fall behind a tree thinking they were safe and suddenly got a bullet through the head from a flank where a sniper was concealed. I had a terribly exciting time altogether, and the next day or two when we held what we had gained was perhaps worse, as numbers of dead bodies, Huns and English, blood all over the place, and a dreadful confusion of blasted trees, scattered brushwood, huge shell holes, bullets, bits of bomb, wounded men, and a perfectly beastly and sickening stink, made life a perfect nightmare, especially as the Huns gave us a terrific day with 8-inch shells, while always unpleasant, was doubly so in a wood where trees just snapped off bodily and* *fell about the place. People all remarked how extraordinary lucky I was, but I know better;* ***it wasn't luck****.*

We lost 17 officers, killed and wounded, and about 300 men. Very few were killed, as in the last push, extraordinarily few in fact. In my company Captain Schreiner was badly wounded, Woulfe was killed and others seriously wounded. I was reported killed and the Sgt Major took command. However I'd only gone off to investigate my position on the flanks as ordered by the CO of the Middlesex [Lt Colonel Maxwell]. Their CO, a VC and DSO and friend of Kitcheners was perfectly splendid. He came up with his Battalion when we'd got most of the wood, and walked coolly about directing operations absolutely calm and cool, in full view of snipers, swinging his tin hat on his arm. A sniper had nearly had me several times and I was lying behind a tree trying to spy him and show him how to shoot, when up comes the CO stands in full view with the sniper firing all the time, beckons me and proceeds to give me instructions and talk for about ten minutes as cool as poss. I didn't like it as I felt I should have a bullet in the head any moment and I'm not that kind of hero. Later on he organised a sort of pheasant drive through the rest of the wood driving the Hun on to a line of men waiting further. Little quarter was given or asked and he himself gave none, shooting several at point blank range with his revolver. The wounded sniped us from shell holes and literally had to drive them from their holes. All wounded who couldn't walk back to their lines were shot off hand. It was a ferocious thing to do but absolutely necessary to preserve valuable lives, as the treacherous way those fellows sniped you was almost inconceivable. As I said, after that we had a nightmare couple of days as others got back behind the lines, where last night we moved back two or three miles to the wood we occupied before the push.

I believe we now go further back and we want the rest badly. Five officers – Hamilton, Lys, Farrell, Major Clark and Woulfe – were killed, 13 wounded. Poor Schreiner, our Captain, got part of his elbow blown away by a bullet and may lose his arm. He was very cheerful with it however and plucky. Fawkes was wounded also. The Bois De Trones was indeed a most bloodily contested place and five hours furious fighting was our part in it. What you see with papers about it was exaggerated. The papers never gave credit in the right place – ***it was us who took it with the Middlesex brigade. It was vital to take this place at all costs****.*

The Hun I will say fought desperately well and their casualties were heavier than ours, as very many of theirs were killed and many of ours wounded. We captured an mg not 20 yards from my final position in a shell hole and several other mg's too, and quite a lot also and an 8-inch Howitzer.

Well, darling, I think I've told you all I can without giving away things of military importance. One amusing thing, the men's trophies, watches, iron crosses, helmets, books, papers, all sorts of things, revolvers, compasses, cameras, prismatic glasses and I never secured one! I am a fool.

Well, sweetie little Tittie, if I think of more to say I will write it in my next letter to Dad. Tons of love to dearest Dad and the kids. I'll write soon

Your loving son
Denzil"

This letter reveals that apparently "dead" Germans would come to life and shoot from the rear. This happened at Boom Ravine in February 1917 and it is possible this is how Heriz-Smith lost his life there.

The letter also reveals some belief in the 6th Northants that they were not given enough credit for their role at Trones Woods.

Experience did tend to prolong survival though chance played a big part too, but he obviously thought that his faith had preserved him so far.

The shooting or bayoneting of wounded German troops was more common than we might suppose, and is to some extent understandable given the ferocity of the battle and some doubt if prone Germans were actually dead or not. There was a real worry about being shot in the back.

July 21st Letter to Mother

Back from the line.

"The country is beautiful here, hills, valleys, woods and endless crops all green and many coloured, and particularly fields of a sort of poppy, made one curse again a war that is as murderous as it is wicked. I confess I fail utterly to see the glamour and excitement that press correspondents see in it, and I don't think many others engaged in it see it either. The only thing that is splendid in war is the fact that men can face its horrors, as they do, ***but to call it glorious and splendid is a lie.*** *One can see the folly of wickedness of it always and especially contrast with nature at a time like this.* ***A very sharp, painful but necessary operation is the only thing it resembles, I think."***

I don't think Denzil would have subscribed to the notion of the "Glorious Dead" that became common after the war.

In the English church in Ypres there is a plaque commemorating Churchill as the "Happy Warrior". This has always seemed inappropriate, and certainly does not describe Heriz-Smith.

The sentence above saying that the only thing that is splendid in war is the fact that men can face it's horrors, seems entirely appropriate to a study of war, the ability of ordinary soldiers and men to be involved in conditions that would be unthinkable before the war, and for human spirit to survive.

After Trones Wood, the Northants moved back out of line for a while.

A "Quiet" period

This rest period allowed Denzil to get on with the letter writing that had been curbed by the incessant war at the start of July.

July 23rd Haazebruck

H-S and company went via Calais and Boulogne to a village near Haazebruck in the Nord and he was billeted at a very nice farm, before being transferred back to the line. On the journey there he saw the cliffs of Dover and became very homesick.

He writes that he would like to stay at the farm for two or three weeks, but it won't happen. He writes as follows — *"The nasty thing is that the battalion is quite altered now with 400 new faces out of 700; most of the NCO's and nearly all the old officers are gone, the new adjutant is an idiot and that is horrid."*

Felt very poorly for several days and was in bed for three. Feverish. Doctor said it was diarrhoea but H-S thinks it was mild dysentery. Not as bad as earlier in the year. Did this hold up promotion at a time when new officers were coming out?

July 29th

Letter to Father – including the usual good-hearted insults they seemed to have!

On arrival at the place we were at, I secured by dint of going ahead early as in charge of a small fleet of cars and motor bikes [to the great interest and enthusiasm of the females in one or two towns, one of whom I distinctly heard say that I was "un beau officer" [just a bit of a slap in the mouth for you after your last comment, which I confess, struck me as merely illustrating your singular lack of taste in matters of aesthetic interest, and that after all my careful training for so many years too], and I was saying I secured a very nice little billet for two of us in a farm with all the modern conveniences in the shape of eggs, milk, beer and ad lib [for a payment of course], and the people were very kind particularly as we arrived without notice at about 1am.

Among the new faces in the division I saw in a certain battalion of the Bedford Regiment, who have lost as many if not more officers than us, a well-known face, WG Lacey an OB, and quite a pal of mine, just come out. In fact the only officer I know out of the original lot is the Colonel, a wonderful old sport, whom we and himself called "Uncle Dudley".

And Denzil shows his political nouse on home affairs. If only more had listened!

The Irish question is ridiculous. Home Rule, as suggested by Lloyd George [with his modifications], during the war and a complete settlement afterwards, is obviously the only thing, and I'll remind you Monsieur Dad, that I have been for three years a home ruler. Another of my little fads comes true.

July 31st

To Mother

Just a line to say I'm alright today, as the enormous mass of letters I had to censor this afternoon kept me from A Coy parade between three and five this afternoon. I feel myself in good fettle and recovered from my poor time last week.

We are getting on apace now though the battalion will never be the same sentimentally or from the point of view of old comradeship, what it was. It will though, I do not doubt, give a good account of itself as usual when it is called upon. I will be a bit nervy I should think, going into the trenches for the first time with many men who have not had that experience before, but I've got no doubt that the old Lads will settle them down.

He complains about the stuffy French smell in billets but says that he prefers it to the abominable smell of a dugout inhabited recently by the Boche!

August 4th

I met an OB acting Staff Captain by the name of Meares, a regular. I knew him years ago and he has been trying to find me. I've seen him often enough but he saw my name and recognised it, as he had seen me have my teeth knocked out [fame] and had been looking for me for some time as he had seen it in the Battalion list of officers.

We soon got talking about the school; he was captain of cricket in 1907 and Head of Cuthbert's when I first entered that house.

H-S delighted to learn that Cuthbert's had won the Senior Championship again for the third time in four years, the first when he was head of house in 1913

August 8th

The CO said he would make me sniping and intelligence officer, as the post, a very decent one, was vacant; but as usual nothing came of it, and he's given it to someone who has only been in the battalion about a month. I'm getting a bit fed up with that sort of thing now, but there is no use fussing about it.

August 17th

It is a bit more trying in the trenches than I thought it would be, as the large number of new men necessitates the officers being very much on the go. I myself am doing rounds all night, as I think it is safer to do so, and to try and snatch a few hours sleep here and there later.

Rumour says that Capt Podmore is coming out again shortly, which is great, as the present officers are nothing like the old lot. I am the senior subaltern of the Battalion by months and months now, but it doesn't seem as if a second pip is much nearer yet! However all in good time I hope!

August 27th

"We had a pretty quiet time in the trenches for just over a week being only troubled by a few of those confounded Minnies, which make such an awful noise, you know, I've described to you, the Sausages.

Apart from that the novelty of being in those new style of trenches, or rather, breastworks.

There have only been one or two incidents I can tell you about. One was a patrol I did one night in No Man's Land, which both amused me and annoyed me at the same time. Amusing because apart from being, comparatively speaking, as safe as houses [I had more fears that one of my new draft would strafe me that the Huns]. I thought I would be out for about half an hour, but when I came in found it close to two hours. There were countless empty tins outside our lines, which made a hideous din, as one couldn't see where one was going, and couldn't help treading on them in the long grass. It reminded me of Bairnsfather's pictures. Another incident was a little strafe our artillery indulged in, which I stood on the fire step watching and enjoying. It was a fine sight but not quite so once they started dropping short for some reason, and one burst just behind us. Shrapnel it was and a perfect hail of bullets drove between my legs as I stood on the step. I speedily jumped down and went to the telephone and stopped the short bursts, but for a time it was unpleasant, though nothing to speak of.

Otherwise we have had a quieter and certainly more comfortable time in the trenches.

We are now back from the lines and in this wretched little village I can't name. But by great luck I've got a decent room and bed which is splendid.

Stokes has recovered from his illness, which caused him to leave the Battalion last March, and is now out here to take command of "A" Coy. He is a decent sort of fellow and one of the old lot, which is a great blessing, when the Battalion is so full with new officers. Our Coy officers are a very decent crowd on the whole, barring one awful washout, but not up to the old standard by a good deal. There are six of us, which is extraordinary.

I hear another of our Battalions has been in a push and several officers I knew in the 8th are killed or wounded.

When I was at the last place, a big town as I've already said, there was a ripping teashop for officers there. It was rather splendid and I had a bit of a beano that afternoon, having tea with two other fellows and then going to the cinema which the Army runs and seeing a good, if rather sensational, show, which certainly made for a pleasant change. A good hot bath completed a trio of notable excitements that day. A thing happened that hasn't happened before. No billet could be found in the village we were temporarily stopping in, so all the Battalion officers slept in a loft above some of the farmhouse. I've never known that in all my stay in France, but I discovered I knew about 25% of the officers of the Battalion well, 50% to speak to and 75% by name, and 25% don't know. In the old Battalion everyone was sort of a member of the family. It's a bit of a change and a sad one too.

I expect we will slap the Boche's face for a third time before I will get leave, and hope it will do him some good and add to his vexations."

23

Thiepval

The War Diary of the Northamptonshire 6th reveals a number of training disciplines in the period in early September up to the assault on Thiepval. The Battalion was based in the Monchy- Breton area in the Pas de Calais close to Arras.

Activities included bayonet fighting, bombing, physical training and rapid loading and firing on the range. and there was also emphasis on practice attack of woods and in digging tunnelled dugouts, as well as following creeping barrages.

There was also considerable work done on forming up after dark and attacking at dawn.

On the 10th September military medals were given to 14 NCOs and men of the battalion for acts of gallantry performed on July 1st and 14th 1916.

Significantly on the 12th based near Arqueves in the department of the Somme, the CO and 2nd in command viewed the lines around Thiepval from various observation posts [OPs].

To Mother Sept 17th

We are in a certain village now, whereabouts unmentionable of course, but still que voulez vous? It's a bad place for billeting, the worse I've seen in France. The men have wretched billets, and as a good billet is never more than a barn with a good amount of straw with no holes in it, you can imagine what a really bad one is like! My platoon's is a broke down house with a few bits of wall missing, a filthy cellar and a floor of dirt. Still, by now of course, it has been thoroughly cleaned and disinfected. It took some time to make it even barely habitable. Still it is better now, clean, if draughty and uncomfortable. In truth one roughs it nowadays, but the poor old Boche, on that sort of thing, must be having the absolute devil of a time. All his previous billets captured, all villages within easy reach of the line under constant and heavy fire of massed artillery, not to mention air raids of planes coming right down and firing at close quarters, and the distinct possibility that one night he may wake up to find one of our tanks knocking on his bedroom door. Oh!

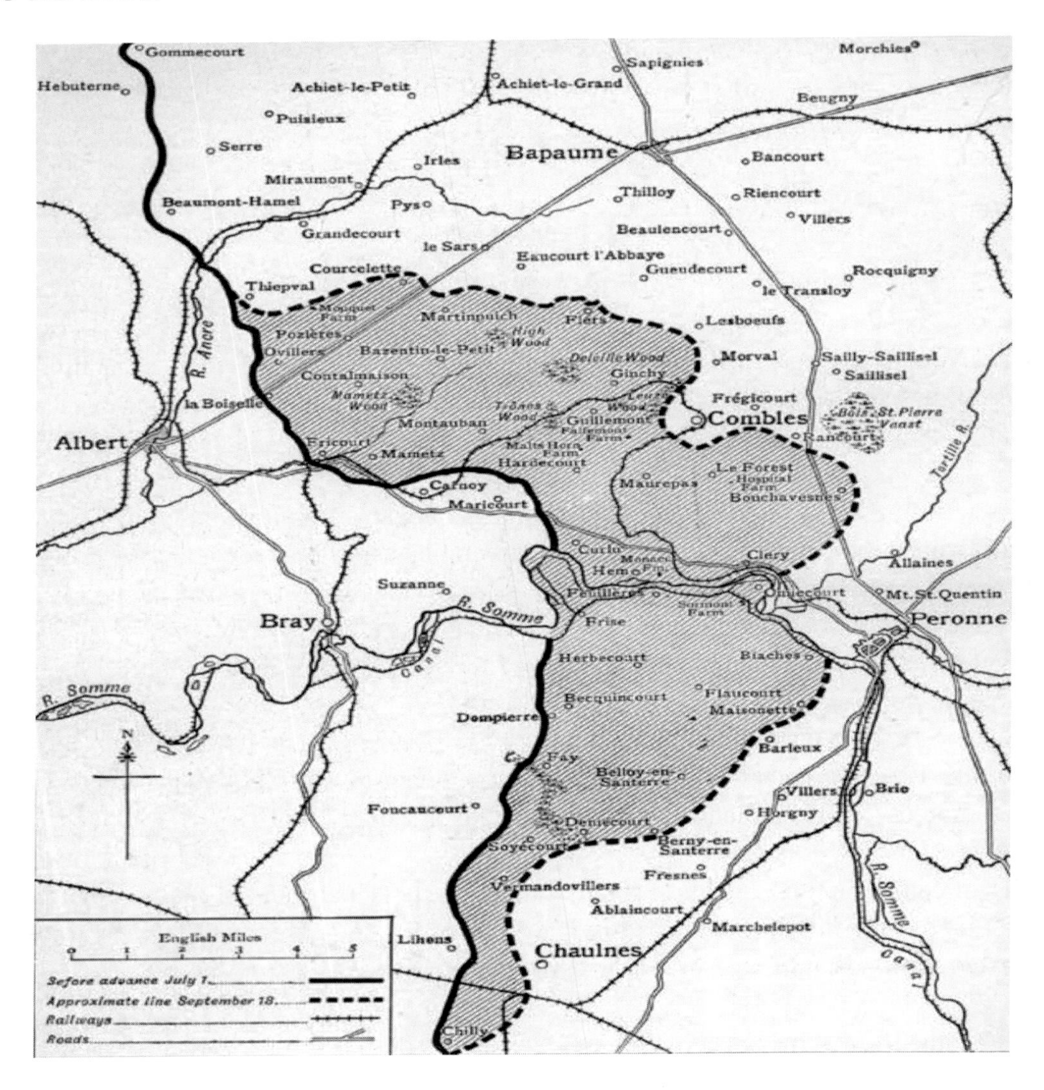

Allied Battlefields on the Somme showing gains made from July 1st to September 18th 1916

It's not a happy life for the Boche, whereas we, when out of the line, have a quiet if uncomfortable time. Our new push has rather put the wind up Brother Fritz, who loathes our guns, hates the infantry, and who runs like the blue blazes when he sees a tank coming. I haven't the slightest doubt myself that we've got him stone cold on this front, and the only things I have slight qualms about is Mackenson in the Balkans.

But, once more to the trenches. We work early and late and have had several games of cricket lately. We have had two matches of Officers v Sergeants in which I played as an extremely effective bowler – when the two real bats of the Sergeants have been dismissed. Then I come on with cunning leg breaks and get quite a bag of incautious hitters. In the two matches in question I have got seven wickets, and yesterday made five runs.

We had a church parade, and then afterwards the old Colonel pinned the Military Medal Ribbon on 16 men in the Battalion to whom it has been awarded for good service, the largest number in our Division. Whilst this was happening, a Boche aeroplane came over, which was being heavily shelled just above our heads by the Archie's, while bits of shell and whole shells occasionally came thudding down all over us and we were expecting a bomb or so to follow. It was a bit hot, but the ribbon ceremony went on all the same, and soon five of our fighters, scouts and battle planes, came tearing after the wretched Boche who skedaddled without waiting a second longer than he could with shells busting around him and our planes after him like hounds after a fox. The Boche, in truth, has no look in at all in the air with us and very little more with the French.

The Basilica, Albert, after the 1st bombardment 1916. It was said that the war would end when the leaning Madonna fell.

Letter to Dad about Northampton medals showing great pride in the performance of the Regiment over the recent months.

September 18th 1916

My dear old Dad

"Quelle vie" as they say! I got yours of the 10th the day before yesterday and very nice it was too. I haven't however, any news to give you I fear. We have had an appalling day of rain, steady and heavy all day, and there is a torrent flowing down the main street of the village from the horse pond at the top. It will be bad enough trying to sleep in wet tents, but far worse for those in the trenches. Apart from being annoying it has put a brake on our operations that were so successful a day or so ago.

As I told mother yesterday we had 16 military medals awarded to our battalion for gallantry on July 1st and July 14th and today I hear that our Coy Sgt Major [Coy Sgt Major Peet] who was with me nearly all the time has been given the DCM, and Schreiner and Shepherd get the Military Cross which both thoroughly deserved. Schreiner is, you know, "A" Coy, and Shepherd I/c "B" Coy. I took over the command of "A" from Schreiner when he was forced to retire to the dressing station with most of his elbow shot away. Not bad for one Battalion Eh? And it is fine as far as the men are concerned.

Other news is almost non-existent and with the heavy rain we have to fill the day and I did no less than four hours lectures to my platoon.

How is mother's lumbago? Etc

The training continued between the 17th and 22nd and brigade and battalion conferences were held, presumably to discuss the forthcoming attack on Thiepval. Inspections of the Battalion were held, as well as checking kit and clothing at Company level

There were a considerable number of route marches, demonstrations of the Stokes Mortar bomb, and practice attacks.

The Battalion was now based at Hedauville close to Albert.

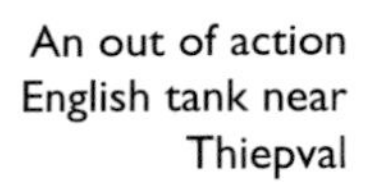

An out of action English tank near Thiepval

From the Battalion diary

25th September 1916, S. Bluff

The battalion paraded at 7.15am & marched to S. Bluff arriving about 10.30am. C.O. and 2nd in command attended Brigade Conference at Passerelle De Magenta at 11am and received instructions for the attack on Thiepval on the morrow.

Another fresh offensive began in September, particularly to the east of Poziòres and involving tanks for the first time.

Thiepval, on the crest of a hill, had a commanding view over the area around Albert and had been fought over for two years but the Germans had always prevailed. In peacetime there had been a chateau on top of the hill but now it was just ruins, ruins that the Germans had turned into a veritable citadel. They were determined not to lose it, and it was close to another big strongpoint, the Schwaben Redoubt. Thiepval in German hands allowed enfilading fire to be put down on the British lines. The Germans had had two years to perfect their defences here, and a captured map showed 144 deep dugouts in the area attacked. These were combined with intricate trench lines and tunnels, and there were numerous snipers and machine gun nests in the vast number of shell holes that were there either because of past or current artillery barrages.

The attack was to be led by the Middlesex Regiment and the Royal Fusiliers, with the Northamptonshire's in support and the 7th Bedfordshire's in reserve. One feature of the 24-hour struggle was the high casualty rate amongst officers, and the necessity, therefore, for leadership by lower ranks. Many of these, from private to Sergeant Majors, did brilliantly and there were a large number of medals awarded from the Victoria Cross down. It was a day that showed that the 54th Brigade, with it's cockney element, could fight and which showed the huge determination of individuals engaged in brutal and bitter small combats.

It is not part of this book to go into military details to any great extent – there are plenty of books that do that very well. It was not a day without cost. In the capture of Thiepval the 54th Brigade lost 19 officers and 176 men killed, and 28 officers and 563 men wounded. In addition 198 men were reported missing.

German losses were much higher. Four officers and 600 men surrendered and it is estimated that well over 3000 were killed or wounded.

It is, perhaps, best to leave it to Sir Ivor Maxse to conclude – "I am convinced that

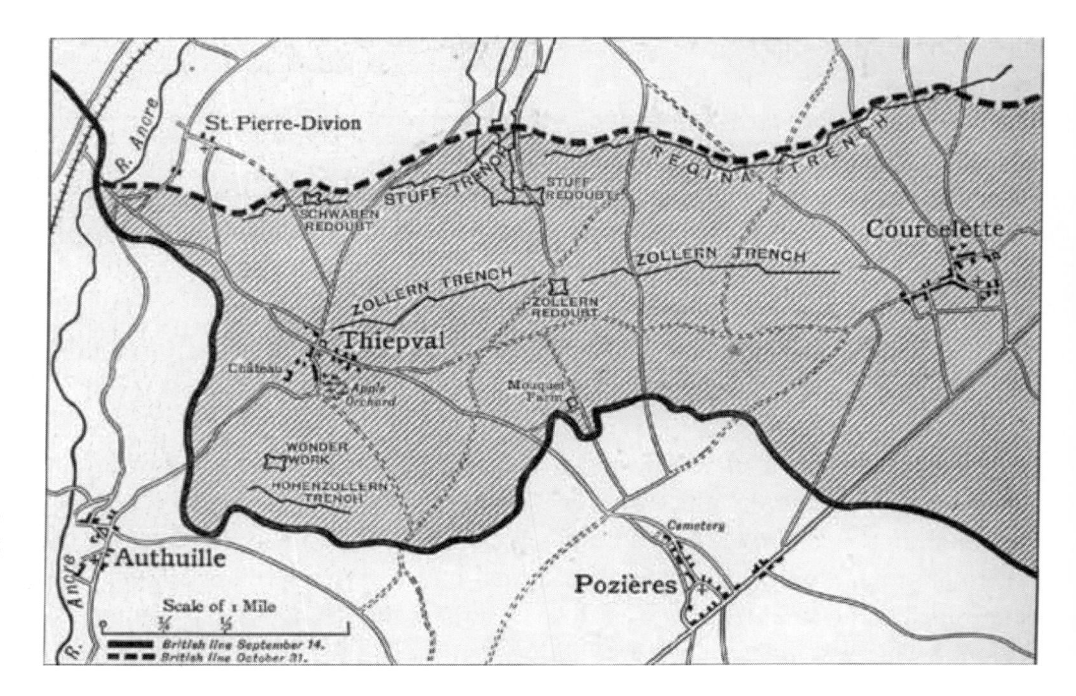

Battle of the Somme showing positions on Thiepval Ridge September 14th to October 31st 1916

Thiepval Park before the attack at the end of September!

if the complete story is ever written of what our men accomplished in the way of hand to hand encounters, from the outbreak of the battle to when Thiepval and the Schwaben Redoubt were captured, their achievements will bear comparison with any similar feat of arms in this war."

The position of the Regina Trench can be clearly seen at the top of the map, and this is where Denzil was killed in February 1917.

Sept 24th

By the time you read this our battalion will have taken Thiepval from the Hun and achieved our third success. As for this child the CO said that as I've been in two little shows I'm to stop behind our first line transport as reserve officer This should mean that I'm not in the battle push but will come up afterwards to replace any casualty or to come in for any counter attacks if made. Well, we shall see. My feelings on the subject are very mixed, though, I must say, very mixed. Still there we are! There will not be much harm in saying this, as I will either be in or out of battle by the time you get this.

Dud English 15-inch shell in trench at Thiepval

26th September 1916, THIEPVAL

"We have just had a few rumours good and bad. One says that we have got our objective all right and are well through it. The other says that the Adj. and Colonel are both wounded, the first badly and the second slightly. The major also, as the tale goes, is wounded.

Whether we shall go up the line tonight I do not know but we probably shall, so I won't be able to write to you again in full yet awhile, though I'll send field cards when I can.

It is an extraordinary sight as I write, in the evening, to watch our planes sailing round literally in swarms. You can count 20 or 30 at a time sailing endlessly over the Boche positions giving them a lot to think about. He fires furiously and uselessly at them now and again, without disturbing them a bit. The only time you ever see a Boche plane is in the quiet times when nothings doing and our planes are more or less quiet. Then they seize the opportunity to fly over our lines for a few minutes and then run like blazes. Ours, when any attack is on as now, are simply the lords and masters of the air. [This was not to last, as, quite soon, the German "Flying Circus" was about to appear].

There really is no news. It is now dark and the sight we can see from our tent door is one of terror and grandeur too. The shells and explosions of both sides are making the horizon a vast sea of fire, and the noise is incessant. It's a terrible thing, war.

"What's the use of worrying, it never was worthwhile
So pack up your troubles in your own kit bag
And smile, smile, smile."

In the words of the song!"

Sept 28th FP
Just a word to say that we've been through the push with small losses, comparatively speaking.

The CO has had his arm broken however, which is unfortunate [as it turned out he was worse than it was thought and he died in England later on in the year] and there are 13 other officer casualties, which is out of all proportion to the men's casualties. Once more I'm temporarily OC Coy. Went up last night and I'm quite well. I will write more later. Push pretty successful too, I'm glad to say. A beautiful day talking of the weather, but not so pleasant in the war.

Send Ousel along when comes out; No more now, but as ever "Beaucoup d'Amour"

Yours
Denzil

Lt. Col. Ripley

Lt. Col. Ripley had been wounded by a stray shell in March 1916 and had been evacuated to England to recover, but despite being on "home service only", he returned to the battalion in June 1916 to "lead his boys over the top", which he duly did on July 1st. He passed through the first day of the Somme unscathed, despite his chagrin at having to be helped across no man's land by his men.

Due to military orders regarding the use of the only CO or second in command in the same attack, he sat out the attack on Trones Wood on the 14th July, but he was back leading his men at Thiepval on September

26th when a German shell landed near him, killing Captain Barkham and shattering Lt. Col. Ripley's right arm. The arm had to be amputated and, after evacuation to England, he looked on the way to recovery until tetanus set in and he died of heart failure in hospital in London in mid October 1916.

Denzil would have enjoyed the poem on Thiepval written by Edmond Blunden.

In comparison to other First World War poets only a small amount of poems written by Blunden during the war have survived. One of them, Thiepval Wood, was written in September 1916 when Edmund was twenty years old. In the poem, the poet is witnessing a battle and describing the devastating affect warfare can have on nature.

Thiepval Wood
The tired air groans as the heavies swing over, the river-hollows boom;
The shell-fountains leap from the swamps, and with wildfire and fume
The shoulder of the chalk down convulses.
Then the jabbering echoes stampede in the slatting wood,
Ember-black the gibbet trees like bones or thorns protrude
From the poisonous smoke – past all impulses.
To them these silvery dews can never again be dear,
Nor the blue javelin-flame of the thunderous noons strike fear.
September 1916

THE SOMME: SOME RECOLLECTIONS ON THE CAPTURE OF THIEPVAL, SEPTEMBER 1916

The capture of Thiepval by 18th Division in September 1916 represents a significant point in the British Expeditionary Force's (BEF) tactical and operational 'learning curve' in the Great War. 18th Division offers a particularly rewarding case study because, in the manner of its raising, in its social composition, and in its battle honours, it was a typical British New Army division, while in its outstanding operational performance it can be seen as a symbol of the improvement of the BEF between 1915 and 1918. Its history shows what could be achieved, following an unpromising and chaotic start, by an "ordinary' Kitchener division which initially possessed neither the social and geographical cohesion of most Pals and Territorial units nor the political and sectarian binding of 36th (Ulster) Division. But what was the composition of 18th Division? There was a strong London presence in the ranks of the Division from the outset, but this had probably been watered down by late September

1916, after the Division had experienced nearly a year of trench warfare in France and had taken part in attacks at Carnoy-Montauban (1st July), Trones Wood (13th-14th July), and Delville Wood-Longueval (19th-21st July) during the early stages of the Somme offensive.

27th September 1916, S. Bluff
The battalion, having been relieved in Thiepval by the 7th Bedfords at 8am, returned to dugouts a S. Bluff at about 10am.

28th September
Have had a very successful push. Division been congratulated by Haig. Lots of prisoners and heavy casualties for the Germans. Our casualties have been light except for officers. Colonel has a mashed arm, Adj. wounded and my OC Coy as well. Total of 14 officer casualties. Am in very good form myself, and as before Temp. OC of the Coy. Came up just after the actual push into our front line. Am now just back a little way.

What Ho for the Water Shoot says Waggles! [I would be very grateful for the origin of this phrase, if anyone knows!]

Good Taag
Yours
D

The regimental diary continues

28th September 1916

There was a reorganisation of Companies. **A Coy was put under the temporary command of 2nd Lt. D. M. HERIZ-SMITH.**

29th September 1916. The battalion left S. Bluff at about 9pm and marched to Mailly Maillet arriving about 10.30pm where the whole battalion was most hospitably entertained by the 12th Middlesex before turning in.

There was an inspection of arms, equipment, ammunition etc

30th September 1916
The battalion was inspected and congratulated by the C.O. on the glorious part it had played in the capture of Thiepval, the strongest enemy position on the Western Front. Numerous congratulatory telegrams were received.

The Thiepval Memorial

Thiepval is the largest, and one of the most emotive memorials for the missing from the Somme Offensive 1916-17. Opened on 31st July 1932 by the Prince of Wales, the Thiepval memorial was and remains the largest British war memorial in the world. The memorial contains the names of 73,357 British and South African men who have no known grave and who fell on the Somme between July 1916 and 20 March 1918. 150ft high and dominating the surrounding area, the memorial was designed by Sir Edward Lutyens. It's brooding presence can be seen for miles around.

24

October to December 1916

Following Thiepval the Northamptonshire 6ths were taken out of the line and went to Mailly Maillet in early October. A Church parade was held in conjunction with the 11th Royal Fusiliers, and Brigadier Shoubridge congratulated the Brigade on the work at Thiepval.

All companies were sent to bathe at Hedauville, and 100 new men arrived to replace the causalities.

There followed much company training.

At about this time Denzil wrote to his mother.

My dear Mother

Just a brief line to say all is well. We are having a quiet time and rest behind the line – quiet but not idle as I'm temporarily in command of my company. I am enjoying the work of organising as I always do enjoy engaging work. It keeps one full with work all day with plenty to think about. My only terror is of having some returning officer very little senior to me, put over my head i/c my Coy, and, since the Colonel left I fear it is more likely, as although the Major is a good chap, I somehow can not quite hit it off with him, ever since a row we had over July 14th. Still, that remains to be seen. Meanwhile I'm thoroughly enjoying leading the company.

Did I tell you that poor old Batty was killed in the last scrap? That means that only one of the four of us who left Waterloo together on that memorable day in December 1915 remain; Batty and Lys are killed, Jackson in England recovering from a serious wound, only myself debout. In the Battalion now are left no combat officer whatever who was in the Battalion in 1914, excluding myself, while the Padre, the Transport Officer and the Quartermaster are the only officers who are left who were in the Battalion but they were not fighting men. I think I told you that the old Colonel had to have his arm amputated, right arm too! The only blessing is that he's too old for foxhunting now and will be a bit of a hero in the home country now. I think he should get the DSO for active service.

Two days have gone astray and I haven't had a letter from home. If the Ousel is out could you send it to me? I also want:

1 A nice new set of braces
2 A good pair of smooth putties
3 A small bottle of Cascaras [very small]. In the army laxatives were often thought to be the best "cure all", for a variety of complaints from coughs and headaches to more serious conditions. The pill was known as Pill No 9 and was carried in all WW1 Field Medical Panniers and was often called Cascara.
4 A few Russian cigarettes
5 A few envelopes white
6 Tooth clean material

A little list this time n'est ce pas?

This list above is a typical one for Denzil asking for practical things that would make life more comfortable.

On October 7th Major Podmore DSO rejoined the battalion [after being wounded at Trones Wood] and was appointed acting 2nd in command.

On October 8th there was a Church parade at 11am but the Corps Commander's proposed inspection in the afternoon was cancelled owing to inclement weather

October 8th 1916
I don't seem to be able to write these days for some reason, because I don't seem to be able to write letters easily now. It is a fact that I have scarcely written at all for about a week. Also there isn't as much news as usual and we are having a comparatively quiet time at the moment, but I don't know how long it will last It is very wet and has poured all night and all morning. There is also a complaint that Scotch is irregular these days.

Podmore turned up yesterday and he is now Major and second in command, as well as a DSO. He is a really fine chap.

During the next week Lt. Price rejoined the battalion [after being wounded at Trones Wood]. He was soon to be appointed acting Adjutant. There were frequent bouts of training, marching and inspection, and some inter company football.

In Mid October the Brigade moved to new billets at Bouzincourt, near Courcelette, and while there practiced attacks. They then moved on to Albert, and prepared to move into new trenches, the Regina and Vancouver trenches.

The regimental diary reports the following for the 26th October:

"Weather fairly fine, but continuous shelling of Regina & Vancouver Trenches especially on left of Regina, which was constantly being blown in. Enfilade of 5.9 guns from direction of Loupart Wood. About 1am two Germans came up to our parapet and gave themselves up."

"""A" Company's H.Q. in Regina trench was twice blown in in the early morning."

The conditions in Regina Trench were very poor, and even in a comparative lull in fighting, casualties were taken.

Letter from Rouen October 27th 1916
He has just returned from a brief visit home and is on his way back to the front.

My battalion is having a thick time of it. We shall be quite bucked to move if they want to rather than stop and be shelled as they are. Found Gotch just down from the line where he had gone already very seedy, now feeling a considerable seedier, in fact, knocked completely up. I think I'm going up tomorrow to take over, but I believe Chantrell has by bad management mislaid most of my battalion. But "Tempus fugit" will show.

29th October 1916, ALBERT
"Battalion was relieved in the morning by the 8th Suffolk Regiment. Day was wet and misty & so even with the bad state of the trenches relief was possible over the top by daylight. Last platoons reached ALBERT at 5pm. Enemy showed no activity in front, but the continuous enfilade shelling which contained few traverses & no dugouts made this a very trying tour in the trenches. Total casualties 52, including seven missing – the garrison of a standing post well out in front of our line; posted in the dark on the first day they must have lost their way in on the next night, and entered the German lines."

Six officers joined the battalion on arrival in billets, including Lt McWha OB.

On the 30th the C.O. presented the Military Medal ribbon to those NCOs & men still with the battalion to whom the decoration had been awarded for gallantry at Thiepval. There were 19 awards in all.

On the same day the battalion had baths, and on the 31st they moved into new quarters at Warloy.

November 4th 1916

Just a line to say I'm all right as usual. I found my battalion in the trenches on arrival but didn't go up as they were coming out again next morning. They had a terrible time with feet of mud and a very unpleasant barrage of heavies and the dugout was buried. Now we are back below but we don't know for how long. All goes well apart from a disappointment, namely the annoying expected arrival of three first hands with the inevitable result that my company is now under a new commander. What's more annoying and rather amusing is that he was in the Under 16 Colts team of the School whilst I was a senior man in the 1st XV. Such are the sweets of slow promotion. But patienza as the Italians say! I will have it yet!

How much longer we stay here I don't know but we are happy as sand boys here. Gotch broke down this time, and the Doc says he fears he will get consumption if he goes up again in this weather, so he's been sent back, probably to Blighty. Two other officers as well as a new Coy Commander have come out making us a party of four, and good company too, and we are very much at home in a French house en famille. Mother and the Mesdemoiselles chatting 10 to the dozen and only me able to understand them

November 12th

We have left that place that was so good to us, and to my regret as it was good to speak so much French there and at such great rate. I became a firm favourite with Madame and the young ladies who almost wept when we left, and I have been invited to Paris after the war [see letter Dec 4th 1916]. *It was good to hear French spoken and not the Somme jargon.*

We have gone back to the place with the leaning figure of the Madonna [Albert], spent a night there and then tramped up to the trenches. We passed through a countless array of guns of all sorts. We went on a big switchback up and down muddy shell holes for a further two miles and then arrived at the trenches. My company was at this time in support and about half a mile from the front line. The trenches were pretty muddy when we got there, no dugouts except for two little ones like cubbyholes to house a few men, and the mud was beastly. However we hadn't have been settled down for more than a few hours when it started to pour. In a few hours the trench from greasy became ankle deep in mud, a few more and it became knee deep, all the cubby holes collapsed leaving no shelter for anyone, and burying bits of kit, and conditions simply became too bad for description. Added to this incessant misery, the men had worked fearfully hard with working and digging parties. Altogether it was four days of abject misery. The officers were a little better off in that Coy HQ had a little dry dugout with room for two to snug down in cramped fashion on the floor, and the other two could sit down on the steps.

To go outside was to get straight away mud up to the knees, and it has to be done. We had a comparatively quiet time from the Hun in our little bit though there were plenty of munitions factories flying about all the time. We got two shells on top of our dugout but luckily they were only small ones, 4.2's. Had it been the 5.9 or larger varieties our shanty would have been blown in about our ears. All movement had to be done over the top, the trenches being impassable, and at night. One night I took a digging party to try to clean up a trench up to the front line, and we had barely got half way there, when instead of the ordinary shells passing over our heads and dropping round us making terrible blasts, we heard numerous shells apparently falling and failing to explode. We laughed a bit at this and joked about Fritz's used up guns, but presently the platoon officer [me] began sniffing a bit. In fact, as Scott says, "He spreads his nostrils to the wind and sniffs before and behind," and sure enough had the smell that had been made so familiar at odd times, in our little redoubt last Christmas, was blown up to us. They were strafing gas shells at our battery and presently I went down the line of digging men making them get out their gas helmets. The stink grew stronger and stronger. I felt a bit sick, and some of the men were coughing and coughing so I warned all the men to put helmets on. I wore mine for the first time since I've been out. The Hun shelled all over the shop with gas, and then shells for hours, but I never heard of any harm being done. At any events, I rather have a gas shell come in my direction than a 5.9 any day. I got back at midnight and I slept on the floor of the "sardinary" quite comfortably despite the Hun except that it was most abominably cold. Well a lot of the men were very done up when we left, and a good few had fearfully bad feet and they were in battle conditions and no shelter was available anywhere. However after a nights rest, personally, I felt as if I'd been to the seaside, only better, and we trotted back to our village some ten miles, only to find that our billets had been moved elsewhere. Fury raged in "A" Coy, but still we had a decent place and have just been there a day or so and have got about a quarter of the mud off their clothes, and beards from our cheeks, and look like men again and not pitiful mud balls when tonight we got marching orders back to the line!

Quelle vie!

This morning, being Sunday, I went to Holy Communion at 11.30 in the village schoolroom, as advertised. When I got there at the appointed hour I found that it had already happened. I was astonished and aggravated, and others ditto. However out here there are no formalities [I confess I like it better as such as it is simpler], and then the padre came up to us when he'd finished the service and asked us if we would like to communicate then, which we did, after the blessing, while the small congregation waited a little. So my service was the shortest I've ever been to – 10 minutes! I'm glad I went and I enjoyed it.

By the way, two more military crosses have been awarded to the Battalion, besides a DCM or two and several military medals. Our little padre has got the military cross, which I'm awfully pleased about. The other thing I'm not so pleased about, as I can't stick the man whose got it! However the Padre has always been splendid and has worked devotedly time after time amidst heavy barrages and all sorts of conditions, tending the wounded, burying the dead etc. We had a big parade, and when the General gave out the decorations to those who had won them, he made a little speech to the recipients, surrounded by the officers of the whole Brigade. He concluded by saying this. "As for you Gentlemen, I won't make a speech." I'll only say that no General could possibly be more grateful than I am for all you've done for the Division. Good morning gentlemen!"

Very theatrical and such a scene as this heart loves, of course, but after all there is this about it, that between himself and the Division, we've got some name in the Army now.

Beaumont-Hamel did fall finally to the British in mid November 1916, 4$^{1/2}$ months after the offensive started. But incessant pouring rain turned the ground into a morass in which men, animals and equipment was trapped. The battlefield became a "foul brown mush, which swallowed everything" [Pierre Loti].

Water overwhelmed the warfare and the armies took to their winter quarters and regrouped.

November 14th to Dad
I hear that Lord Luke is missing. He is an OB, of course. Ha! The Huns have just put a shell into this town. There goes one! There's only one gun that shells us and I believe he has got a naval gun. We call it Whistling Walter. No, my serenity is not disturbed yet because they are going at least 200 yards away so I shan't panic! I shall only say, " Poor tag, old man, poor tag!"

What else? My servant, Chantrell, is going on leave soon, lucky fellow. Not only does he get his leave but he misses this show, which is not so dusty is it? But one cannot begrudge the chap as he has been out here for 16 months without any leave at all.

November 20th to Mother
When I last wrote to you we were in huts not a great distance behind the front line, amidst a waste of shell holes and surrounded by 8 inch and 9.2 inch guns which did their best to make sleep impossible and we are further favoured by a fearfully cold snap, which was, nevertheless a pleasing change from the mud that has been

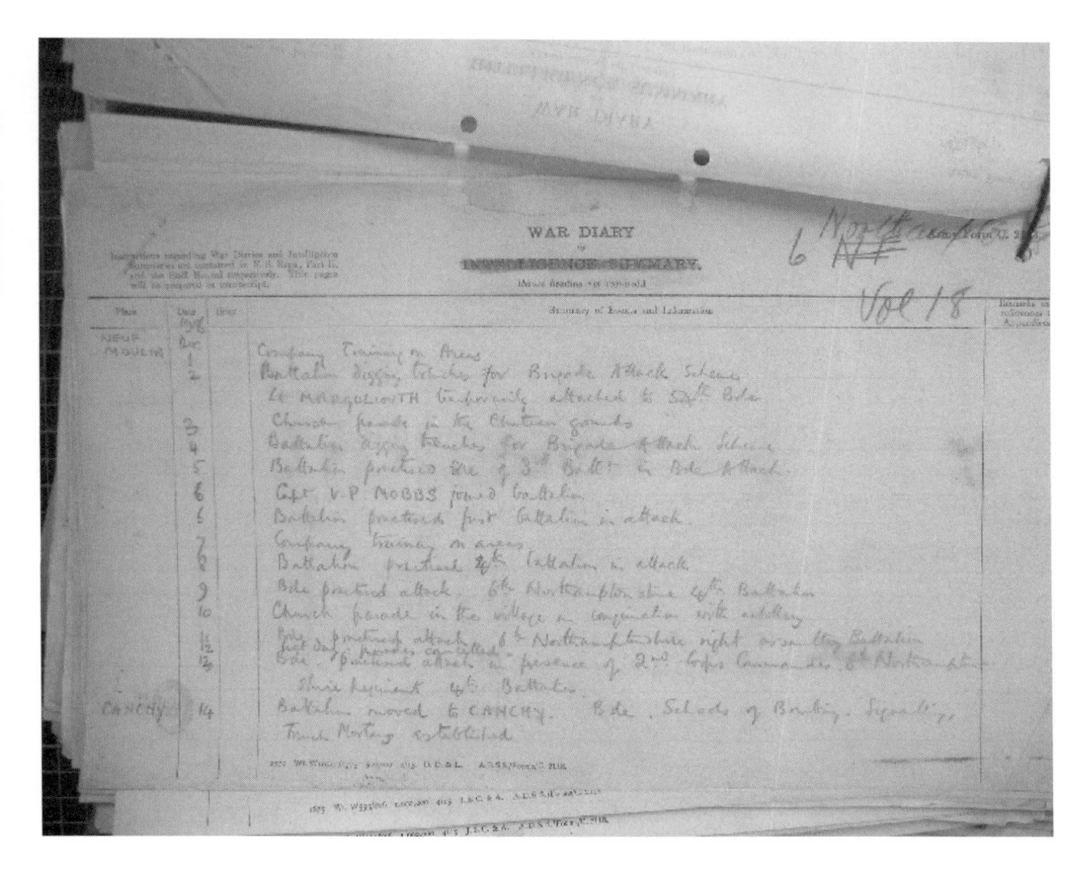

WAR DIARY

6 NF

Vol 18

Place	Date 1916	Summary of Events and Information
NEUF MOULIN	Dec.	Company Training on Areas
	1	
	2	Battalion digging trenches for Brigade Attack Scheme
		Lt MARGOLIOUTH temporarily attached to 53rd Bde
	3	Church parade in the Chateau grounds
	4	Battalion digging trenches for Brigade Attack Scheme
	5	Battalion practised role of 3rd Battn in Bde Attack.
	6	Capt V.P. MOBBS joined battalion
	6	Battalion practised first Battalion in attack.
	7	Company training on areas.
	8	Battalion practised 4th Battalion in attack
	9	Bde practised attack. 6th Northamptonshire 4th Battalion
	10	Church parade in the village in conjunction with artillery
	11	
	12	
	13	Bde practised attack in presence of 2nd Corps Commander. 6th Northamptonshire Regiment 4th Battalion.
CANCHY	14	Battalion moved to CANCHY. Bde. Schools of Bombing, Signalling, Trench Mortars established

War Diary
December 1916

here. Well, you can imagine us wandering round with sand bags tied around our legs, balaclava helmets under our tin hats, leather jerkins over our tunics, and coats over that, mittens on our hands and a pair of the new gloves which are leather outside and wool inside with no fingers, and hanging round your neck by a tape, so that you can put your hands in and take them out quickly and yet not lose the gloves on those.

After various rumours all jobs were cancelled at the last moment. We were suddenly attached to another Brigade of our Division and set up to be support for that Brigades attack. The night we went up the weather changed completely and we ploughed our way up into the teeth of an icy wind and blinding sleet and made our way to the trenches allocated to us, very slowly and with some difficulty, and waited. In the grey of the morning a barrage opened up at the allotted time. It was a fine sight! The whole of the horizon in a vast semi-circle around you suddenly stabbed into a blinding flash by the reports of a thousand guns all going off together, and thereafter for a long time the fierce sounding flashes and crashes from everywhere and the rushing of the shells overhead to the German line, whilst amid the inferno, one could hear a steady dull "cry-ump, cry-ump" of the German counter barrage on our line. No shells came very near to us though, I mean within 50 yards or so, as the Hun only shelled our front and support lines and the batteries. Meanwhile ahead of us the Brigade we were support to, and the other battalions of our division, went over to the Huns and within a few hours, amidst the steady German crumps, filed back lines of prisoners. Four German youths looking quite decent lads of 18 or so came in carrying one of out troops who had lost an arm, on a stretcher. I was quite pleased with this as they took a lot of trouble to jolt him as little as possible. We did not capture large numbers of prisoners, as it was not a large action, merely being the capture of a single trench in a front of a moderate size. We got along with other brigades about 600 prisoners and 15 officers. Our battalion was not wanted as the objective was found, but we were ordered to go up and dig a communication trench between the captured trench and the original front line, about 400 yards.

However it was a terrible slog through a pitch dark night in feet of mud and in nasty rain; falling into shell holes and getting smothered with mud. When we got a few yards from our destination the whole thing was suddenly cancelled, as there were still snipers to be cleared out. So we went back into the trench. We had a dugout 30ft deep, we'd completed with only room for just two at the bottom, and someone sitting in the steps, but it was better than nothing. We were just settled moderately comfortable for sleep and sitting positions when suddenly the weather changed from frost to driving sleet in the night and then during the day it changed once again to a pelting down pour of rain. We heard an ominous drip, drip, drip, so up we rushed to find the trench 2ft deep in water and slopping over into our dugout. No measures we frantically took were useful and presently a stream of water came trickle, trickle, trickle down the steps. In half an hour we had to abandon the dugout and a lot of our kit that had been irretrievably wetted, and betake ourselves to shiver wakefully all the rest of the night over a brazier.

November 25th to Dad
Repeating some of the things he had mentioned to his mum.

We got a total of 840 prisoners in the last raid. After a night of wet misery we were relieved to go back to our huts not far behind. We are doing this in easy stages. The first stage was about six miles, the second to a nice little town about 13, and the next about 10 to another place, then this morning in drenching and continuous rain that sopped us all, a further seven miles until we got to the place whose Church I inspected mentioned in an earlier letter — Amiens? We hope to have a good rest and training here before we resume Hun strafing.

The 18th Division has just completed it's seventh successful going over.

The British advance after 4 and a half months of battle was about 12 kilometres. Of approximately three million men in line, some 1.2 million were killed, wounded or missing. The Allied objectives of December 1915 were not attained.

November 30th. At rest. To his father
Not much news to relate. We're having all sorts of competitions initiated. Brigade soccer, Divisional boxing, Pierrot troupes, Gymkhanas, Cross-country races, and goodness only knows what not! Unfortunately they have just cancelled the rugger, which is aggravating as several battalions had challenged us and we can produce "some" rugger team.

Dec 2nd to Dad

Not much news but discussion about cigarettes.

I have smoked so many "stinkers" when in the line that my under finger and second are not the colour they should be, being to wit, stained yellow. This aggravates me and has led to my temporary abstention from "stinkers". I have resumed my usual ration of three "Three Castle" per day. Mrs Lambert has sent me a parcel containing De Reszkes, [as smoked in the Hounds of the Baskervilles] so that's all right. The Russians Mother sends me I don't really care for. They won't remain alight and I'm afraid my taste gravitates at the moment to common or garden kinds of cigs—Gold Flake or three Castles, State Express etc

Dec 4th to Mother
Do you know I will have had my commission for two solid years by the end of the day, and in another fortnight I will have been at the front for a whole year.
The next letter in French [to test you out!], and its translation were related to the period in November when Denzil and others were billeted with a French family. He and his French obviously made a good impression!

Warloy-Baillon-Somme
4 December 1916

Cher Monsieur

Nous avons rècu votre lettre avec un très grand plaisir. Nous sommes heureuses de savoir que vous avez eu da la chance et nous souhaitons que vous ayez un lon repos pour vous remettre de vos fatigues.

Certainement, si vous repassez par ici, nous espérons vous revoir. Et perhaps aussi après la guerre, si vous venez à Paris.

Ou êtes vous à pròsent? Fòterez-vous Noòl et le Jour de l'an loin des tranchòes? Pour one foes vows aurez le droit de faire zigzag.

Non, j'oubliais que vous étiez très sobre. Vous ûtes seulement très taquin avec votre ami, le grand officier; et il trop timide, je crois, pour vous en faire autant.

Maman a été très touchée de votre reconnaissance et elle me charge de vous remercier pour elle. En ce moment elle a beaucoup de travail avec les officiers que nous logeons. Leurs ordonnances boivent la provision de whisky des lieutenants' en sans maman les pauvres officiers n'auraient souvent rien à manger. Aussi pardonnez-lui si elle ne vous répond pas elle-même.

Vous avez sans doute su que depuis votre depart, les boches avainent jeté deux bombes sur notre village. Elles sont tombées à 80 mètres de chez nous. Vous voyez notre peur car nous n'en avons pas, comme vous, l'habitude. Elles n'ont tué que cinq prisonniers et ont blessé 7 autres [para?t –il]. Tous les carreaux furent brisés aux alentours; une vielle femme reçut une fenêtre dans les bras, et une vache en eut la jaunisse. Les dég?ts ne sont pas énormes vous voyez.

Dans tres semaines nous aurons ici mon père et mes frères et souer. C'est trés chic.

J'espère que nous aurons encore quelques nouvelles de vous et de vos amis.

Comment va votre famille? Vos parents ont-ils toujours des officiers chez eur? Donnez notre meilleur souvenir aus les lieutenants qui ont logé chez nous.

Et acceptez pour vous-mûme nos voeux de bonne chance et nos amitiés.

Melitza

Dear Sir

We have received your letter with great pleasure. We are glad to know that you have been lucky and we hope you have a long rest to recover from your exhaustion.

Certainly if you are passing this way another time, we hope to see you again. And perhaps also after the war in Paris.

Where are you at the moment? Will you celebrate Christmas and the New Year far from the trenches? For once you are entitled to make zigzags! [probably translates as "indulging yourself in a riotous time"].

No, I was forgetting that you were very sober. You just like to tease your friend, the big officer; and he is too shy, I think, to do the same back to you.

Mother was very touched by your gratitude and she has told me to thank you for it. At the moment she has a lot of work with the officers that we are billeting. Their batmen drink the Lieutenants' whisky supply, and if it weren't for mother the poor officers would often have nothing to drink. So forgive her for not answering you herself.

No doubt you've learnt that since your departure the Jerries had dropped two bombs on our village. They fell 80 metres from our house. You understand how afraid we are because we aren't used to it. They only killed five prisoners and injured 7 others it appears. All the windowpanes round about were broken; one old woman had a window land in her arms and **a cow got jaundice from it**. *The damage is not vast as you see.*

In three weeks time we'll have my father and my brothers and sisters here. It's very nice.

I hope we will hear a bit more from you and your friends. How is your family? Have your parents still got officers with them?

Remember us kindly to the Lieutenants who stayed with us.
We wish you the best of luck and send you our best wishes.

Melitza Tarnoy

December 22nd to Dad
I have not written for some time, and since then things have happened.

Amongst other things I am on a grenade course two to three miles from my battalion. We are having a good time and the officer in charge is a good pal of mine though outside my battalion. Every officer has to go on a course and I had a choice between Divisional School, Grenade School, Trench Mortar School or a Lewis Gun course, and I chose the second, having been on all the others before.

A match between Possibles and Probables for the Divisional side is coming shortly and three out of the four OB's are playing for Probables and one for Possibles.

three more of our officers have been awarded the MC, one DSO, One VC, about seven DCMs or more, and umpteen military medals to the Battalion. I can tell you that we have four VC's now in the Brigade.

On Monday we are having a regular slap up Battalion dinner that should be good fun.

It should be a distinctly more pleasant Christmas than last year when we spent Christmas morning, Captain Willows and myself, pulling one leg after another in five feet of slushy mud in that redoubt I once commanded, and I shan't forget it to my dying day. The mud got worse and worse and so did the language, I fear, till we arrived fed up and dead beat at the Observatory. The only relief to a terrible morning was that one of our planes looped the loop over Boche lines and every time they fired at it. I shan't forget that morning in a hurry! And in the afternoon the Bache dropped some shells into our village, and in the evening I had to take the ration party to the front line through indescribable mud and all the way flopping on our faces every now and then in the darkness with bullets whistling by and occasional MG fire. Ye little Gods and fishes, it was some day!!

This certainly looks as if it is going to be better than that this Christmas.

Today is the anniversary of me going to the Battalion out here and of our last Christmas dinner before being marched into the trenches to be raided on December 29th!

Quelle vie!
The period between December 1916 and February 1917 was a relatively quiet one, a saving of breath after the Somme battles starting on July 1st.

In December there was company training including digging trenches foe a practice Brigade attack. There were also Company training course in bombing, signalling, trench mortars and range finding. The senior NCO's did bayonet practice.

On the 14th December they had moved to Canchy.

On July 7th they were all fitted with new box respirators, and on the 8th medals were presented by Major General Maxse to those men who had been awarded medals but not yet received them.

On the 9th Th Battalion moved up towards West Miraumont and occupied trenches there for a period. Heriz-Smith noted the increasingly severe frosts that made duckboards very slippery and that men wore sand bags over their feet. They established a supply dump in part of Regina Trench.

Casualties were quite few and shelling not severe but there were casualties of the attritional nature associated with trench life – such as the man who put his pick through a live shell.

Towards the end of January men were sent into Authuille Wood to get timber, as coke was very scarce.

On the 30th January there were discussions at Brigade level to plan the proposed attack near Boom Ravine.

Robert Graves concludes his analysis of the effective life span of an officer by saying that after a year or so an officer can become worse than useless, and that this was partly for a medical reason – neurasthenia, whereby the thyroid gland fails to pump it's sedative chemical into the blood. Without this assistance a man could become apathetic and rather "doped".

Once again there is little evidence for this in Denzil's case though early 1917 saw him tired and run down. The war was not ending as soon as he thought, but there is no evidence whatsoever that he ceased to be an effective officer.

25

Boom Ravine K.I.A.

On the Somme battlefield the period between the British offensive of 1916 [that petered out in the late autumn], and the German attacks of the 1918 Spring Offensive, is not as well covered, and the Boom Ravine offensive of February 1917 is not well known. Yet it was an important and costly action and there are still debates as to its necessity, for the German were already beginning a secret withdrawal to prepared positions twenty miles to the rear. In a few days, the British could have taken Boom Ravine with no cost.

The actual Ravine itself was one of the most spectacular features of the Somme battlefield, and the Germans took full advantage of the ravine's defensive possibilities, and inflicted heavy casualties on successive waves of British attackers.

The Brigade had another three days out of the line for rehearsals, and on the night of February 15th-16th took over the battle front for the operations on the 17th. These were part of a big attack on both banks of the Ancre, to seize the high ground giving observation over the upper Ancre Valley.

The British plan was to take the sunken lane opposite Baillescourt farm. The lower part of this lane, approximately 100yards, was in British hands. What was needed was to take the rest of this lane and link with troops to the north. Once this lane had been taken, strong points were to be formed 50 yards in front of the sunken lane. On the southern flank, the 18th Division was attacking northwards, at 90 degrees to the Royal Naval Division. On their right flank, the 2nd division was also attacking Boom ravine northwards towards Pys and Petite Miraumont. The purpose of all of these attacks was to take this high ground and remove a bulge in the British line west of Courcelette/ Pozieres.

The 6th Northamptonshire war diary makes mention of Heriz-Smith and his fate, but not the details. It was almost certainly from fire from the "Tongue" a part of the ravine that protruded further south than the rest. It was around 6am

From the Northamptonshire War Diary:
"The first two waves of the centre company (A) got over Grandcourt trench with

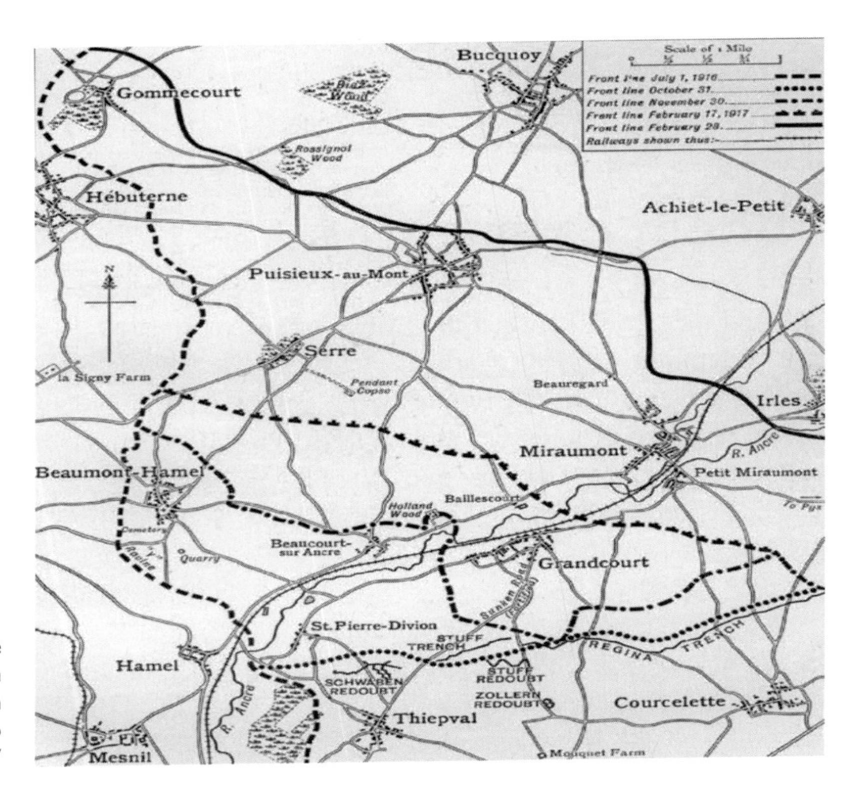

The Battles of the Ancre; British advances from October 1916 to February 1917

little opposition but were then met by heavy machine gun & trench mortar fire from their left from a large body of Germans holding the Tongue in the Boom Ravine.

It was necessary to clear this point before advancing: during the operation A/Capt. McWha [Also an OB], and Lt. Heriz-Smith became casualties. The rear waves of the centre company were met with considerable opposition in Grandcourt trench. It is not clear if the opposition was present when the first two waves went through or not: but the 4th wave encountered machine guns in the wire of Grandcourt trench."

Major Hugh Podmore April 6th 1917

That could leave it open to be rifle, machine-gun or trench mortar fire that delivered the fatal wound. It is surmised that he was wounded below the waist because of the very good condition of the possessions he would have been carrying in his jacket.

The location of Lt. Heriz-Smith's mortal wounding is of course an estimate (and presumably A/Captain McWha was wounded around there somewhere). "A" Company had reportedly crossed the wire and South Miraumont Trench (the box-

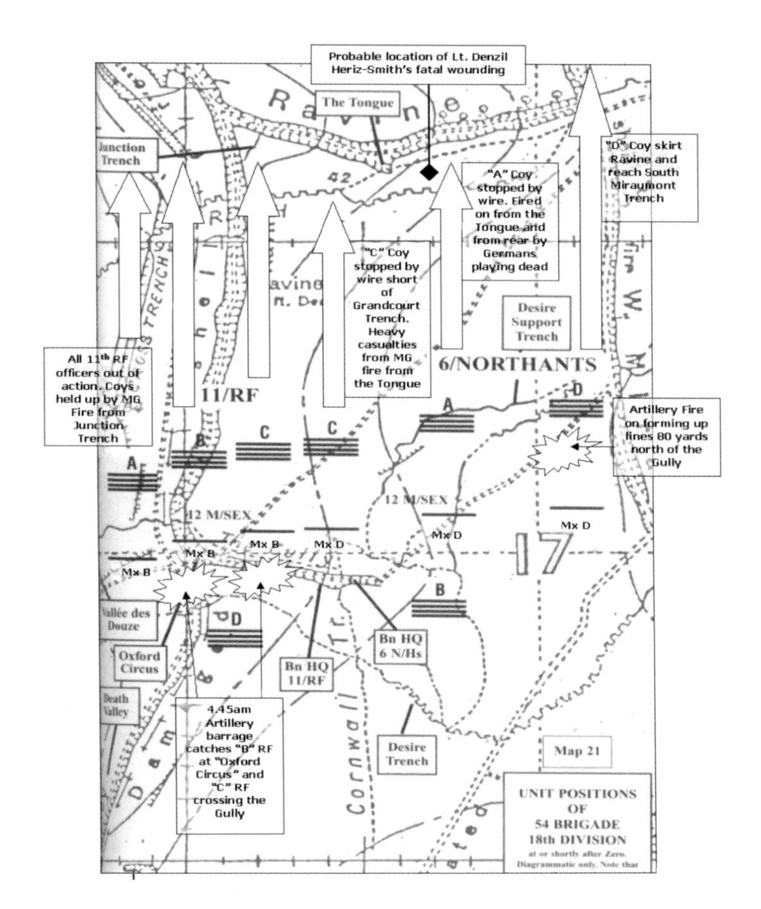

Boom Ravine

type line south of the Ravine, on the map) with the Tongue on their left.

The first two waves of the centre company (-A-) got over Grandcourt Trench with little opposition but were then met by heavy machine gun and trench mortar fire from their left a large body of Germans holding the Tongue in the Boom Ravine The newspaper report states that he died before reaching the regimental aid post, so presumably he was on his way back to the gully, either on a stretcher or under his own steam when he died.

Lt. Heriz-Smith is mentioned as being killed, though it leaves open the possibility that he was killed before crossing the wire in front of South Miraumont Trench.

Mention must be made of the employment of German prisoners as stretcher-bearers. The Fusiliers had captured about 100 prisoners. By keeping them constantly at work, all the Brigade casualties were evacuated within a couple of hours, though it was a very long carry over heavy ground. The difficulties that the medical service had to grapple were indeed very great. Stretcher cases were carried

2,400 yards from regimental aid-posts in Boom Ravine to tram head at Hessian Trench, and then pushed along the tramline 2,300 yards to the advanced dressing station. The carry was uphill all the way, under fire, and over ground all churned up by shells and knee-deep in mud. In the opinion of the medical officers it was the heaviest work that the bearers ever had to perform. None who survived that day would forget the gallantry of Lieutenant C. G. Kemp, the medical officer, whose cheerful and unceasing work, in spite of many casualties to stretcher-bearers, got the battlefield cleared in such short time.

Mention must also be made about the servant of Heriz-Smith, Private Charles Chantrell. He was the servant of the officer commanding the leading wave. When Heriz-Smith and most of the NCOs became casualties, before reaching the ravine, he at once took charge of the platoon, lead them against a number of the enemy, whom he cleared out, reorganised in the ravine, and proceeded with the advance.

When Grandcourt Trench was reached, many Germans were found lying in front, apparently dead. It occurred to Private J. W. Walsh to lift the cap from one of them. The man at once jumped up and held up his hands. The rest of the Germans who were also playing dead were promptly dealt with. A machine gun and a number of rifles were lying by them, and but for Private Walsh's action the whole company would have been shot in the back [This tactic was reported successful in a different part of the line].

It was about this time – apparently about 8.30am – that a strong German counter-attack was delivered from Petit-Miraumont and the Gully. This appears to have been the main attack, though parties also advanced from the brook in (on the Grandcourt – Miraumont Road) It appears from captured German orders and statements from prisoners that these were specially trained counter-attack troops, who had been brought up as soon as the information of our coming attack reached them on the previous night: they consisted largely of marksmen and machine-gunners. The fire was extremely accurate, while in the majority of cases British rifles & Lewis & Vickers guns had become clogged almost from the start – owing to lying in the mud in the dark before the attack & the bad ground traversed during the advance.

Whatever the exact cause, the British line seeing no appreciable effect produced by their fire on the advancing Germans began to fall back, chiefly on the right and then all along the line. It was at that point that Lt. Price (Adjutant of the 6th Northamptonshire's) displayed most conspicuous gallantry. He moved to and fro along the line steadying the retirement. Then, perceiving that the right was being left in the air and thinking our left comparatively safe, he formed the whole Northamptonshire body of survivors into a defensive flank on the W Miraumont Road and this was done by him personally under heavy rifle & machine gun fire & done most successfully. In this position they stayed from about 9.00am to 9.30am: at this time fire began to be opened on them from their left and rear, i.e. from S. Miraumont Trench with both machine guns and light trench mortars. After suffering heavy casualties for some time, Lt. Price decided to swing back his line to the original front: this was also carried out under heavy fire and at about 10.00am the battalion was occupying a position about 100 yards North of Boom Ravine.

There had been a number of additional reasons why the attack stalled in some areas.

The morning was extremely dark (heavy clouds obscuring the moon that should have risen about 4.20am), the ground was very soft and slippery – the thaw after nearly a months heavy frost having just commenced and altogether conditions could not have been more unfavourable to forming up for an attack absolutely without trenches.

Just why the weather had such frequent pro-German moods during the war is a question to be discussed in a more scientific book than this. But the fact remains that the hard frost, which would have given almost ideal ground to attack over, broke on the night of the 16th, and most of the troubles were due to the appalling mud, which resulted from the untimely thaw.

The forming up place was just in front of a depression known as the Gully, and from the Gully a sunken road ran into Boom Ravine. The junction of this sunken road with the Gully was known as "Oxford Circus", facing Miraumont, and not a healthy spot in the darkness of the early hours of Feb 17th.

Every step made had to cope with shell-holes and churned up ground, knee deep mud, and a deadly hail of shrapnel and high explosive, with rifle fire and machine-gun fire to sweep every yard of the advance.

"*It was discovered afterwards from captured German officers that they had learned full details of the proposed attack, and knew the approximate hour at which it was to be launched.*" From the 18th Bde Diary. Brigade report April 1917, though this was surmise rather than fact.

One platoon of the Northamptonshire Regiment was almost entirely wiped out as it was led up to the forming-up place.

Both the assaulting battalions suffered heavily in this bombardment, especially the Fusiliers. Crowded together in the Gully and Oxford Circus, the men had no shelter. It was in the pitchy dark hours before dawn, rain was falling, the ground was deep in slippery mud, and there were no trenches to guide to the forming-up line. That they coped with this hell was due very largely to their gallant and skilful handling by officers and NCOs and to the courage and discipline of the men themselves, many of whom lay in the mud for three to four hours under heavy shell-fire, awaiting the order to go over the top. Actual casualties among the lines actual formed up and lying down were extremely few, but the test of discipline was extremely severe. The greatest credit is due to 2Lts Boulton and Higham for the success of the forming up, that, after the terrible ordeal before dawn, they fought their way forward so well as to snatch a very large measure of success out of what might have been utter disaster speaks volumes for their doggedness and dash.

The men had no difficulties in following our barrage up to Grandcourt Trench – though the light was very poor till after 6am but at arrival at the wire they found in many cases that it had not been cut. Only a few very narrow passages were to be found and the delay in finding these gave the enemy time to get into position again both in Grandcourt Trench & also on both sides of Boom Ravine. This movement along the wire to find gaps was also largely responsible for the loss of direction and mixing up of companies which took place in the case of the left company (-C) the first two waves & those behind were held up by machine gun and rifle fire in Grandcourt Trench which delayed them at least half an hour & caused heavy casualties.

The killing or wounding of the entire D Coy Lewis Gun team was a bad blow.

The whole battalion was position by 4.50am. The enemy shelling continued heavy till 5.30am and then slackened a little. It was afterwards discussed that the enemy had received information of the attack six hours previously from some deserters (or prisoners) from the division on the right, who had told them everything except that they put the zero hour at 5.15am instead of 5.45am. The barrage was certainly much heavier than the previous morning and on this occasion was accompanied by S.O.S. in great profusion.[33]

On arriving before Grandcourt Trench it was found that much of the wire was still uncut, and the delay in finding the gaps gave the enemy time to get away and take up fresh positions beyond the trench and on both sides of Boom Ravine. The movement along the front of the wire to find gaps also led to some loss of direction and mixing up of companies. It must be remembered that it was still dark. Not until

6.50am was there light enough to see more than a few yards. On the whole, the wire was better cut in front of the Fusiliers than in front of the Northamptonshire Regiment. In the case of the latter, the left and centre companies were held up by rifle and machine gun fire at this point so long as to "lose the barrage". Soon after this, about 8.30am, a strong German counter-attack was delivered from Petit-Miraumont. From captured German orders and statements by prisoners, it appears that these were specially trained counter-attack troops, brought up as soon as news of our intended attack reached them the previous night. They consisted largely of marksmen and machine gunners. Their fire was extremely accurate, while we were in poor plight, most of our rifles and Lewis guns being clogged, owing to the lying in mud in the dark before the attack and the bad ground that had to be covered in the advance.

Both in the Fusiliers, and the Northamptonshire Regiment, the early loss of practically every officer threw a heavy responsibility on the other ranks, and they rose splendidly to the occasion.

This position was maintained till the afternoon when, in conjunction with 11 Royal Fusiliers, the line was pushed forward almost to the west of the hill and occupied by a series of rifle and machine gun posts.

This line was handed over to the 8th East Surrey Regiment on the evening of 18th.

The conclusion in the Brigade History that the attack was a success is more than a little optimistic. While the first line at Boom Ravine was certainly taken, the attack failed in reaching its objectives and indeed several enquiries were held into its failings.

Indeed, there is much controversy concerning the action of Boom Ravine and whether it was necessary. It does not seem to have been seen as the start of a new British assault, even more so because it was February and with notoriously poor weather. British intelligence seems at fault. The Germans were actually about to move back from this area 20 miles or so to the east of Bapaume, what became the Hindenburg Line, where new defences were being constructed.

But there are different points of view about the necessity of Boom Ravine.

The Germans did defend their old front line fiercely as the 6th Northant's found to their cost.

A summary of casualties is attached. Brigade casualties were heavy, losing in all

14 officers killed, 25 wounded, and 2 missing. Of other ranks, 115 were killed, 423 wounded and 161 missing.

A visit to the site today enables you still to see the commanding view there was there, over miles of country.

There are justifications of the action

Firstly, whether there was a breakdown in intelligence or not, there was no knowledge of the retreat. The action was well underway before there was a realisation of this. After all the Germans were in a prime defensive position and had always made a fight of it, so offensive action to remove them was worthwhile.

Secondly, even if a withdrawal was known about, an offensive would make life very difficult for a unit trying to disengage and retreat. The withdrawal was probably underway, and this attack probably made life very difficult. The observation position gained as a result of this attack would have certainly made the Germans very uneasy.

Thirdly, had there been treachery that enabled the Germans to deal with the British attack?

Just before the attacks of these units the assembly trenches were badly shelled and many casualties resulted. Captured Germans stated that they knew the attack was coming and had planned for it and that the information came from a deserter. General Gough ordered an immediate enquiry, the results of which are not known as records cannot be found. Afterwards, commanders were asked about men missing the attack but all these are subsequently accounted for.

There probably wasn't any treachery and the Germans would have known an attack was in the offing through aerial reconnaissance.

The barrage that caught troops assembling may have been a lucky hit – as happened elsewhere during the war. Knowing that an offensive was in the offing, most started at the first light so a speculative barrage at sunrise would always be worth attempting. The report about a traitor was probably political and spread by the Germans. The enquiry into this wasted much of the time of senior officers at this time.

It has been suggested that from the British point of view this was the Dieppe raid of the 1st WW, to find out how strongly the enemy would react. One month later the Germans moved eastwards, and the charnel house of the Somme belonged to the British.

They also inherited a great swathe of scorched earth where every house had been pulled down, every tree uprooted and the water supplies polluted, and booby traps abounded.

The battle would be resumed next spring in what became known as the Battle of Arras. Little consolation to Heriz-Smith and the many other OB's who died on the Somme, but they would not have questioned the cause or their part in it.

This was Denzil's last letter home, written the day before his death. There is a certain war-weariness not apparent in letters about the Somme, Trones Wood, or Thiepval in 1916. He does not refer to the "Tiddly old Push" he did last July. There seems to be some cynicism, entirely understandable, about the effort required to finish the war.

As with most of his letters, this one runs from the mundane, though important, references to socks and buttons, to the foreboding of going over the top one more time.

The letter is in it's full state.

BEF
16-2-17

My darling little Mother

What am I going to talk about my wee Tit? Here we are just sitting in a dugout, and some dugout too, waiting with what patience we may for the moment to go over and give Fritz as nasty a smack as we can. It won't be pleasant, of course, and of course we are not exactly bucked with life just at present, but it all goes towards finishing the war, which is the great thing, isn't it? That is about all the news there is really, as since I last wrote we have done nothing very much, beyond working parties and such like. I have been recovering from my attack of cold, cough, no voice etc, which process is pretty slow and not quite finished yet, though I am a good deal better than I was. Still if we are lucky we may get a rest sometime and then we shan't be long doing a complete recovery. Meanwhile we go on much as usual. I hope with luck to get a letter from home ce soir, which will be nice if it comes. I got a letter from Dad on the 6th, some from you on the 7th, both of which, of course, were very welcome. Yes, I got the socks, buttons etc all safely, the former especially just in a nick of time, as washing is a distinct problem nowadays on this front. The Tommie cooker etc came in very handy too and is doing yeoman work. I haven't had an Ousel yet, but I imagine it cannot be easy to do shopping etc with all the invalids! And how are all the invalids now? I suppose you have gone to

Caversham by now, and I hope everyone else is in good health, or as a Corporal who came here last night said of some Boche prisoners he was escorting down; when asked whether they were wounded or not, said " oh my they are in fine condition." It made me laugh some; as a matter of fact they were a very draggled tailed looking lot!

I met a man whom I came back from leave with last November, yesterday; the lucky beggar had had another on January 11th already. I fear I've still got five people in front of me, which is aggravating. One of our fellows is back in Bedford at the moment of writing, a fellow who played in the St Paul's team against our "B", but he only joined the Battalion the day after I got back from my last leave. Yes, I'm reduced to the weather now! As a matter of fact it is more important to me by far than at home, as it does affect one's comfort seriously. It is not half as cold now and the snow has started to melt a bit which makes the roads a bit greasy to say the least.

Well, I'm going to stop as I can't, for once in a way, think of a single item of news, and also I have some 'bizz to enact of a somewhat important character. Worse is I cannot get hold of field cards, and for the next day or two writing a letter will be extremely improbable to say the least, so don't get alarmed if you don't get a "pukka" letter for a little time.

Tons and tons of my love, my darling and bestest of mothers, to you and the same to my old Pa, to whom I hope to write as soon as poss. I'm not forgetting the kids, one and all.

Your lovingest son
Pops

At about the same time Denzil wrote to a friend, "we are billeted in a ramshackle old village just within sound of the guns and will be moving up to our killing warrens in a few days."

Daily Telegraph
Monday February 26 1917
BOOM RAVINE
BATTLE IN THE FOG
A GRIM STRUGGLE
From PHILLIP GIBBS
BRITISH HEADQUARTERS [France]

Saturday

"In broad outline I have already described the heavy fighting which took place last Saturday morning [Feb 17th] across a gully called Boom Ravine and up the slopes towards Miraumont. The history of the attack deserves to be told more fully. In difficulty, in grim human courage, in all the drama of fog, and darkness, and shell fire, and death, it seems to me to hold more of what the war means to individual men - all that can be asked of them in such hours. Some of the young officers who went through and beyond Boom Ravine and had the luck to come back again - described their adventures as though they were just a nightmare from which they has awakened, laughing.

It was very dark, pitch black before dawn and heavy in fog when daylight failed to come. The thaw had just set in, and the ground was soppy, which was bad luck. In spite of the thaw, it was horribly, damply cold, but the men were given a good meal before forming up for the attack, and officers brought up the rum ration in bottles, so that men could attack with some warmth in them. In the utter darkness, unable to make any glimmer of light lest the enemy should see, the brigades tried to get into line. Two companies lost themselves but got into touch again in time. It was all black and beastly. A great fire of high explosives burst over our assembly lines. The darkness was lit up by the red flashes of these exploding shells. Men fell, wounded, and dead. One Battalion was specially tried, and their Brigadier wondered whether they would have the spirit to get up and attack when the hour arrived. But when the moment came they rose and went forward, and fought through to the last goal - splendid and wonderful! They were the first to get to Grandcourt Trench, which lay between them and Boom Ravine. The wire was not cut, and there was a hammering of machine guns and the swish of machine gun bullets.

LOST ALL ITS OFFICERS

This Battalion had already lost all its officers, who had gone forward gallantly, leading their men and meeting the bullets first. A sergeant major took command, shouted to his men to keep steady, and found a gap through the wire. They forced their way through past Grandcourt Trench, and with other men dropped into Boom Ravine. That place is a deep gully almost parallel with Grandcourt Trench, and Miraumont Trench beyond. It was a ravine of death. Our shellfire had smashed down all the trees, and their tall trunks lay at the bottom of the gully, and their branches were flung about. The banks had been opened out by shell craters, and several of the German dugouts built into the sides were upheaved or choked. Dead bodies or human fragments lay among the branches and broken woodwork. A shell of ours had entered one dugout and blown six dead men out of it's doorway. Inside were six other dead. From dugouts not blown up or choked came groups of German soldiers, pallid and nerve-broken, who gave themselves up easily enough. One man was talkative. He said in perfect English that he had been coachman to an English Earl, and he cursed our artillery, and said that if he could get at our blinking gunners he would wring their blighted necks - or words to that effect. Another man was an ex-waiter of the Trocadero, and after the battle he was kept for making coffee, which he did as though he loved it.

GERMANS SHAM DEATH

But the battle was not over yet. It had only just begun. While Boom Ravine was being cleared of it's living inhabitants by the first wave of English soldiers [they were men of London or the southern counties], other waves were coming up; or rather, not waves but odd groups of men, dodging over the shell craters, and hunting as they went for German snipers, who lay in their holes firing until they were pinned by bayonet points. Their bodies lie there now, curled up. Some of them pretended to be dead when our men came near. One of them lay still with his face in the moist earth. "See that man is properly dead", said an officer, and a soldier with him pricked the man. He sprang up with a scream and ran hard away—to our lines. Six prisoners came trudging back from the Ravine, with a slightly wounded man as an escort. On the way back they found themselves very lonely with him, and passed some rifles lying in their way. They seized the rifles and became fighting men again, until a little Welsh officer met them, and killed everyone with his revolver.

Behind the troops who went up to the Boom Ravine was a colonel and a young adjutant with a whimsical way of hiding his courage. "We'd better get up to Grandcourt Trench", said the colonel. "I feel a bit anxious". They went up picking their way among the dead. "There's a lot of machine gun firing," said the young adjutant, whose ears, since Loos, were trained for it. "We had better get down". "I want to see what's going on", said the colonel. He did not see much for presently he was hit by a bullet and dropped. The adjutant went on with an Intelligence officer, who afterwards led an attack on a German strongpoint. On the way, this Intelligence officer with six men of a machine gun team lay in a shell hole to escape the scythe of bullets cutting the ground around them. When it seemed time to get out and get on again, all six men fell and only the officer escaped. He took command of another party and attacked the strongpoint, and captured it by rifle grenade.

"A DEFENSIVE FLANK"

The young adjutant made himself busy in the Ravine. There was a mixed crowd here and he got them together and started towards South Miraumont Trench. The sergeant-major, who had reorganised the first wave, had gone ahead with ten men and pushed out to within eighty yards of that ditch, where he was joined by the adjutant and the supporting troops. The Intelligence officer was working up with another group on the left. Machine gun fire was sweeping down from high ground near Petit Miraumont, and by this time it was lighter, so that the enemy could see our men coming over the slope. Outside South Miraumont trench the wire was solid and uncut, but here and there the enemy had left a gap for working parties, and on the left the Intelligence officer got through with six men, while a little to the right the adjutant rushed through with twenty men. Between then were the Germans. It was a dangerous situation anyhow. It became enormously dangerous when, owing to German counter-attacks, troops were forced to fall back on the extreme right of the attack, leaving the adjutant and his men naked and exposed on the side. He is just a boy, this officer, though he would not like one to say so. But he thought quickly and remembered tactical lectures by his Divisional General on the subject of defensive flanks. "A defensive flank sounds alright", said the adjutant, and he proceeded to make one with three hundred men – "a party of all sorts"–along the West Miraumont road. It seemed just the place with a high bank as good as a parapet.

The defensive flank, with their rifles over the bank, felt safe and easy until after a while they found bullets coming from behind. Several men were hit in the back of the head and fell. The others began to feel white about the eyes. "Pineapple bombs" were exploding behind them. "This defensive flank seems to be played out" said the adjutant, and he decided to withdraw his men and form them up at right angles to the West Miraumont road on a line running parallel to Boom Ravine. It would have been easy to swing them into their new position by the ordinary movement but for the machine gun fire, and he had to withdraw them down from shell crater to shell crater, and then let them crawl out in the same way by the left. Later in the day a retirement was made to the Boom Ravine, but, after reorganisation, the line was advanced again to the reverse side of the last slope, with snipers shooting down into South Miraumont Trench, and supported now by strong bodies of men on the right and left so that they were in a good defensive position. The Intelligence officer who had done so gallantly as a leader of men was one of those who did not come back, though all day long the stretcher-bearers went searching for the wounded. This is the story of the battle of Boom Ravine"

This graphic account by Philip Gibbs would not have been published earlier in the war, as it would seem to be too shocking for the reading public to take in. It pulls very few punches, and would have been censored before July 1916. The authorities, though, began to realise that they couldn't disguise what was going on, or to an extent at least. The lists of casualties that appeared daily in the press, returning soldiers tales, and the local devastating effect of what happened to Pals Battalions on the Somme, meant that the public were "mature enough" to be presented with something like what actually happened.

The Times followed this up in an article on February 23rd, saying that the Germans were bound to try to win the land lost back, and that he launched his men in waves in his old determined style, but that our shrapnel caught them out in the open. With that and the Lewis machine guns the attacks simply faded away. They evaporated in fire before they got near our defences.

It was a gallant effort; but after the first attacking wave was obliterated, a stupid and wasteful one on the parts of its directors.

This attempt at a counter attack does raise doubts about whether the Germans were about to withdraw, but more likely it was carried out as withdrawal could be dangerous with the British holding the Boom Ravine area.

26

Letters and Obituaries concerning the death of Denzil

Feb 22nd 1917

Dear Mrs Heriz-Smith,

I cannot tell you how deeply grieved I am at your loss, and Denzil was more to me than just a pupil; he was a friend whom I loved and to whom I was bound not only by our own common work for the School but by the affection I felt for a boy of so manly, generous and kindly a nature. He was head of the best set of Monitors I have ever known – and a worthy head –for his influence kept all together in the right road, without fuss or self seeking or ostentation ; it just spread quietly and did it's work because he was what he was. 1913-14 was the happiest year I have had in my schoolwork – I shall never have such another – nor indeed will this life ever have the same promise of happiness. So many of my old school friends have gone, and of all the boys I have known, his loss touches me most deeply. We must thank God for the gift of him, and try not to grieve overmuch; he died as he lived, doing his duty, and all is well with him now. You will tell me sometime about his end and where he is buried.

The School is deeply affected by the news of his death; he was honoured and loved by all – for them as well as for myself. I offer to you and Mr Heriz-Smith our great sympathy. Words fall short of what I mean, but you will understand.

Yours sincerely
Reginald Carter
5 Pemberley Crescent
Bedford

Feb 22nd 1917

Dear Heriz-Smith

I simply can't come in to see you today, and I expect you can't wish to see anyone.

Not having any immediate relative of my own, I had centred all my interest and prayers on Denzil, as if he felt like my own son. You are too good a churchman to lose your faith, but it seems perfectly diabolic why the best men, only sons and those marked out for Holy Orders, should be taken.

Perhaps this is not so, and if we were able to do percentages we should find that others who are not such valuable lives, have been taken in equal measure, but I can't but feel the frightful loss of such a splendid fellow as Denzil to his home, his church, and his country

One can only feel that he, with his friend Lambert, will be one of those that Lord Roberts will welcome, for I do believe that Kindred souls will find each other in Paradise.

The world can have very little to offer to those of our generation, and the sooner we pass the better, and let the children who don't realise these sorrows, build a new world. These things are "the beginnings of travail", and often in the pain of these days a new era will be born. But it is hard for those who have to endure the birth pains of a new order.

I write just what I feel. I cannot say there is any consolation to you in this, but indeed you all have my greatest sympathy and friendship

Yours Sincerely
Richard Howes

Feb 22nd

"Dear Sir
It is with the greatest regret that I write to inform you of the death from wounds received in action of your son Lt D Heriz-Smith of this battalion. He was severely wounded in an attack on the German positions on the morning of the 17th and died before reaching the dressing station.

I knew your son well both in England with this battalion and also out in France, where he joined us last December year. He was a fine soldier and I cannot speak too highly of his coolness and gallantry in action and of the affection with which his men regarded him. He led them through two big actions in July with distinction and came through unscathed, and it is indeed hard luck that his wounds this time should have been so severe that he died before reaching the dressing station. Our regimental doctor did all he could for him, but he could not stand the journey back.

Any words of consolation of mine would be an impertinence, but it will I hope be a source of comfort to you to be assured [though you must be certain of this already], that he died doing his duty and leading his men to victory as he would have wished.

Yours sincerely"
H Podmore [Major]

Postcard from OB's to Denzil 28-1-17

Dear Heriz

Thanks for your Christmas card. I lift my hat to you for going over the top so many times; you appear to have blushed unseen a little bit. Still out here and in peace we lift our hats to you. We salute you.

Mudford, Walker and I send greetings. Here's to our next merry meeting. We are ever your pal.

JTM

NB A FS card was sent to his Parents says that he is wounded and in hospital

25-2-17
Letter to Heriz-Smith parents from Cyril Cook re Denzil's death

Dane Bank
Northwich
Cheshire

Dear Mrs Heriz-Smith

Your letter containing the terrible message of Denzil's death reached me on Friday, and Oh! How I wish I could write down all I feel.

It was the saddest news I could have, news that I had never expected, for like you I had implicit faith that God would bring Denzil home again. Oh! How I have prayed for him, now these prayers seem to have come back to me. It looks as though all our prayers have failed. Denzil has gone forever from this world, but his journey is not a long one. It is just the passing from the darkness to the light, just the pathway of the sun, from the still, cool air of tonight to the bright happy morning of tomorrow, And he'll be so happy now but, he would be sad, too, if he looked down and saw us clothed in sorrow. The blow is very hard to bear, but may God be very near to you all.

Mother wishes me to express her deepest sympathy for you.

Yours very sincerely
Cyril B Cook.

The Ousel
March 17th 1917

The Late Lieutenant D.M. Heriz-Smith

Lieutenant Denzil Mitford Heriz-Smith, Northamptonshire Regiment, was severely wounded on February 17th, and died before reaching the dressing station. Born in 1894 he was the sole surviving son of Mr C Mitford Heriz-Smith, P.W.D, Madras, India [retired].

He was educated at Bedford School where, when Head of the School, he received from Lord Roberts a special prize, presented by the Field Marshall "for the best all round boy in the School".

He entered at Queen's College, Cambridge, with the intention of taking Holy Orders, but immediately war broke out he joined the Public School's Battalion, the Royal Fusiliers, receiving later a commission in the Northamptonshire Regiment. He went to the front in December 1915, and saw much fighting, and was one of the very few original officers of his Battalion when he died. His Commanding Officer writes — "I cannot speak too highly of your son's gallantry and coolness in action, and of the affection with which his men regarded him. He had been through two big actions with distinction. He died doing his duty and leading his men to victory, as he would have wished." The Times.

Heriz-Smith was the Head of School in 1913-14, a year of pleasant memories. His service to the School will be remembered with gratitude and affection. He had many accomplishments, and one single purpose, to do his duty. A lover of peace and home, he would have devoted his life to work for his country in the highest service of all. Of him the words written by a soldier in the trenches are singularly true.

Lover of life we pledge thee Liberty

And go to death calmly, triumphantly.

Bassinghome
Abington Park
Northampton
31 March 1917

Dear Mr Heriz-Smith

It was only last night in the Independent I found out what your address was. I was longing to be able to write to you and express my very deep sympathy with you on the loss of your son. I was in the same company as he was while I was out there for two and a half months and had a lot in common with him especially after Thiepval, he and I were the only two left in the same company.

I can assure you that all his men loved and respected him as did all of us officers. He was a fine soldier and awfully easy to work with, so helpful and cheerful under all difficulties. The Battalion has undoubtedly sustained a great loss in him. His men always came first with him and he was never content unless he was sure that they were as comfortable as circumstances could possibly permit.

I'm afraid that this letter is too inadequate in expressing how much I feel for you under your tragic loss and how deeply I sympathise.

I am

Yours very sincerely

D Ingle Gotch

Northampton Independent 31-3-1917

Died for their Country

Lt. D. M. Heriz-Smith
The Head Boy of Bedford School.

There is great sorrow among all ranks of the 6th Northamptonshire Regiment over the death in action of Lt. Denzil Heriz-Smith for there was no officer more beloved in the battalion than he. He was within a few days of his 23rd birthday, but he crowded into his all too short career a record of good and gallant service united with a nobility of character, which will make his memory tenderly cherished. He was the only surviving son of Mr. Charles Mitford Heriz-Smith, of St. George's Lodge, Bedford, late of the Public Works Dept., Madras. The first few years of his life were spent at Cornard Magna, Sudbury where his parents resided before coming to Bedford in 1904. A nephew by marriage of Mr. E. C. Ransome of the firm of Messrs. Ransome, Simms and Jeffries of Highwood, Ipswich, lately Mayor of that town, he came into association with the late Colonel Ripley whose brother, Mr. Phillip Ripley is managing director of that firm. At Bedford School he greatly distinguished himself, winning many form prizes and in 1913-1914 he attained the position of "Head of the School", a position in which his abilities and affectionate disposition found full scope for helpful service. By nature gentle and unobtrusive, his manly and generous nature working in concert with a great love of boys and boyhood made him an ideal "Head of School". He formed many close friendships and it was a great grief to him to have lost so many companions in the war. One of his most intimate friends was the late Lieutenant Lambert (the first officer in the battalion to fall) who received such high tributes from the late Colonel Ripley. An accomplished athlete, Lieutenant Heriz-Smith received at Lord Robert's hands a special prize given by the Field Marshal himself, for the best all round boy, consisting of the book "Forty-one years in India" on the first page of which in the Field Marshall's own handwriting and over his own signature is the following inscription:

"Presented to Denzil M. Heriz-Smith, the best all-round boy in the school. Head of the School, awarded a special Exhibition of Classics at Cambridge, Captain of the Gymnasium, in the Football XV, a member of the Officer Training Corps, and of the School VIII. – F.M. Lord Roberts. Bedford, 27th July 1914.

Left behind when his battalion went to the front, he underwent prolonged training at Bedford, Colchester and elsewhere rejoining his battalion in France in December 1915. From that time onwards he went through the usual experience of life in the trenches varied by spells of training in rest camps, during which time he took great interest in the games and recreations of the men, playing himself in several inter battalion "rugger" football competitions.

In July 1916 the forward movement began and the battalion played a memorable role in the two important actions that took place in that month commencing with the attack on July 1st and then that of Trones Wood in which the casualties were high including the gallant Colonel. Through these actions and a good deal of subsequent time he was lucky enough to pass unscathed but in the battle which took place of February 17th of this year he received his fatal wound as he was leading on his men towards the objective, and succumbed the same day. "He did splendidly in the battle getting right forward with his platoon" writes one who was there. "He was a great sportsman and a true English gentleman" In writing of his death. Major Podmore says, "He was a fine soldier, and I cannot speak too highly of his coolness and gallantry in action, and of the affection with which the men regarded him."

Another officer writes: "He was one of the very few remaining original officers of the battalion at the time of his death. He had been through many fights unscathed and I think no other officer in the battalion has a bigger record of battles, but now we have lost him." The Chaplain says "I cannot say what a loss he is to us."

The School paper, the "Ousel" in a tribute to his memory adds: "His service in the School will be remembered with gratitude and affection. He had many accomplishments and one single purpose – to do his duty. A lover of peace and home, he would have devoted his life to work for his country in the highest service of all.

Northampton Independent 14-4-1917
From the Front, April 5.

Seeing about the late Denzil Heriz-Smith's death in your last week's paper, I thought it would interest you to know that of the four that fetched him out of the barrage, two of us, Privates Whyman and Silvester of "D" Company, 6th Northants, are still here. I am sorry to say that the others are killed. We got him to our Regimental Doctor. After that four more took him to the R.A.M.C. station. We had to carry him about 700 yards to safety. We have also written to the late Lieutenant Smith's family.

3/10297 Pte. Whyman, "D" Company. 11608 Pte. Silvester, "D" Company.

Pte. Frederick Whyman, ex 1st Battalion, was gassed at Loos, MM LG 18-7-17

It will be remembered that the bereaved father of the gallant officer (Mr. C. M. Heriz-Smith of St. George's Lodge, Bedford) who has thus lost his only son, wrote to me concerning these gallant stretcher bearers in the hope of tracing them and added: "Their names will, I suppose, never be known but they offer farther prove of their gallantry and fearlessness of our Northamptonshire fellows, and my heart goes out to them for their devotion and bravery."

OFFICERS OF THE 6th NORTHAMPTONS.
Back row—Lt. L. Gordon Crook, Lt. J. D. Unwin, Lt. H. M. Margoliouth Lt. R. B. Fawkes, Lt. R. W. Spencer, Lt. P. Knight, Lt, F. G. B. Lys, Lt. R. J. Mackay, Lt. J. A. F. Morton, Lt. A. H. Burrows
Second Row—Lt. S. Le Fleming Shepherd, Lt. J. F. Arnold, Lt. D H. S. Gilbertson, Lt. W. Askham (k) Lt. D. H. Heriz-Smith (k) Lt. F. A. C. Wilcox, Lt. C. C. Hoare, Lt. N. C. Hamilton, Lt. J. N. Beasley Lt. R. A. Webb, Lt. H. J. Loughlin, Lt. W. H. Bird,
Seated—Capt. H. B. Simpson, Capt. G. M. Clark, (k) Capt. H. Podmore, (k) Capt. R. W. Beacham, (k) Capt. W. T. Wyndowe, Col. Ripley, (k) Major B. Hickson, Capt. G. W. Willows, Capt. F. S. Neville, (k) Rev. E. A. Bennett, Lt. H. C. Grace.
Seated on Ground—Lt. G. Shangster, Lt. E. F. Stokes, Lt. O. B. Palmer, Lt. O. D. Schreiner, Lt. G. L. Woulfe, (k) Lt. W. H. Fowler.

OB's in the Photo

Unwin, Lys, Burrows, Gilbertson, Heriz-Smith, Hamilton, Beasley, Webb, Loughlin, Simpson, Beacham, Neville, Grace, Shangster, Stokes, Palmer, Fowler

This is a letter to Sybil from the French family whom he billeted with a few months before.

Warloy Baillou/Somme
11 April 1917

Dear Miss

It is with sorrow that we have read your letter
We had leant indirectly that two officers, who had slept at home, were died. But we do not know their names.
It is just as seeing the silence of Mr Smith that we have confectured him to be died.
And your letter was confirmation.
I assure you that we have been very pained and we take a big part in your pain.
The esteemed man, your dear brother, although he has lived with us just some days. Indeed he had a splendid temper and you could be proud of him because he was a brave one.
But you knew him better than us.
My mother and all at home; we will keep his good remembrance.
When he has departed from here, he was going in the trenches. He told us "I will take Miraumont and will be able to sleep inside." He was very happy to put out the Germans, and we had gave him our best wishes of good luck!
But that was in vain.
If we can go to Miraumont later, and if we can find his grave, be sure that we shall carry some flowers.
As for you, Miss, I believe I know you by a photograph.
If you come to France after this terrible war, our invitation will always be like in remembrance of your dear brother. I hope you will accept it. You will find in my family sincere friends.
Now I stop because I have no words for appeasing your pain.
Please give our sympathetic condolences to Mr and Mrs Smith and to your sisters.
And accept for yourself my friendship.

Melitza Tarnoy

36 Royal Parade
Eastbourne
April 17th 1917

Dear Mr Heriz-Smith

I'm sorry that you have not heard from me before, and I do not think you will have thought that any delay was due to want of sympathy with me in your great loss which is our loss too.

I have just read the account of your son in the Ousel. The war has brought great losses to my college. We had expected quite the best year since I have been

This cross is now in the School Chapel

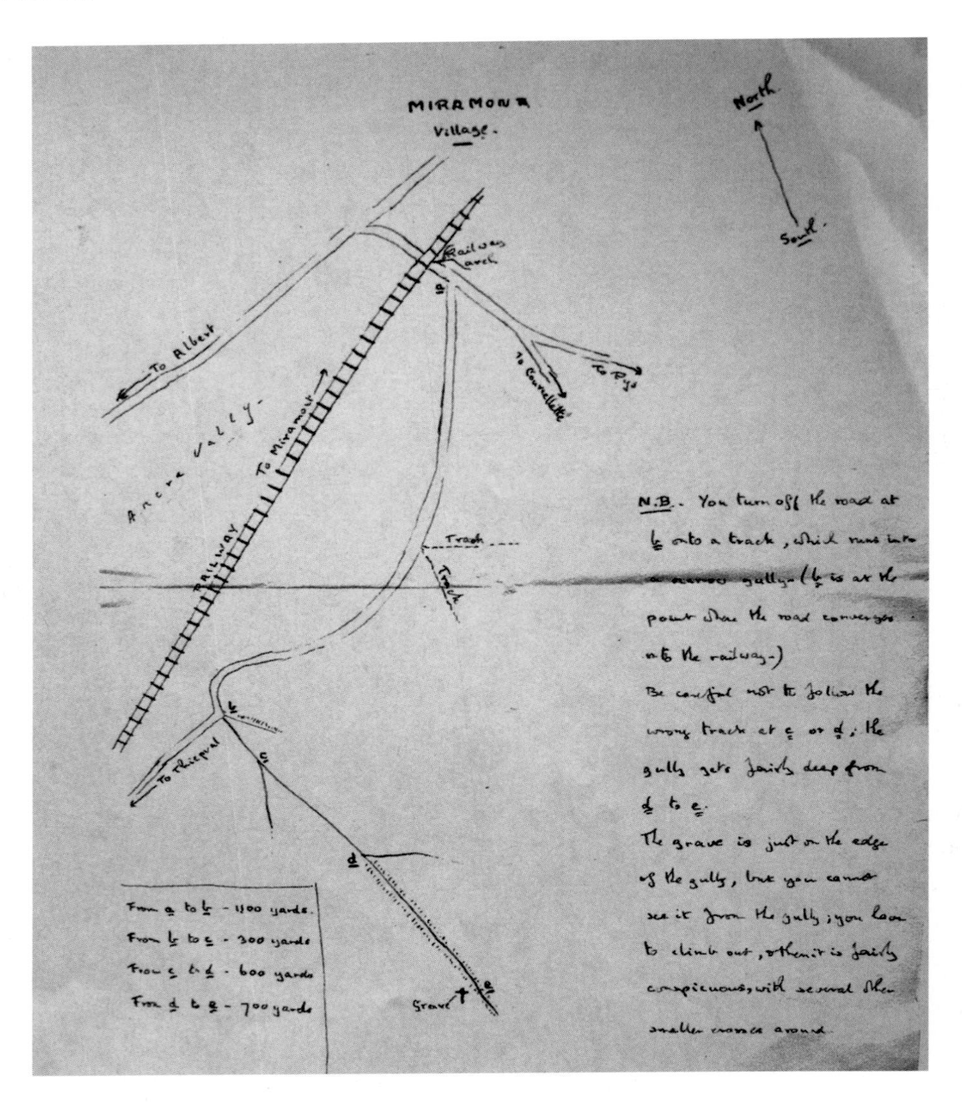

President of Queens[34] to come up in autumn term 1914, for it contained the Head Boy of four Public Schools. Of course we have seen none of them. I was looking forward with particular pleasure to the arrival of your son from my old School, partly because of what I have heard of him from Mr Carter, partly from the experiences of our meetings. The loss of the best in any life is grievous and nowhere is this felt more than universities where the loss of friends and pupils is so great.

With deep sympathy

T C Fitzpatrick

Trenches trip 1998. Boys placing a wreath on the grave in Regina Trench Cemetery

19-11-18
My Dear Mr Heriz-Smith

You will be glad to hear I have visited Denzil's grave, to see if it was alright after the Hun retired. I found that the cross had been broken off apparently from a shell, but it has been laid on the grave, so I just erected it again, and it is all right though it is about a foot shorter than before. The other names that I noted in pencil are still quite clean.

I have made out a rough map, which I think will make it easy for you to find the right grave should you be coming to France. It is in the middle of the most desolate place imaginable. As I stood by the grave I saw dozens of little crosses dotted about the shell holes, and I could not help thinking how thankful we ought to be that this great sacrifice of all our best and noblest has at last been justified, and by their deeds they have won security and peace for those of us who remain. It is a grand thing to die for an object like that. I am returning to my job next term, all being well, I have had some strange experiences since I left Bedford.

Please remember me very kindly to all your family.

Yours very sincerely
HG Perry

Attached 10th wing RAF
BEF

27
Conclusion

So another young live was snuffed out, one of over 750,000 who were of British or Commonwealth origin, and another family was distraught. At the age of 22, Denzil was almost middle aged compared to many victims of that brutal war.

Who knows what he would have gone on to become, after all, his sisters lived over sixty or seventy years longer. Of his close comrades from school or in the regiment, one went on to be knighted for services to the country, and another became the leading anti-apartheid judge in South Africa. Who knows what he would have done, but he would have been very successful, of that I have no doubt.

He was keen to get to the front and behaved in the manner that was expected of him; Lieutenants were always right in the firing line and faced a strong chance of death or injury. His complaints in the Army were always about incompetence and he had little time for those who were not up to the mark, but he never complained about the cause, and he never doubted that he should be out there. 1917, the year of his death, saw quite widespread mutinying in the French Army and there was some restlessness in some British units, interestingly enough not by those at the front. He was war weary but it would never have occurred to him not to do his duty.

By the time of his death his writings reveal a certain possibility that he was going to the "killing warrens" once too often, but his patriotism and his belief in God ensured that he would do what was expected of him. No one ever doubted that his first priority was the welfare of the men who fought alongside him.

The archives that have been left let us look at the lives of the 2,500 boys from the School who fought in all areas of the Great War.

It is a pleasure to say that Denzil would recognise the School as it is today, it's routines are remarkably similar in some ways. I've a feeling he might have become Head Boy!

Endnotes

1 On July 27th 1918 the School received the unprecedented honour of a visit by the King and Queen. They were greeted by the Head Master and his wife, and an inspection of the Corps followed. Then school songs were sung in the Great Hall and there followed a speech by the King who paid tribute to the splendid record of the School in the War. He asked the Head Master to give the School an extra weeks holiday because of this.

The Old Bedfordian Club erected a Memorial Hall to the honour of the Four Hundred and Sixty-Three Old Boys who were killed in the Great War. The building, which was placed to the west of the main School building, contained a Hall, Library, Storerooms and Cloakrooms. It was opened by HRH Prince Henry on July 26th 1926. In the unavoidable absence of the Bishop of St Albans, the Memorial was dedicated by the Lord Archbishop of Dublin, Dr JAF Gregg, an Old Bedfordian. The architect was OP Milne Esq., FIBA, the head of the firm of Messrs S.F.Foster, the builders, and he and the general foreman, Mr R Robinson, were presented to his Royal Highness.

The Library occupied the lower floor of the building. Placed around the Hall, which was

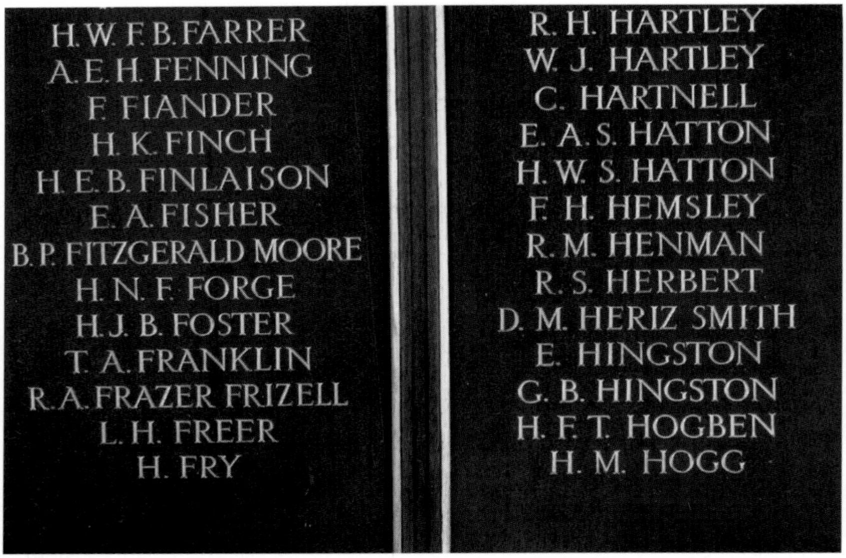

H. W. F. B. FARRER
A. E. H. FENNING
F. FIANDER
H. K. FINCH
H. E. B. FINLAISON
E. A. FISHER
B. P. FITZGERALD MOORE
H. N. F. FORGE
H. J. B. FOSTER
T. A. FRANKLIN
R. A. FRAZER FRIZELL
L. H. FREER
H. FRY

R. H. HARTLEY
W. J. HARTLEY
C. HARTNELL
E. A. S. HATTON
H. W. S. HATTON
F. H. HEMSLEY
R. M. HENMAN
R. S. HERBERT
D. M. HERIZ SMITH
E. HINGSTON
G. B. HINGSTON
H. F. T. HOGBEN
H. M. HOGG

Extract from the Memorial Boards in the Memorial Hall

on the first floor immediately facing the staircase, was panelling on which were written the names of the Fallen. The panels were in blue with gold lettering; five were situated on each side of the central panel, on which the following inscription; "In memory of Old Bedfordians who gave their lives in the War 1914-1918" was written. On either side of this inscription were the names of the Countries and Battlefields in scroll design.

This entailed a blank wall in the upper part of the North Gable, and there, outside, was a niche for a statue of St George; under this niche were two Doric columns resting on a base stone with the dates "1914-1918" upon it. The alcove had a shell pattern canopy of fine design; the South Gable carried the School Arms, while over the inside of the Memorial Hall doors, in letters of gold was the one word, "Remember".

Two thousand three hundred and fifty Old Members of the School served in the Great War.

2 The School name, **Bedford Grammar School**, was dropped in 1918, to become simply, Bedford School

3 The Ousel was the school magazine so loved by Heriz-Smith and other OB's. It is still going strong and is now produced as a bumper review of the year at the end of the Christmas Term.

4 **Academic school life** in early 20th century

The School was split into two in the upper school

1. Classic side, about 190 boys
2. Civil and Military side about 190 boys, and a subsection for 40 boys-Mercantile

and London Class

There were 17 classic teachers
12 Modern languages
13 Maths
1 Arithmetic
1 Chemistry
2 Physics and Natural Philosophy
1 Writing
1 or 2 drawing
1 Botany
1 for music
1 for violin
1 Sergeant in charge of gymnastics and drill
1 School Engineering Corps
3 Prep School

5

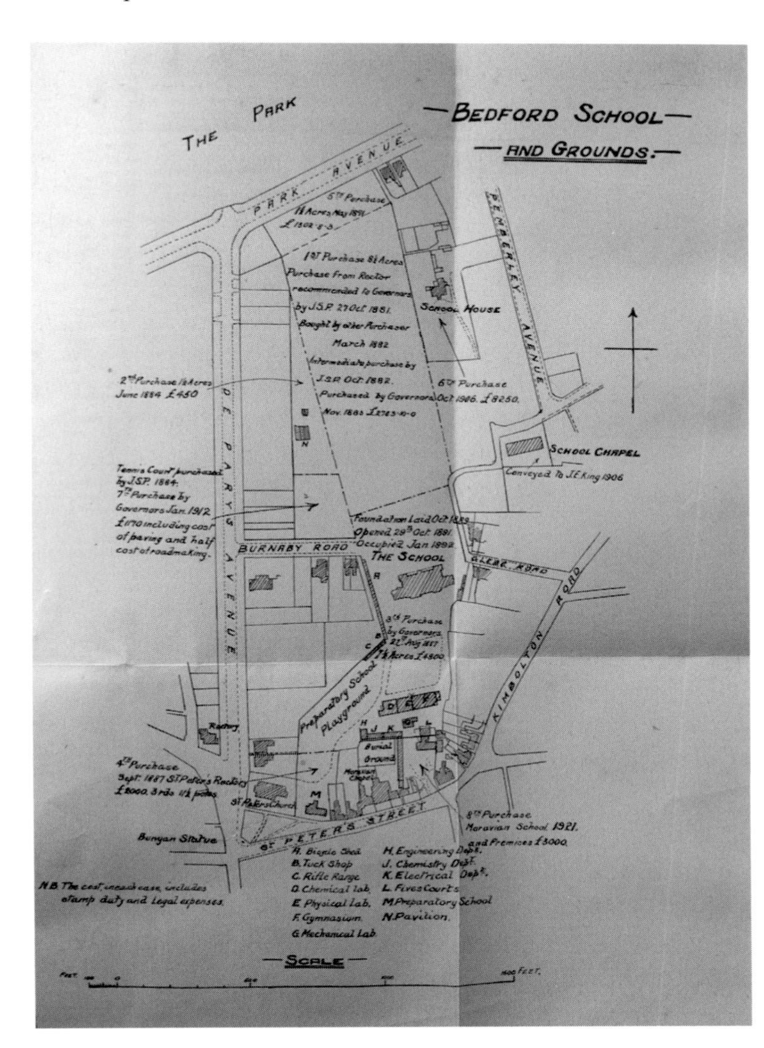

6 **Mr J E Nixon**

A classics teacher and a Cambridge man. He kept up many correspondences with Cambridge combatants in the early stages of the war. He had been active in reorganising the music in Kings College Chapel, and for the founding of Kings College Choir School. His death was announced in the Times.

7 Matador. A card game similar to poker that Denzil played frequently at Cambridge with Mr Nixon. When in the army he frequently played coon·can, a card game for 2 players using 40 cards that is an early version of rummy.

8 **Learning to play the game of Life**

The ideal schoolboy did not have to be academically bright, but if he had 'grit', if he was a 'sport', if he believed in his country, he would soon learn to respect and use authority. As a fag in his first few terms he learned to submit; as a prefect he learned to rule, in accordance with the system established by Dr. Arnold

The Headmaster of Rugby had, in the 1830s, increased the authority held by the schoolboys themselves. As the historian and political George Trevelyan wrote "The real education of a civil servant consists in the responsibility that devolves on him at an early age."

On the playing field, the public school-boy learned the importance of teamwork and fair play. "It would be terrible to think what would happen to us if from our public school system were swept away our Athletics and our Games", said Eustace Mile, amateur tennis champion of the world in 1899- an apt sentiment from one who believed that the best proof of a man's fitness to rule India was to have been Captain of Games at school. These were the traditions that built up the unshakeable belief among Victorian public schoolboys that the British held a god-given monopoly of wise rule, the traditions that created in Trevelyan's words "the fire of zeal which glows in every vein of an Indian Official". The tradition was remarkably long lasting.

9 **The 1914 XI**

As the 1914 XI ambled through the lengthening shadows towards the Old Pavilion at the conclusion of play on the 23rd July 1914 one wonders with what emotions they packed their skeleton pads, donned their striped blazers and headed for the future.

It was late in the school year – the term was actually to end on July 28th – the summer had been long and hot and, whilst there was the inevitable sadness of finality, the future beckoned. The season had been disappointing 'the worst, so far as records go, for many years' and the OB 'XI' had just beaten them in convincing fashion. There can, however, have been little time for melancholy, for ahead lay their future, and the future that lay before a public school leaver in the early part of the twentieth century was one of challenge and opportunity.

World events, however, were quickly to smother any seeds of optimism and within seven days of leaving the School, any semblance of self-determination had been torn

from them. By August 4th the World was at war and these young men were destined to be facing a far bigger challenge than that for which the foibles of cricket had so far prepared them.

Records tell that within four years of leaving School, five of this XI were dead. Their names are engraved for prosperity in gold on the boards of the School Memorial Hall; their lives are outlined briefly in the Memorial books written following the Great War. W F Garraway, J E D Lambert, E N Mitchell, C W S Robinson and J W De H Larpent were all to be killed in the massacre that greeted their valediction.

Garraway, from Paulo-Pontine, was a keeper who had averaged just 15 with the bat and had been criticised in the Ousel for lacking judgement. Serving with the 82nd Punjabi Regiment of the Indian Army he had drowned in 1916 whilst attempting to rescue some of his men who had got into difficulty erecting a pontoon.

Lambert, serving in the Northamptonshire Regiment and commanding a bombing party, was killed by a sniper within a year of leaving school. He had been 'a rather stiff bat with a solid defence, a somewhat uncertain catcher. E N Mitchell of the 8th Battalion of the Bedfordshire Regiment was killed on the 15th February 1916. He was caught by machine gun fire at a listening post in the British Front Line. After his death Mitchell's mother had received a letter from an old form mate of her son who had been present when Mitchell had been stretchered in. His last words had been, 'I know I am dying, send my love to my Mother.' Mitchell had headed the batting averages in 1914.

C W S Robinson was 'a very fair medium paced bowler' in his time at School. His School record had been tarnished somewhat by an episode of cheating when he and a friend had been caught out by matching wrong answers. He died of wounds in August 1918 whilst serving in the RAF.

The rather refined sounding J W De H Larpent has no known grave. He was buried where he fell in August 1916, killed by a shell in Pozieres and is commemorated on the Thiepval Memorial. At School he had been 'a very fair fastish right hand bowler, rather plain.'

The tragedy of these five young men is a story told in countless schools around the world. Brief lives recounted in faded scripts, promising futures randomly snatched. 'Spectator' summarising the season in the 1914 Ousel writes, 'If we profit by our disasters there is every reason to hope for a better season in 1915.'

There is an irony in these words.

This article kindly presented by Mr Guy Fletcher, OB, the current Head of Cricket at the School.

10 **Percivale Liesching** joined the Honourable Artillery Company at the start of the War, later was in the Machine Gun Regiment and finally was a Captain in the Tank Corps. He survived the war and went into the upper echelons of the Civil Service, ironically something Heriz-Smith had been trying to qualify for. He became Sir Percivale Liesching and was Permanent Under-Secretary, Ministry of Food, 1946–1948, Under-Secretary of State for Commonwealth Relations, 1949–1955, and High Commissioner for the UK in South Africa between 1955 and 1958.

His portrait is in the NPG

11 **The Llanelli Riots of 1911**

The tragic events in Llanelli surrounding the 1911 railway strike riots shocked the nation: on 17 August two men, both innocent bystanders, were shot and killed when troops were called out. It is an episode which still rankles in the town.

The five or so years running up to the First World War were a time of industrial turbulence – it has become known as the Great Unrest. But for the war, there might have been a savage general strike. There are theories that syndicalism, which was advocating the use of strikes to overthrow the capitalist order, was at work here. The syndicalism movement flourished principally in France and to a lesser extent in Spain and there were ripples of it England and Latin America.

In Britain in those years there were strikes in the coal mines, on the railways and in the docks. The Liberals, who were in power at the time – with Winston Churchill as Home Secretary – thought the very stability of the state was threatened. There is, however, insufficient evidence of any great and coordinated subversive plot. The truth is that wages and living conditions for working people were abysmal and getting worse. Wages had been static for ten years but the cost of living had risen considerably. A pound a week was not enough to live on.

The merchant seamen and dockers at Southampton, Goole, Hull, Liverpool and Southampton went on strike, as did the miners in the Rhonda Valley and railwaymen all over the country. Churchill was willing to allow heavy-handed troops to be called in if things were deemed to have got out of control, and that is what is thought to have happened at Llanelli after just two days.

12 **Lord Roberts**

Frederick Sleigh Roberts

Field Marshal Lord Roberts of Kandahar, V.C., K.G., K.P., G.C.B., O.M., G.C.S.I., G.C.I.E.

"Bobs", Lord Roberts of Kandahar. Hero of the Afghan and Boer Wars, and the most famous soldier in England. He was to die in France in November 1914.

13 **Casement, Sir Roger David, 1864-1916, Irish revolutionary**

While in British consular service, he exposed (1904) the atrocious exploitation of wild-rubber gatherers in the Congo (thus helping to bring about the extinction of the Congo Free State in 1908) and later exposed similar conditions in South America. He was knighted for these services in 1911. Although an Ulster Protestant, Casement became an ardent Irish nationalist. After the outbreak of World War I he went first to the United States and then to Germany to secure aid for an Irish uprising. The Germans promised help, but Casement considered it insufficient and returned to Ireland in Apr. 1916, hoping to secure a postponement of the Easter Rebellion (see Ireland). Arrested immediately after his landing from a German submarine, he was tried, convicted, and hanged for treason. To further blacken his name, some British agents had circulated his diaries, which showed him to be a homosexual. The diaries were probably genuine, but the manner of their use helped to inspire controversy about the possibility of forgery.

14 **Kessingland**

As the map shows, Kessingland is about five miles south of Lowestoft and the same distance north of Southwold, and it was where the extended family spent what seem to have been blissful summers.

Before the War, the family lived at a house called the Moorings, a house that is still extant and recognisable. Four Winds was not built until the early 1920s.

Denzil wrote extensively about his time spent there and it is sufficient here to give a snapshot of this. It was time spent with frequent walks, with frequent visits from other relatives, with study of local nature, with the collection of bird's eggs, and with daily comments about the weather.

On April 5th 1911 the family went to Kessingland, and were met by a dreadful blizzard

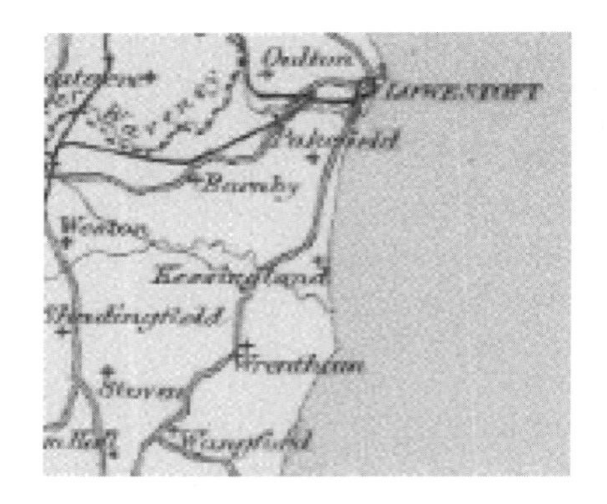

on arrival and with snow thick on ground.

On the 6th he went to the Sluice in the morning and the Lifeboat station in the afternoon.

During this Easter break they were visited by Uncle Ted, Auntie Flossie, and Auntie Cicely. [Flossie seems a particular favourite and she sent him frequent food parcels when he was at war in France].

They were also visited by Uncle Eddie, Tessie and Phylis who often drove down from Ipswich and whose car seemed to frequently suffer from punctures.

On August 23rd in the same year Denzil walked with the family to Southwold. He went with Gilly on the pier, and then they all had tea in a restaurant after which the family went on the pier and caught the steamer to Lowestoft. They then walked back "Splendid fun" was how he described it!

On 31st August Denzil set out for the Lake District and arrived at Penrith at 6.30pm and half an hour later was in Keswick, where Uncle Ted met him. The next day they started from the Keswick hotel in a charabang and went over the Honister pass which was described as a very steep and exciting ride. They also climbed Bannerdale Knot at 1160ft.

On the 2nd he went fly fishing on Crummock water with Uncle Ted after a lesson in the art. He caught nothing!

He then climbed Whiteless Pike with his Auntie and Uncle. They walked up to 2159ft, a walk that was over two hours up and 45 minutes down. He comments on a lovely view of the Solway Firth.

On September 3rd he attended Matins in Buttermere Church that was described as a tiny Church but with a good service.

On Monday 4th they went to Wastwater over Scar Gap and Black Scar passes. This was a stiff walk of 20 miles around. Wastwater is said to be a rather disappointing lake but Emmerdale was nice.

He remained in the Lakes till the 16th and obviously had a great time with Uncle Ted based in a hotel in Keswick.

[Unfortunately whilst there he heard he had not passed his higher certificate].

On 22 September the new term started

On April 4th 1912 Denzil went to Kessingland, but missed the Cambridge connection and did not get to Lowestoft until 8.30pm. He was met by his family who had cycled there but his light went out, and as he had no matches he had to walk and eventually went to bed at 1am.

This holiday much time was spent clearing the land, filling in holes and planting potatoes. April 16th was the only decent day so far weather-wise, and much time was spent chopping fire logs and clearing the land. He also found a peewit's nest with four eggs — he took one.

By April 27th he had earnt 2/- working in the garden at 1d an hour!

On August 1st They returned to Kessingland, and the next day watched Territorials fire from the beach at a target 600 yards into the sea.

On August 13th he heard, or rather read in papers, the tragic news that Bill Anderson, who had been one of his best friends at school during the last eight years, was killed by the Paris-Basle express whilst he was crossing the line at Hesdigneul near Boulogne.

On August 22nd there was the Kessingland regatta – sailing races, rowing, sculling and swimming for residents and visitors, then some athletic sports chiefly for the young of the community, followed by a fireworks display on beach.

The weather was bad from the 24th to the 26th August and he stayed in working on *Noon Star.*

On September 7th he was happy to hear that Uncle Ted had been made Mayor of Ipswich for another year.

On April 9th 1913 he returned to Kessingland.

He played a lot of croquet, learnt new card tricks, chopped fire wood, walked up to the sluice, found whinchat eggs and went into marshes to look for more, repaired the tennis court, worked on maths and history, went on excursions to Southwold and the pier, and heard the first cuckoo of year

He stayed till 25th and then went to Ealing.

He returned on Tuesday 6th August 1913. He played croquet and tennis, and sung unaccompanied part songs and snatches with "somewhat dismal results".

He walked to Rocky Point, the sluice and the boathouse with Dad.

On the 9th it rained all day, so he spent the afternoon composing a ghost story, pretty morbid thing too, for Noon Star, but he was "doubtful it will get in pages of that respectable paper"!

On the 13th he swam to the boathouse and half way back – this was about 1,000 yards and only his fourth swim of the year.

On the 15th he cycled to Lowestoft for breakfast and then sailed up river from Oulton Broad to Burgh Church with Rev HC Perry. They went very slowly due to complete lack of wind, and got tangled up in a Yacht race it being regatta time – described as a "very anxious moment!"

On the 18th after lunch he catalogued the library of 62 [6th edition] novels.

On September 4th the results of exams into the Intermediate CS arrived – failed again! He was about 36 places and 800 marks more than last time, coming 49th with 9,114 marks. Greek, Latin, History, French and Maths improved but English rather worse

On September 17th he went back to Bedford and term started the next day.

On April 14th 1914 he went down to Sweetlands soon after breakfast, and was met at Cambridge by Robin and Auntie Blanche. They cycled round the Backs before going to Shelford. He had a tennis set with Auntie and then a long paddle in canoe with Robin [his cousin].

On the 15th there was more Canadian canoeing up and down the Backs that were "looking lovely".

He also went for a long walk with Uncle Walter.

On the 16th he took the train to Lowestoft.

He obviously had an excellent time at Kessingland in good weather for the next 10 days or so, going on walks, searching for bird's nests, and swimming and reading. As he said about the 27th, it was a "perfectly heavenly day".

15 **Heligoland Bight, 28 August 1914**

The first significant naval engagement of the First World War. The German High Seas Fleet was based in Jade Bay, on the short German north sea coast. The bay was approached through the Heligoland Bight, the area of sea off the mouth of the Elbe, named after the island of Heligoland, thirty miles off the coast. Early in the war, the Germans put a pattern of patrols in place, where each evening, a destroyer flotilla, escorted by light cruisers, would arrive at Heligoland. The cruisers would then return to harbour, returning in the morning to escort the destroyers home. This was intended to detect any British night time attack on the High Seas Fleet. News of this patrol soon reached the British. Two Royal Navy officers, Commodore Roger Keyes in charge of the Submarine force, and Commodore Reginald Tyrwhitt, commander of the destroyers and light cruisers at Harwich, put forward a plan to intercept these forces. The original plan was to send forward a decoy force of very light cruisers and destroyers to draw the German heavy ships out into a submarine ambush, aided by three battle cruisers from the Grand Fleet, committed after Tyrwhitt impressed Winston Churchill, First Lord of the Admiralty. The Admiralty then decided to send six light cruisers, and up to battle cruiser force to five, this time without informing the original forces. The Germans guessed a raid was planned and increased their cruiser force. When combat was joined, the British force only managed to sink one German destroyer, before German cruisers started to do serious damage. At this point (11.50 am) the first British reinforcements, the 1 Light Cruiser squadron, arrived and saved the destroyers from a mauling, managing to sink the German cruiser SMS 'Mainz'. Luckily for the British, the heaviest German ships were trapped behind the sandbar at the mouth of Jade Bay by low tide, and could not join the battle. However, heavier German cruisers were despatched at speed to join the battle. Finally, the British battlecruisers, under Rear Admiral David Beatty, were engaged (12.30 am), and quickly sank the German cruisers SMS 'Koln' and SMS 'Ariadne' (which managed to leave the battle, but capsized at 3.10 PM). Only the mist, which limited visibility to at most 4–5 miles allowed the remaining German cruisers to escape. The battle was portrayed as a major victory in Britain, the Royal Navy having sunk three cruisers and a destroyer for no loss, just off the German coast. Its main impact was to confirm the Kaiser in his determination not to risk the High Seas Fleet in any major encounters, and thus to confirm British control of the North Sea, and the security of the blockade of Germany.

16 **Colonel Ripley**

Colonel Ripley was well loved by his men and was an Officer of the old school. He died as a result of injuries sustained at Thiepval on the 26th September 1916. He lost an arm as a result of shellfire, and though invalided home died later in England.

He had been their CO of the 6th Northants since its formation and though designated for Home service, after being wounded previously in March 1916, insisted in returning to France to lead "His Boys" in their first full offensive action. He had been with the Northamptonshire's since 1884.

On July 1st 1916 he endeared himself to his men by distributing hard boiled eggs as a boost for morale in the forthcoming battle!

17 **Reed Hall**

In 1904 the government bought Reed Hall and Bee Hive farms, comprising together 785 acres. southwest of the garrison. In 1914, when between 30,000 and 40,000 men were in training in Colchester, wooden huts were put up at Reed Hall. A military airfield was established on several acres of land at Blackheath; after the war it was transferred to Friday Wood. Between 1926 and 1933 large areas of Berechurch parish, including Berechurch Hall, were bought for the army. During the 1930s Kirkee and McMunn barracks were built at Reed Hall; Roman Way and Cherry Tree camps were established southeast of the main camp. In 1939 emergency barracks were built on various sites in the garrison area including the Abbey field, at Blackheath, and at Berechurch

18 **SMS *Blücher*** was the last armoured cruiser of the German Kaiserliche Marine and was considered an intermediate stage toward the future German battlecruiser. The ship was built at the Imperial Shipyards in Kiel, between 1907 and 1909 and commissioned in October 1909.

When World War I began, *Blücher* was posted in the Baltic, but was soon transferred to the North Sea station where she participated in artillery raids on Great Yarmouth (3 November 1914) and Hartlepool (16th December 1914). During this second raid she was hit by a coastal battery, but returned to port under her own power.

On 24th January 1915 *Blücher* was part of the German squadron commanded by Vice Admiral Franz Hipper that was surprised by a superior British force of five battlecruisers, under Vice Admiral David Beatty on HMS *Lion*, at the Battle of Dogger Bank. Due to a misunderstanding of Beatty's orders, the British ships concentrated their fire on *Blücher*, the slowest and rearmost ship of the retreating German line of battle. At 11:30 am *Blücher* suffered a major hit which caused her speed to drop to 17 knots. To save the rest of his squadron in the face of superior force, Hipper had no choice but to abandon *Blücher*. She was bombarded by heavy fire from four of the five battlecruisers and finally sunk at 13:13 pm by torpedoes. 792 of her crew went down with her, 260 were rescued by Beatty's ships.

S.M.S. Derflinger

A German battle cruiser laid down in 1913. On December 6th 1914 she fired on Scarborough, and she took part in the Battle Of Dogger Bank, January 14th 1915, where she received one hit.

In April 1916 she fired on Lowestoft and Yarmouth, and she was in the Battle of Jutland, May 31st 1916, during which she sank H.M.S. Queen Mary and Invincible, and received seventeen heavy calibre hits and four medium calibre hits; she returned to Wilhelmshaven under her own power, although she carried over 3,000 tons of water.

She was interned at Scapa Flow in November 1918 and then scuttled in June 1919.

19 **Ivor Maxse**

Before the Great War, Maxse had followed the standard career of a professional soldier, taking part in the wars in Egypt and the Boer War. At the outbreak of war in 1914 he commanded the 1st Guards Brigade that went to France as part of the BEF in August.

In October 1914 he became a Major-General and commanded the newly formed 18th Division. He began the training of this new formation using innovative techniques that emphasised the need for independence and initiative in both junior officers and NCO's. This was called "Drilling for initiative", and all tactical movements that could be foreseen were rehearsed before hand.

In the spring of 1915 the 18th went to France, and it spent the winter of 1915-16 on general duties in the trenches. He believed that training should be relentless and this made the 18th one of the best prepared by the time of the Somme in July 1916. They were based in the Albert area. In the period July 1st to 13th they did well, but Maxse had encouraged his officers, if conditions indicated, to ignore the instructions of Sir Henry Rawlinson, the 4th Army commander. Maxse wanted rapid advance by the 1st wave with a mopping up done later, as opposed to the broad general advance. He also used the creeping barrage, though he didn't invent it, as he had said. After the German spring offensive of March 1918 he was controversially dismissed as CO of the 18th Division and went back to England as the Inspector-General of the BEF.

He is considered by many to have been the best trainer of the British Army, and also the best tactician, but he remains one of the least known.

20 **Codford**

Before the First World War this was a village of about 500 people, which was eventually taken over by the military. Because of the rail connections in Codford, thousands of Kitchener's 'new army' came to this area and camped around different parts of the village. The camp was laid out in 1914 at Manor Farm, which is between Salisbury and Warminster. It was particularly used by British and Anzac troops, and having been shut down in 1919 was reopened in the Second World War and was used extensively by US troops.

21 **Swedish Drill**

The boarding schools organised games and competitive sports for their pupils, for example, rowing, rugby, hockey, football, tennis, cricket and polo. The military drill was based on the idea that many soldiers, or in this case pupils, could march, drill and so on. This way many pupils could exercise for a very low cost, as it required only one instructor and an open space. This military drill idea was followed by the Swedish Therapeutic Gymnastics in the Ling tradition, this change occurred in the 1870s. Ling gymnastics was also based on military drill, though with a more therapeutic approach, and during its first thirty odd years part-time, ex-army, non-commissioned personnel often taught it.

22 **Deaths of Old Bedfordian friends of Heriz-Smith**

Acting Major	S Atkinson	17-2-18	Royal Field Artillery	York
Captain	G Batty	27-09-16	Northants	Thiepval
Lt	F Bolster	4-4-17	RGA	Arras
2nd Lt	L Brereton	29-4-17	Beds	Cairo
Captain	A Burrows	13-3-16	Northants	Carnoy
2nd Lt	R Cameron Killed same time and place as brother Neil	25-9-15	Cameron Highlanders	Loos
2nd Lt	E Carrington	18-10-16	Wiltshires	Guedecourt
Lt	M Colson	25-9-17	Royal Field Artillery	Ypres
2nd Lt	H Copeman	03-18-16	Ox and Bucks	Guillemont
2nd Lt	P Curlett	3-7-15	King's Liverpool	Ypres
2 Lt	H Forge	20-11-17	Bedfordshires	Touillet Wood
2nd Lt	D Fowler	26-9-19	RAF	Winchester
2nd Lt	W Garraway	5-11-16	IA	Tigris
Captain	H Grace	2-9-17	Northants	Flanders
2nd Lt	G Gilbertson	28-11-17	Bedfordshires	Ypres

Acting Captain	W Griffiths	30-3-16	Royal Welsh Fusiliers	Ypres
2nd Lt	L Halliday	31-7-17	Northants	Ypres
Lt	K Hore	25-9-15	City of London	Loos
Lt	WK Humfrey	26-08-14	Lancs Fusiliers	Le Cateau
Rifleman	B Jackson	22-3-1918	The Rifle Brigade	Arras
2nd Lt	T Kilpin	15-6-17	RFA	Nieppe
2nd Lt	J Lambert	1-11-15	Northants	Fricourt
Captain	B Maclear	24-5-1915	Royal Dublin Fusiliers	Ypres
Lt	E Mitchell	15-2-16	Beds	La Brigne
Lt	H Moberley	25-5-15	Punjabi Infantry	Neuve Chappelle
Captain	G Peel	17-7-17	Bedfordshires	Flanders
Lt	C Sanderson	27-4-18	RE's	Mendinghe
2nd Lt	W Smith	25-6-16	Royal Munster Fusiliers	Loos
2nd Lt	O Stokes	5-3-17	Royal Munster Fusiliers	Somme
Lt	O Tancock	17-3-18	RFC	Aubigny
Captain	A Tanqueray	30-7-15	KRRC	Ypres
Guardsman	H Tanqueray Willaume	31-3-15	Coldstream Guards	Richebourg
2nd Lt	G Thomson	19-5-17	Kings Liverpool Regt	Ficheux
2nd Lt	J Thornton	9-11-16	RFC	Carrick
Sub Lt	A Tisdall	10-5-15	RNVR	Gallipoli
Lt	E Walker	22-8-16	Royal Fusiliers	High Wood Somme
2nd Lt	N Wemyss	27-7-16	Bedfordshires	Longueval
Captain	J Yarde	21-9-18	Bedfordshire's	Palestine

23 **Letters of Affection and the language of 1914**

In the vast range of letters that Denzil wrote and sent there are terms of endearment that would not be used now!

Frequently he refers to his mother as His "Wee Tit" or "Tittie" and I wonder whether this refers to her size, and is a cross reference to a titmouse. Does it come from Gilbert and Sullivan and the Mikado? We know he sung in this at school and could the song "Tit Willow" be the inspiration? The photos of her, which exist, do not show her to be very small.

Undoubtedly his Father was an influence on his letter writing style as can be seen by this extract from a letter in February 1914.

Dad to son

He describes a railway carriage on the way home from Europe via Harwich.
"There were a great deal of foreigners boarding at Harwich, and we had in our carriage an alert and lively Italian Gent, a very shabby, malignant looking old man of the same nationality, a sleeping grey haired nonentity, and a sulky looking yellow haired young man with elegant brown boots, and a wee cage of canaries which he kept on his knees and which he devoured now and then with an anxious gaze"

Father also loved receiving letters from Denzil, as can be seen from this extract. from a letter from PPF to son Feb19th 1914, wishing him a happy birthday.

"Do write one of your topping letters soon. I'd have given my new electric bulb to speak to you tonight, and that is a most valued possession of mine!

I think of you in your cosy study and wonder if you think of me in my freezing bed sitting room".

In early correspondence between the two Denzil writes to "Daddy" or "Dad", but as age increased his nerve so his address was less formal, with to "My Dear Old Dad" being a common one. But in these letters Denzil fills with frequent references to his Dad's "appearance; for instance "Nightie pyhtie my little Tittie, even if the old dad has got a face like a frenzied mackerel in a blizzard, it's not his fault!"

Also the letters PPF frequently are used sometimes by Father and sometimes by son. I think they come from the Latin phrase "Pater pater familias" i.e. Father of the Father who is the Head of the family. This could refer to the position held in the family by the only son, and that he was considered to be male head of the family in his Fathers absences.

What is not in doubt was the very close relationship Denzil had with both parents.

The language of 1914!

It is reassuring to know that many of the caricatures about speech in the early 20th century are true!

Ripping
Topping
Bucked
Fed [up]
Blaggard
Splendid
Wheeze
Scragged

There is also a prolonged correspondence between H-S and Podmore as to whether both damn and dash are swear words and if so which is worst! The answer is damn that is close to a mortal sin.

Good manners and behaviour are frequently discussed to the point of absolute stuffiness by our own standards, as is the need to inculcate them in the young.

A word I cannot explain is the frequently used one **Poortaag.** I think it means "bad show" or "bad luck" but I cannot trace it's derivation. This affectation appears only in Denzil's letters to his family.

24 On the 5th October 1915 the Northants Battalion was inspected by the Brigadier and on the 6th by General Sir C Munroe, commanding 3rd Army, who expressed his opinion in the following words "An admirable battalion, I am proud to have you under my command."

This is mentioned in Lambert's last letter.

25 **Smoking and the War**

Having worked on two sets of diaries about the 1st World War, it becomes clear that whether an officer or from the ranks there were 3 real common factors. Firstly there was the fear of death, or worse in a way, maiming. Second was the squalor of the conditions troops had to fight and live in, and lastly was boredom. Boredom was the result of the fact that war rarely happened along all sectors of the Western Front at the same time, and because time had to be filled in there were repetitive drills and fatigues. such as filling sand bags and trench digging. When they were actually in the front line trenches there was a lot of standing around waiting for something to happen – be they officers or men.

Smoking had been prevalent amongst armies since the 17th century and the authorities saw the morale boost of ensuring that the supply of cigarettes reached the men serving at the front, either from the canteen or from home. Many who had never smoked before the war took up the habit during, and the majority smoked.

The most popular cigarette was the Woodbine, though plenty rolled their own using Rizla cigarette papers.

Undoubtedly tobacco became a "comfort" in a very harsh world, and there was little discussion about the health consequences of this. Also, cigarettes were shared round and became a means of the development of friendships and morale.

Soldiers more and more cupped their smokes to avoid the sniper and the 3-match trick they had.

The biggest short-term consequence of smoking was if the soldier had been gassed, and the dreadful consequences of both on the lungs.

26 **Mons Medal**

This is the least common medal of the war, and one that was highly coveted, and it is popularly but erroneously known as the Mons Star. This medal was awarded to all officers, warrant officers, non-commissioned officers and all men of the British and Indian Forces, including civilian medical practitioners, nursing sisters, nurses and others employed with military hospitals; as well as men of the Royal Navy, Royal Marines, Royal Naval Reserve and Royal Naval Volunteer Reserve, who served with the establishment of their unit in France and Belgium between August 5th 1914, and midnight of November 22/23rd, 1914.

The decoration consists of a lacquered bronze star, the uppermost ray of the star taking the form of the imperial crown. Resting on the face of the star is a pair of crossed swords, and, on them, is a circular oak wreath. A scroll winds around the swords: it is inscribed with the date Aug–Nov 1914. The ribbon is red merging into white and then into blue.

A bar inscribed "5th Aug to 22nd Nov 1914" was given to all those who served under fire. Since the same ribbon is used with the 1914-15 Star, holders of the earlier award were permitted to wear a small silver rosette on their ribbon when the decoration itself is not worn. On the medal index cards this is usually noted as the "Clasp and Roses".

27 **War work and Bedford School**
There are several references to Bedford School and the War in letters and diaries.

With very few exceptions, all boys of military age during the years 1914-18 left school and joined one of the three services, the great majority of them getting commissions for which they underwent special training at School under the OTC officers.

But the energies of the School were not confined to active service, and there were several more ways it contributed to the war effort.

At the beginning of August 1914 the Gymnasium was taken over by the Beds Yeomanry, and the last of their horses had barely left the field when the 4th Seaforths took up their quarters there. They used the Hall and classrooms of the building during the holidays for sleeping and two rooms for office work, while the Gym was used for store room, and portions of the field for drilling, cooking, canteen and Sunday Services up to November 5th when they left for the front.

After the Seaforths left, the fields were used by many other battalions and military units, e.g. for Officer Cadet Training, Sunday services and some sport; and a general review of some thousands of volunteers was held there by Field Marshall French. During the holidays members of the School guarded the Armoury of the OTC from possible attack.

In the School workshops, too, much valuable work was done, largely under the supervision of Mr W Davison, the Engineering Instructor of the School, who was released from the Army in 1915, and returned to organise the shops for war work. Under his guidance, a contact was completed for submarine valves, and boltings for turbine casings for Messrs Yarrow and Co, of Clydeside. Thus, when the call for ammunition came, the shops were further fitted up for the manufacture of 13lb shells. Mr Davison, ably supported by Mr Phillips, made the cutting tools, and organised his squads of young and old workers so well that work was soon in full swing. The shells were accepted as first class work by the HM Inspector of Munitions.

To some extent the task was complicated by the fact that the boys could only work for short periods. The vacant times were filled by Masters, Master's wives, and other residents, men and women, who volunteered. Some of these passed on' after their basic training, to larger factories elsewhere. Different gangs per day were thus employed, so as to keep the machinery full time. The work went on even during Mr Davison's absence at the Hackney Marshes Projectile Factory. Tools were also made for the manufacture of shells in 1917, and work was done for Stoke's Bombs in 1917 and 1918. Clearly the school has a record here which is not well known and in which it should have just pride.

But good and useful work happened in other areas. Squads of boys helped in farm work round Bedford under the general direction of Mr Dasent; a portion of the fields were divided into house allotments for growing vegetables; more than a ton of chestnuts was collected, used in the manufacture of munitions.

Conkers were needed by the Ministry of Supply and 7/6 per cwt was paid for the immediate delivery of chestnuts. At the beginning of the war cordite – the smokeless powder used as propellant in small arms ammunition and artillery – was mainly imported from the USA, but when blockages and submarine warfare made shipping difficult Britain needed to produce it's own cordite. One of the ingredients required for making cordite is acetone, a volatile liquid compound used as a solvent. Acetone is made from starch and Britain looked for supplies of this, at the beginning of the war relying on imported maize and even potatoes.

When supply routes were cut, Lloyd George, the Minister of Munitions required that starch came from closer at home. Professor Chaim Weizman of Manchester University, and a leading Zionist, came up with an alternative method to make acetone, not only from maize but also from horse chestnuts – conkers. Factories were built in Poole and

Bedford School fitting shop

Kings Lynn producing as much as 90,000 gallons of acetone per year. When maize began to run out it was supplemented by conkers collected by children, with the factory locations being top secret.

It was said that so many conkers were collected that there were transport problems, and piles of rotting conkers were left at railway stations.

Conkers were, however, used again in WW2.

A subplot of this is that Lloyd George was so grateful to Chaim Weizman for this that it led on to the controversial Balfour declaration in 1917 which set out British approval for the establishment in Palestine of a national home for the Jews – the state of Israel!

In August 1918 a squad of 15 boys and three teachers assembled near Spalding to help in the potato harvest, and soon to be joined by 18 others. They toiled for seven hours per day for six days per week on this heavy task.

28 Maconochies Bully Beef was staple issue to troops in WW1. It was a bit like Irish stew and it was often added to with biscuits, onions or curry powder. Probably Maconochies and Tommy Tickler's jam were the most famous British army food.

29 **Mortars**

Mortars, which lobbed a shell a relatively short distance, were widely used in trench fighting for harassing the forward trenches and for cutting wire in preparation for a raid or attack. In 1914, the British fired a total of 545 mortar shells. In 1916, they fired over 6,500,000 shells.

The main British mortar was the Stokes mortar, which was the precursor of the modern mortar. It was a light mortar, but was easy to use, and capable of a rapid rate of fire by virtue of the propellant cartridge being attached to the shell. To fire the Stokes mortar, the round was simply dropped into the tube, where the cartridge was ignited automatically when it struck the firing pin at the bottom.

The Germans used a range of mortars. The smallest were grenade-throwers (*Granatenwerfer*) which fired "pineapple" bombs. Their medium trench-mortars were called mine-throwers (*Minenwerfer*), dubbed "minnies" by the British. The heavy mortar was called the *Ladungswerfer* which threw "aerial torpedoes", containing a 200 lb (90 kg) charge, over 1,000 yards. The flight of the missile was so slow and leisurely that the men on the receiving end could make some attempt to seek shelter.

30 **Captured dugouts and redoubts**

If the problem of capturing these was not enough, it was not much easier to hold on to them. The Germans reinforced the dugouts much more on the side facing the Allies. On the other side – the reverse – the concrete and protection was nowhere near as thick, leaving them vulnerable to German artillery. This was seen as a problem both at Ypres and on the Somme.

31 The Commanding Officer was Lt. Colonel Frank Maxwell V.C., C.S.I., D.S.O. (Victoria Cross, Companion of the Order of the Star of India, Companion of the Distinguished Service Order). He had taken over command of the 12th Middlesex Regiment on the 31st May 1916. Lt. Col. Maxwell had won the Victoria Cross at Sanna's Post during the South African Campaign (Boer War) on the 31st March 1900. When Frank Maxwell was appointed Commanding Officer of the 12th Battalion Middlesex Regiment, his personality exerted a tonic effect upon the morale and fighting qualities of the Battalion. In temperament, and in every other attribute physical and mental, Lt. Col. Maxwell was fitted for the task assigned to him. There was a steely quality in his personal bravery that seemed accentuated by the almost studied tranquillity of his speech and general manner. Frank Maxwell was killed by snipers whilst reconnoitring in No Man's Land near Ypres, Belgium on 21st September 1917

32 **Philip Gibbs**
Before the war Gibbs was a journalist and an author

In 1914 he was sent by the Daily Chronicle to France to report the 1st WW. The War Office wished to control the news that appeared in British newspapers. When Gibbs continued to report the war he was arrested in Le Havre and sent back to England.

Yet in 1915 he was one of five journalists selected by the government to become official war correspondents with the British Army. Gibbs had to submit to the censor CE Montague.

He continued to argue the case for greater press freedom though he knew there would have to be some censorship.

One of his greatest opponents had been Earl Haig. He had the old cavalry officers' prejudice against war correspondents and "writing fellows", and made no secret of it. When he became Commander-in-Chief, he sent for the correspondents and said things which rankled. One of them was that "after all you are only writing for Mary Ann in the kitchen."

He was not allowed to get away with that, and he was told that it was not only for Mary Ann that they were writing, but for the whole nation and Empire, and that he could not conduct his war in secret, as though the people at home, whose sons and husbands were fighting and dying, had no concern in the matter. The spirit of the fighting men, and the driving power behind the armies, depended upon the support of the whole people and their continuing loyalties.

There was an idea, still lingering, that the war correspondents of the First World War were "spoon fed", and just wrote that they were told. That was partly due to an arrangement they made among themselves. They decided to pool all information, in order to give the fullest record of any action, reserving only to oneself personal impressions and experiences.

The limitations of censorship were of course irritating. They could not give the figures of our losses – the immense sum of our casualties, as on the first day of the Somme battle. That was inevitable because that was what the enemy would have liked to know, but the worst handicap they had was the prohibition of naming individual units who had done the fighting.

33 **DF** – Defensive Fire – was a pre-registered artillery target that is located on likely enemy approaches and FUP's (Forming Up Places/Points). It is sometimes called DFSOS – defensive fire save our souls. The infantry commander would assess likely approaches and FUP's, plot a grid reference and give the DF a call sign. The gunners would plot it and work out all their bearings, elevations, etc. If time permits, they might even put a few rounds down to confirm the target. Then, if the enemy are seen, or are thought to be, near the DF the infantry commander could call for artillery support by simply radioing in the call sign for that DF, and adjust fall of shot if necessary. The whole idea was to save time when calling in artillery support. An FPF – Final Protective Fire – is a DF registered on the most likely enemy approach. The guns are meant to be in direct support of the infantry but there were many cases of friendly fire, as described in this book.

34 **To Cambridge Men Serving in the War**
Extracts from an Address delivered by the Vice Chancellor, Dr James, on resigning office October 1st 1915.

The University has shrunk to less than one third of it's former numbers. It's buildings – labs, lecture rooms, Examination Halls – have been filled with soldiers. Colleges have been converted into schools of instructions for officers, into head-quarters for it's military staff, into lodgings for nurses, into billets for men.

A great military hospital now covers one of the largest college fields. Many Professors, readers and lecturers have out of residence to take up scientific work, or commission as officers. Others, still with us, are devoting themselves to tasks not less useful to the common welfare. Yet again, others have engaged in work in government offices, and have placed their attainments, linguistic, economic, and historical at the service of their country

The policy of the university in this crisis has been to render all employment of it's resources, material and intellectual, for the benefit of the country, as easy as it can be made. It is not indeed conceivable that we should other wise than grant leave of absence in every possible place, and keep open all temporarily vacated posts.

We know that of Cambridge men not less than 10,000 are fighting or preparing to fight for their country, that 700 have been wounded, and that over 300 have won distinctions in the field. We know, too, that the whole number 2,000 to 3,000 would in the ordinary course still be living and studying amongst us. To these we stand in a special relation.

We are debtors to all, but to them we have some means of showing that we recognize the great sacrifice they have made. What has been the found possible to do for them I will not go into details now but the aim has been to secure on the one hand, for those who have completed some part of their residence, an easy passage to a degree, mainly by allowing of as many as four terms, and by counting time spent on active service as the equivalent of the Special Examination in Military Subjects. For those who have yet to come into residence the policy is to let them enter forthwith into the subject study for which they have been selected. Already more than 100 degrees have been conferred on those currently at the front. We cannot, of course, estimate the number of those who were to come here, who wish to take it up, or in what mind they will return to us.

We pass to the thought of the many who will not return. More than 470 Cambridge men have fallen, 150 of them at least who should be with us now. For these no privilege that we can devise avails. Yet the University bears them upon it's heart, and will not, I know, neglect to perpetuate the memory of them in such sort that it may speak to the youth of England in times to come.

Dr James mentions from his own college Rupert Brooke, whose name had started to pulse through all England. His name will always bring back, besides the thanks due to the true poet, images of beauty, nobleness and affection

If I should die, think only this of me: That there's some corner of a foreign field that is forever England. *The Soldier* (1915)

Rupert Brooke caught the optimism of the opening months of the war, with his wartime sonnets 1914 (1915) expressing idealism in the face of death that contrasts strongly to poetry published later in the war and after his death. They brought him immediate – albeit posthumous – fame.

35 **Extract from Denial's extensive address book.**

ADDRESSES

Gerrard J.H. 88 Cawood Rd. Cradock. Cape Province
Jarling R.E. Haileybury College. Herts.
Jarling E.J. 1 Milton Rd Bedford
Simpson M.Y. 6th Yorks Regt. Grantham
Simpson [illegible]. Mia-mia. Pemberley avenue Bedford
Perry Rev. H.C. 17 Devon Rd. Bedford
Batterbury T.K.C.B. Burnaby House Bedford
[illegible] E.H.B. Burnaby House Bedford
Carter. R. School house. Bedford.
Ozanne R.T. 64. Kimbolton Rd Bedford
Henderson. H.A. 66. Kimbolton Rd Bedford
Atchison. G.T.A. 19. Cornwall Rd.
Bull G.G.C. Mandora Barracks Aldershot
Copeman K.G.H. 23 Miles Rd Epsom (Temp)
Peel G. 23 Miles Rd Epsom (Temp)
Drayton R.H.
Trott. J.W. 'C' Coy IInd Batt P.S. R.F. Epsom
Jolly A.J. 'C' Coy IInd Batt. Royal Fusiliers Epsom
O'Brien F.P. 21. Parkside. Wimbledon
Hole M.C. 11th Batt. West Riding Regt Halifax
Lacey W.G. 9th Batt. Beds. Regt. Harwich
Griffiths W.P. 10th Batt. R.W.F. Wimborne Rd Bourne[illegible]
[illegible] A.W. 15th Batt RWF. W. Rd. Bournemouth

Epilogue

Thanks from the French Marshall Joffre for the contribution of the School to the 1st WW, dated December 11th 1918.

This would seem to be an appropriate way to pay tribute to Bedford School for the huge contribution it made in the 1st World War.